TEACHING
WITH POWER

TEACHING WITH POWER

DRAWING YOUR FAMILY AND OTHERS TO CHRIST

TAD R. CALLISTER & KATHRYN S. CALLISTER

SALT LAKE CITY, UTAH

© 2021 Tad R. Callister and Kathryn S. Callister

All rights reserved. No part of this book may be reproduced in any form or by any means without permission in writing from the publisher, Deseret Book Company, at permissions@deseretbook.com. This work is not an official publication of The Church of Jesus Christ of Latter-day Saints. The views expressed herein are the responsibility of the authors and do not necessarily represent the position of the Church or of Deseret Book Company.

Deseret Book is a registered trademark of Deseret Book Company.

Visit us at DeseretBook.com

Library of Congress Cataloging-in-Publication Data
CIP on file
ISBN: 978-1-62972-973-2

Printed in the United States of America
Lake Book Manufacturing, Inc., Melrose Park, IL

10 9 8 7 6 5 4 3 2 1

Contents

An Overview of Teaching

1. What Is the Mission of Every Teacher? 1
2. Every Leader Is a Teacher 6
3. Parents: The Prime Gospel Teachers of Their Children 12
4. Everyone Can Teach 22

Teach by the Spirit

5. Prepare and Teach by the Spirit 31
6. Create a Lesson Plan 44

Teach the Doctrine

7. The Power of the Doctrine 51
8. How Can I Best Teach the Doctrine? 63
9. Focus on Doctrinal Principles, Not Rules 75
10. Putting Together the "Gospel Puzzle":
    Doctrinal Relationships 81
11. How Should We Interpret the Scriptures? 86

CONTENTS

Teaching Skills That Support the Doctrine

12. The Power of Repetition 99
13. The Power of Discourse, Stories,
    Parables, and Object Lessons 107
14. The "Like Unto" Principle 117
15. Responding to Difficult Questions 127
16. A Testimony Seals the Truth of the Doctrine 138

Edify One Another

17. Set High but Loving Expectations 145
18. What Makes for an Inspired Question? 151
19. How Can I Lead an Inspired Discussion? 162
20. Extending Inspired Invitations 170

Love Those You Teach

21. Loving Those You Teach 177
22. Reaching Out to Those Who Do Not Attend 186
23. Making Teaching with Technology More Personal 196

Parents: The Prime Gospel Teachers

24. Teaching Ideas for the Home 201
25. Informal Teaching Moments 215
26. Teaching Our Children to Recognize the Spirit 221
27. Teaching Our Children Morality 229
28. The Refining Influence of Culture
    in Our Homes and Classes 245

Learning

29. The World Is Our Classroom 261
30. What Responsibilities Do I Have as a Learner? 264

CONTENTS

Conclusion: How Can I Honor My Calling
   as a Teacher and Parent?............................. 279

Notes 283

Works Cited 295

Index 304

AN OVERVIEW OF TEACHING

CHAPTER 1

What Is the Mission of Every Teacher?

A GREAT TRUST

On one occasion a good brother sat in President David O. McKay's office, where he received a call to preside over a mission. He thanked President McKay for this great honor. President McKay, "with his kindly but piercing eyes, looked into the appointee's soul and replied, 'No, not a great honor. It is a great trust!'"[1] Likewise, it is a great trust to be a teacher of the gospel of Jesus Christ, at both home and church.

Inspired teachers honor this trust. They do not teach the doctrines of men, nor do they advance their own philosophies or agendas, however intellectually stimulating or entertaining they may seem. They recognize that they are on the Lord's errand and thus are fiercely loyal and true to teaching His message. The Apostle Paul gave this related caution and command: "Speak thou the things which become sound doctrine" (Titus 2:1). Ernest L. Wilkinson, former president of Brigham Young University, reminded us where our doctrine comes from: "Our roots spring from Palmyra rather than Cambridge."[2] In other words, it is spiritual doctrine, not secular philosophy, that is the foundation of our teaching.

In the early days of the Church, the Lord instructed His elders to say "none other things than that which the prophets and apostles have written, and that which is taught them by the Comforter" (D&C 52:9; see also D&C 43:15). It was a call to arms—a call to use the spiritual weapon that trumps all others—the word of God as taught by the prophets and as directed by the Spirit. That is the sacred trust we as teachers are expected to honor, both at home and at church.

In order to put our teaching at home and church in proper perspective and priority, our leaders have counseled us that our gospel learning and teaching should be home-centered and Church-supported. President Russell M. Nelson spoke to this point: "The Church is to assist and not to replace parents in their responsibilities to teach their children."[3] As we fulfill this parental responsibility, we become instruments in God's hands.

LIFTING OTHERS TO HIGHER GROUND

For a moment consider three leaders who had an incredible impact on the world: Adolf Hitler, Joseph Stalin, and Genghis Khan. If you were to grade them on vision, commitment to their cause, organizational skills, ability to delegate, and demand for accountability, what grade would you give them? No doubt, they applied many MBA leadership principles with remarkable skill. They were effective leaders in the sense that they got the job done.

These men knew how to motivate people. Imagine if one of them were in charge of ministering in your ward—what would your ministering percentage be? Motivation alone, however, is not our goal as Church leaders or teachers. The devil *motivates* people.

What Is the Mission of Every Teacher?

Rather, the mission of every leader and teacher is to *inspire* others to become more like Christ.

Most leadership and teaching in the world is *horizontal*—it motivates people to acquire knowledge, money, fame, physical pleasure, and power. Leadership and teaching in the Lord's kingdom, however, is *vertical*—it lifts people up and inspires them to be more like Christ.

President Harold B. Lee explained how this principle works: "You cannot lift another soul until you are standing on higher ground than he is."[4] That is a powerful truth. While many in the world use style and charisma to motivate people, only spiritual substance can elevate them. That is why the Savior's principal leadership style has never been to push or prod, but rather to "draw all men unto him" (2 Ne. 26:24).

Although each President of the Church demonstrated different leadership and teaching styles, a common thread ran through each of their lives—they were men of profound spiritual substance—they were Christlike. Christ was the foundation and core of their lives and the source of their inspiration and power. Likewise, while each of us may teach with a different style, it is our spiritual substance that allows us to teach with power and authority from God—to lift others to higher ground.

OUR MISSION AS TEACHERS

Every teacher has the responsibility to diligently live the gospel of Jesus Christ so he or she can teach the doctrine by the Spirit in such a way that builds faith in Jesus Christ and brings about lasting conversion. In essence, the goal of teaching is much more than just facilitating learning or even doing—it is about helping those we teach to become converted disciples of Jesus Christ, meaning to become more like Him. That is the mission of every teacher.

Everything else is a distant second—the sports analogies, the videos, the flowers, the visual aids can all be helpful, but they are never a substitute for this objective. When we understand this purpose, the questions we ask, the discussions we lead, and the invitations we extend will all be designed to further this mission.

It has been said of the famous orator Cicero that when he spoke, the people applauded, but when Demosthenes spoke, the people took up arms. Hopefully, teachers' lessons will be so stirring, so filled with the doctrine and Spirit, that they will be a call to arms to walk in the footsteps of the Savior. In support of this, President Dallin H. Oaks stated: "In contrast to the institutions of the world which teach us to *know* something, the gospel of Jesus Christ challenges us to *become* something."[5] And that something is to become like Christ (see D&C 11:30). Inspired teaching is a divine catalyst that promotes and fosters such a pursuit.

A TEACHER'S INFLUENCE CAN HAVE ETERNAL IMPLICATIONS

President Dallin H. Oaks also described how we might measure the success of a teacher: "A gospel teacher . . . will measure the success of teaching and testifying by its impact on the lives of the learners. A gospel teacher will never be satisfied with just delivering a message or preaching a sermon. A superior gospel teacher wants to assist in the Lord's work to bring eternal life to His children."[6] This means that our teaching, when inspired, can have a powerful and permanent impact on the souls of those we teach, even throughout eternity. That can be our legacy as teachers.

CHRISTLIKE ATTRIBUTES AND SKILLS

As teachers we are to follow the example of the Savior—meaning, we are to seek after and acquire His attributes and develop His teaching skills. After all, He is the Master Teacher. As we do so, we invite the Spirit into our lives in the fullest measure possible. Christlike attributes and teaching skills complement and supplement each other. For example, humility facilitates our learning of divine teaching skills. And loving our students heightens our appetite to improve those skills for their benefit.

Some may believe teaching skills or techniques are mechanical or secular tools. These skills, however, when developed, allow the Spirit to choose from a variety of options that can best meet the needs of individual learners. For example, who is more productive—the man who attempts to cut down a tree with his pocket knife or the same man who utilizes a chain saw? In both cases it is the same man with the same strength and character, but in the latter he is so much more productive because he has better tools at his disposal. Teaching skills become divine tools in the hands of the Spirit, allowing the Spirit to be more productive and influential as our skills increase.

CONCLUSION

Hopefully this book will help us acquire a greater measure of the Spirit and those skills we need to be effective instruments in the hands of God. Then perhaps, it might be said of us as it was said of the sons of Mosiah: "And when they taught, they taught with power and authority of God," and "by the power of their words many were brought before the altar of God" (Alma 17:3–4; see also Mosiah 13:6).

CHAPTER 2

Every Leader Is a Teacher

THE PERFECT EXAMPLE

The Savior set the example of the perfect leader, in large part because He was and is the Perfect Teacher. President Boyd K. Packer made this observation: "The Lord is our example. It would be hard to describe the Lord as an executive. Let me repeat that. It would be hard to describe the Lord as an executive. He was a *teacher*! That is the ideal, the pattern."[1] President Gordon B. Hinckley observed, "*Effective teaching is the very essence of leadership in the Church. Eternal life will come only as men and women are taught with such effectiveness that they can change and discipline their lives. They cannot be coerced into righteousness or into heaven. They must be led, and that means teaching.*"[2]

If anyone questions that teaching is the essence of leadership, then that person should read the number of times the New Testament refers to Jesus as a teacher or shows Him engaged in the act of teaching. This occurs about thirty times in the four Gospels.[3]

So vast were the Savior's teachings to the Nephites that the scriptures record, "And now there cannot be written in this book even a hundredth part of the things which Jesus did truly *teach* unto the people" (3 Nephi 26:6; emphasis added). Teaching was at the heart of His leadership. That is why He instructed His Apostles to "go ye therefore, and *teach* all nations" (Matt. 28:19; emphasis added). That is why His Apostles "ceased not to *teach* and preach Jesus Christ" (Acts 5:42; emphasis added). That is why Paul said, "A bishop then must be . . . apt to *teach*" (1 Tim. 3:2; emphasis added) and why he further instructed Timothy to prepare "faithful men, who shall be able to *teach* others also" (2 Tim. 2:2; emphasis added).

In our dispensation, the Lord has given similar instructions: "Teach one another according to the office wherewith I have appointed you" (D&C 38:23). On another occasion He said, "When ye are assembled together ye shall instruct and edify each other" (D&C 43:8).[4]

The Book of Mormon prophet Jacob referred to himself and his brother Joseph as "teachers of this people" and then spoke of their sacred duty to fulfill this responsibility: "And we did magnify our office unto the Lord, taking upon us the responsibility, answering the sins of the people upon our own heads if we did not teach them the word of God with all diligence" (Jacob 1:18–19).[5] Jarom described the leaders in his day as "mighty men in the faith of the Lord; and they taught the people the ways of the Lord" (Jarom 1:7).

President Boyd K. Packer made this observation: "The prophet is a teacher; his counselors are teachers; the General Authorities are teachers. Stake presidents and mission presidents are teachers; high councilors and quorum presidents are teachers; bishops are teachers; and so through all of the organization of the Church. *The Church moves forward sustained by the power of the teaching that is accomplished.*"[6] And we would add—all women's leaders are teachers.

President Packer also addressed when and where leaders should teach: "Leaders have a responsibility to teach, whether they are in councils or interviews or worship services."[7] In other words, great leaders are constantly teaching, whether in formal or informal settings, whether in large groups or one-on-one situations.

Over the years we have been blessed to associate with many great leaders. As we reflect on the ways they have helped us, we do not recall the audit reports they submitted in a timely manner or the numerous agendas they prepared. Rather we recall the visits they made to members' homes, including our own, the counsel and training they gave us and others, and the constant expressions of gratitude and encouragement. It always seemed to be the one-on-one teaching and ministry moments that left the greatest impact.

WAYS THAT LEADERS CAN TEACH

It has been said, "Don't die with your music still in you." Another rendition of that thought might read: "Don't die with the gospel still in you." In other words, teach the gospel to every person at every possible opportunity. We have many wonderful examples of leaders who have demonstrated this principle. One such example was shared by President Thomas S. Monson:

> As I approached my 18th birthday and prepared to enter the mandatory military service required of young men during World War II, I was recommended to receive the Melchizedek Priesthood, but first I needed to telephone my stake president, Paul C. Child, for an interview. He was one who loved and understood the holy Scriptures, and it was his intent that all others should similarly love and understand them. Having heard from some of my friends of his rather detailed and searching interviews, I desired minimum exposure of my scriptural knowledge; therefore, when

I called him I suggested we meet the following Sunday at a time I knew was just an hour before his sacrament meeting time.

His response: "Oh, Brother Monson, that would not provide us sufficient time to peruse the scriptures." He then suggested a time three hours before his sacrament meeting, and he instructed me to bring with me my personally marked and referenced set of scriptures.

When I arrived at his home on Sunday, I was greeted warmly, and then the interview began. President Child said, "Brother Monson you hold the Aaronic Priesthood. Have you ever had angels minister to you?" I replied that I had not. When he asked if I knew I was entitled to such, I again replied that I had not known.

He instructed, "Brother Monson, repeat from memory the 13th section of the Doctrine and Covenants."

I began, "Upon you my fellow servants, in the name of Messiah I confer the Priesthood of Aaron, which holds the keys of the ministering of angels—"

"Stop," President Child directed. Then, in a calm, kindly tone, he counseled, "Brother Monson, never forget that as a holder of the Aaronic Priesthood you are entitled to the ministering of angels."

It was almost as though an angel were in the room that day. I have never forgotten the interview. I yet feel the spirit of that solemn occasion as we together read of the responsibilities, the duties, and the blessings of the Aaronic Priesthood and the Melchizedek Priesthood.[8]

Not only did President Child interview President Monson but, perhaps of equal importance, he also taught him. Leaders have many such opportunities to teach. For example, when bishops set apart Aaronic Priesthood quorum presidents or Young Women class presidents, they might teach them how to receive and recognize revelation.

Elder Bruce R. McConkie once came to our stake and observed that many youth wait too long before receiving their patriarchal blessings—waiting until they go on missions or are married in the temple. He then taught that they should receive such a blessing at the earliest date they would be spiritually mature enough to appreciate it. He then explained why—there was much in that blessing that would add to their self-confidence and spirituality. Patriarchal blessings often define some of the gifts and talents they possess. They remind them they are children of God. In addition, they often encourage the youth to be morally clean, to prepare for a mission, and to enter the temple. He emphasized that patriarchal blessings address many of the key challenges that teenagers face on a daily basis. Elder McConkie then observed that if young people waited until a mission or marriage, they would miss this inspired guidance and encouragement at an age when they may have needed it most. Parents and bishopric members can likewise teach and implement these truths before it is too late.

As leaders immerse themselves in the scriptures, the Holy Ghost will bring to their memory the doctrinal principles that will be most helpful as they counsel and teach those in need. Tad recalls a temple recommend interview with an older sister who lamented that she had never married. She had some very good friends, however, who had been a great source of joy to her. Nonetheless, she recognized she could not be sealed to them. With some anguish she asked, "What will happen to those friendships?" Fortunately a scripture came to Tad's mind. They read together D&C 130:2: "And that same sociality [friendship] which exists among us here will exist among us there, only it will be coupled with eternal glory, which glory we do not now enjoy." She was overjoyed. "President," she said, "that is what I needed to know."

CONCLUSION

It seems that most needs can be addressed by principles taught in the scriptures and by the words of the living prophets. On multiple occasions the Lord has commanded, "Teach one another" (D&C 38:23; 88:77). Leaders have almost limitless opportunities to teach gospel principles. Sometimes it is easy for leaders to get trapped in the administrative mode, when in reality the most important aspect of their work is ministering and teaching. The Savior was and is our great exemplar, again and again, in this regard.

CHAPTER 3

Parents: The Prime Gospel Teachers of Their Children

THE RESPONSIBILITY OF PARENTS TO TEACH

It was the year 1833. The First Presidency of the Church had been reorganized, composed of Joseph Smith (the Prophet), Sidney Rigdon (First Counselor), and Frederick G. Williams (Second Counselor). One might wonder what new truths, what divine disclosures, what breathtaking insights would be revealed to this newly called First Presidency. Certainly, glorious truths were revealed, as recorded in the revelation today known as Doctrine and Covenants 93, but the climax of this revelation focused on the basics of the gospel—the family.

The Lord began by reprimanding Frederick G. Williams: "You have not taught your children light and truth." And then He added, "*Set in order your own house*" (D&C 93:42–43; emphasis added). The Lord then turned His instruction to Sidney Rigdon: "In some things he hath not kept the commandments concerning his children; therefore, *first set in order thy house*" (D&C 93:44; emphasis added). It was then Joseph's turn to be counseled. The Lord said: "Your family must needs repent and forsake some things, and give more earnest heed unto your sayings" (D&C 93:48). And finally the Lord addressed Bishop Newel K. Whitney and said that he "hath need to be chastened, and *set in order his family*" (D&C 93:50; emphasis added). The message was clear and consistent—as leaders of the Church, their first responsibility was to set in order their own homes. The message to these men likewise applies to each of us—we must first set in order our own homes. Parents play the pivotal role in accomplishing this aim.

The scriptures speak repeatedly of the role of parents—they are to be the prime gospel teachers of their children. In the Old Testament the Lord admonished parents: "Thou shalt teach [God's word] diligently unto thy children, and shalt talk of them when thou sittest in thine house, and when thou walkest by the way, and when thou liest down, and when thou risest up" (Deut. 6:7).[1] During Book of Mormon times, parents were instructed similarly: "Ye will teach them to walk in the ways of truth and soberness; ye will teach them to love one another, and to serve one another" (Mosiah 4:15).[2] That parental duty remains preeminent in our dispensation. The Lord has commanded parents to teach their children "the doctrine of repentance, faith in Christ the Son of the living God, and of baptism and the gift of the Holy Ghost. . . . And they shall also teach their children to pray, and to walk uprightly before the Lord" (D&C 68:25, 28).

In 1999, the First Presidency accentuated the parents' responsibility to be the prime gospel teachers of their children:

> We call upon parents to devote their best efforts to the teaching and rearing of their children in gospel principles which will keep them close to the Church. The home is the basis of a righteous life, and no other instrumentality can

take its place or fulfill its essential functions in carrying forward this God-given responsibility.

We counsel parents and children to give highest priority to family prayer, family home evening, gospel study and instruction, and wholesome family activities. However worthy and appropriate other demands or activities may be, they must not be permitted to displace the divinely-appointed duties that only parents and families can adequately perform.[3]

While all gospel teaching, whatever the location, is helpful, the Lord established the home as the prime forum for teaching His divine plan. Parents are entitled to discernment to know the needs of their children. They are in the best position to know the weaknesses and strengths of each child, and they possess the power to maximize agency or impose restraints as needed. As part of teaching in the Lord's way, parents have the responsibility to lovingly correct their children when they go astray. Speaking of this parental duty, King Benjamin taught, "Neither will ye suffer that they transgress the laws of God" (Mosiah 4:14).

It is parents who control the atmosphere in which the gospel is taught—evidenced by the pictures on the wall, the music that is played, the television shows and other media that are viewed, the conversations that are spoken, the scriptural discussions that are held, the family prayers that are offered, the books that are read, and the service that is rendered.

If parents do not become the prime gospel teachers of their children, then their children will most likely experience a famine in the home, "not a famine of bread, nor a thirst for water, but of hearing the words of the Lord" (Amos 8:11).

Parents: The Prime Gospel Teachers of Their Children

THE PROFOUND INFLUENCE OF PARENTS

Parents can have a profound influence on their children. Ben Carson's mother, a single parent, was Ben's prime teacher, and what a difference she made. Ben said of himself, "I was the worst student in my whole fifth-grade class." One day Ben took a math test with thirty problems. The student behind him corrected it and handed it back. The teacher, Mrs. Williamson, started calling each student's name for his or her score. Finally, she got to Ben. Out of embarrassment, he mumbled his score. Mrs. Williamson, thinking he had said "nine," replied that for Ben to score nine out of thirty was a wonderful improvement. The student behind Ben then yelled out, "Not nine! . . . He got none . . . right." Ben said he wanted to drop through the floor.[4]

At the same time, Ben's mother, Sonya, faced obstacles of her own. She was one of twenty-four children, had only a third-grade education, and could not read. She had married at age thirteen, was divorced, had two sons, and was raising them in the ghettos of Detroit. Nonetheless, she was fiercely self-reliant and had a firm belief that God would help her and her sons if they did their part.

One day a turning point came in her life and in the lives of her sons. It dawned on her that successful people for whom she cleaned homes had libraries—they read. After work, she went home and turned off the television that Ben and his brother were watching. She said in essence: "You boys are watching too much television. From now on you can watch three programs a week. In your free time, you will go to the library—read two books a week, and give me a report."

The boys were shocked. Ben said he had never read a book in his entire life except when required to do so at school. They protested, they complained, they argued, but it was to no avail. Then Ben reflected, "She laid down the law. I didn't like the rule, but her determination to see us improve changed the course of my life."

And what a change it made. By the seventh grade he was at the top of his class. He went on to attend Yale University on a scholarship, then University of Michigan Medical School. Afterward, at age thirty-three he became chief of pediatric neurosurgery at Johns Hopkins School of Medicine and a world-renowned surgeon. Later he became a presidential candidate. How was all this possible? Largely because of a mother who, without many of the advantages of life, magnified her calling as a parent.[5]

As parents, we are to be the prime gospel teachers and examples for our children—not the bishop or the Sunday School, Young Women, or Young Men teachers or leaders, but the parents. As their prime gospel teachers, we can teach them the power and reality of the Savior's Atonement and of their divine identity and destiny. In so doing, we will give them a rock foundation upon which to build.

The home is the ideal forum for teaching the gospel of Jesus Christ. This fact was greatly impressed upon us while on assignment in Beirut, Lebanon. While there, we learned about a twelve-year-old girl, Sarah. Her parents and two older siblings had converted to the Church in Romania but were then required to return to their homeland when Sarah was just seven years of age. In their homeland there was no Church presence, no organized units, no Sunday School or Young Women program. After five years, this family learned of a branch in Beirut and, just before we arrived, sent Sarah, accompanied by older siblings, to be baptized. While there, we gave a devotional on the plan of salvation. On more than one occasion, Sarah raised her hand to answer the questions we asked.

After the meeting, and knowing of her almost nonexistent exposure to the Church, we approached her and asked, "Sarah, how did you know the answers to those questions?" She immediately replied, "My mother taught me." Her family did not have the Church in their community, but they did have the gospel in their home. Her mother was her prime gospel teacher.

Helaman paid a great tribute to the mothers of the two thousand stripling warriors: "*They had been taught by their mothers*, that if they did not doubt, God would deliver them. And they rehearsed unto me the words of their mothers, saying: We do not doubt our mothers knew it" (Alma 56:47–48; emphasis added). What a powerful witness those mothers must have borne to their sons! And what finer tribute could a child pay to a parent than Enoch did of his father: "My father taught me in all the ways of God" (Moses 6:41).

It was Enos who said, "The words which I had *often* heard my father speak concerning eternal life, and the joy of the saints, sunk deep into my heart" (Enos 1:3; emphasis added). Alma the Younger had a similar experience. In the moment of his extremity, "racked with torment," he "remembered also to have heard [his] father prophesy unto the people concerning the coming of one Jesus Christ, a Son of God, to atone for the sins of the world." As his "mind caught hold upon this thought," he pled for the mercy of Jesus Christ, and then the miracle came (Alma 36:17–18). What if in these moments of readiness, even desperation, there were no words of eternal life taught by their fathers and mothers to draw upon, no reservoir of doctrine to drink from because there had been no home evenings, no scripture discussions, no preaching in the home? Fortunately, however, their fathers and mothers were their prime gospel teachers, and when their hearts were receptive, the power of the doctrine bore deep into their souls.

The family proclamation explains why it is so important for parents to teach the gospel in the home: "Happiness in family life is most likely to be achieved when founded upon the teachings of the Lord Jesus Christ."[6] What an example Alma is to all parents in this regard. The scriptures record, "He caused that his sons should be gathered together, that he might give unto them every one his charge, separately, concerning the things pertaining unto righteousness" (Alma 35:16). In personal, intimate, one-on-one encounters, he counseled his children and bore his irrefutable testimony to them. No doubt this inspired teaching became the bedrock upon which their testimonies grew and their lives of service were built. Helaman was of like mind as he taught his sons "many things" (Hel. 5:13).

Tad remembers his father stretched out by the fireplace, reading the scriptures and other good books, and then Tad would stretch out by his side. He remembers the cards his father would keep in his shirt pocket with quotes of the scriptures and Shakespeare that he was memorizing and new words that he was learning. Tad recalls wanting to do the same thing. He remembers the gospel questions and discussions at the dinner table, the many times his father played catch with him before dinner, and all the ball games he came to—from Little League baseball through high school basketball. It seemed like his father was always there, rooting and cheering his son on. Tad never wanted to do anything to hurt or embarrass his father. He remembers the many, many times his father took him to visit widows—how they would stop by to pick up ice cream for one or a chicken dinner for another and his father's final handshake with some money enclosed. Tad remembers the good feelings he had and the desire to be just like his father.

Tad also remembers his mother, at age ninety or so, cooking in her condominium kitchen and then exiting with a tray of food. When asked where she was going, she replied, "Oh, I am taking some food to the elderly." Tad thought to himself, "Mother, you are the elderly." In truth, she must have cooked hundreds of meals for the needy.

Kathy's father unexpectedly passed away from a heart attack

when she was in high school. At the time he was the principal of an elementary school. He had previously converted to the Church while in the military and was a big, strong man with a gentle and loving disposition. Like the Savior, he went about doing good—doing small but continual acts of service and kindness. He loved his wife immensely and treated her like a queen. He had a wonderful sense of humor. He loved children, and they knew it. Kathy knew he was a man of God. He taught her the gospel and set an example for her that she wanted to follow.

Kathy remembers her mother, a widow at age forty-five, teaching school full-time and managing and cleaning apartments so she would have the financial means to raise four children at home. During these difficult times, with the utmost kindness and patience, her mother taught Kathy and her siblings the value of hard work. At the same time, Kathy's mother served in many Church callings, including ward Relief Society president. With the early and unexpected death of her beloved husband, the faith of Kathy's mother never waivered. She was a rock upon which Kathy could build her own testimony of faith.

We can never express enough gratitude for our parents, who were our prime gospel teachers and examples.

WHAT IS THE QUALITY OF TIME WE SPEND WITH OUR CHILDREN?

While the quantity of time spent with children is certainly important, it is no substitute for the quality of such time. President Harold B. Lee tells of a meeting with President Russell M. Nelson and his wife Dantzel at a time when President Nelson was a sought-after heart surgeon. He asked Sister Nelson how her husband could have time for home and family with such demands placed upon him. She replied, "When he's home, he's home!"[7] If there were ever a time for fathers and mothers to come back home and fulfill their prime responsibility as examples and teachers to their children, it is now.

TEACHERS AT CHURCH CAN HELP

Teachers at church can help parents in their divine role of teaching their children. These teachers can instruct with the understanding that they are encouraging and providing materials for parents to teach at home. Alma taught this principle to his son Corianton: "Now, my son, this was the ministry unto which ye were called, to declare these glad tidings unto this people, to prepare their minds . . . *that they may prepare the minds of their children*" (Alma 39:16; emphasis added).

CONCLUSION

We do not know in the life to come if titles such as "bishop" or "Relief Society president" will survive, but we do know that the titles of "husband" and "wife," "father" and "mother," will continue and be revered throughout eternity. That is one reason it is so important to honor our responsibilities as parents here on earth, so we can prepare for those even greater but similar responsibilities in the life to come. We might all ask ourselves: Do our children and grandchildren receive our best spiritual, intellectual, and creative efforts, or do they receive our leftover time and talents, after we have given our all to our Church callings, hobbies, or professional pursuits?

We were touched as we read about the life of one great man who had served as director of the CIA, US ambassador to the United Nations, and vice president and then president of the United States. In reflecting on his illustrious life, he said, "The three most rewarding titles bestowed upon me are the three that I've got left—a husband, a father, and a granddad."[8]

Parents: The Prime Gospel Teachers of Their Children

As parents, we can proceed with the assurance that God will never abandon us. God never gives us a responsibility without offering divine aid—of that we can testify. In our divine role as parents, and in partnership with God, we can, and should, become the prime gospel teachers of our children. We should teach and "exhort them . . . with all the feeling of a tender parent" (1 Ne. 8:37).

CHAPTER 4

Everyone Can Teach

THE MASTER SCULPTOR

Have you ever wondered, *Can I teach? Do I have anything of worth to say? Can I be an instrument in God's hands to help change lives?* The answer is a resounding *yes*! Peter may have thought he was nothing more than a simple fisherman; or Matthew, a despised tax collector; or Paul, a tentmaker. Yet with the help of Jesus, each became a powerful leader and teacher in His Church.

This ability of the Lord to mold and shape us is not unlike the experience Michelangelo had sculpting one of his statues: He sought the finest marble block available. From this he would eventually shape and mold what is considered by many the finest work ever fashioned by the hand of man—*The David*. No doubt he looked for a piece that was flawless, but it was not to be found. Instead, in the course of his search, he found a two-thousand-pound column, seventeen feet in length. It was the right height and width, but there was a problem. It was severely flawed. Two sculptors, Agostino di

Duccio and Antonio Rossellino, had both tried their artistic touch on this marble column but to no avail. There were just too many imperfections. Finally, they each gave up. Michelangelo saw these same imperfections, but he also saw beyond them. He saw a living, breathing, majestic form of David that would cause onlookers to gasp in awe at first sight.

Likewise, God sees in us our imperfections, but He also has the vision to see beyond them. He has the ability to work within them and eventually to help us overcome them. He can see in our flawed body of flesh and blood a spirit that can be shaped and sculpted into a divine-like image. With that vision and divine insight, the Lord knew what was in Peter. He knew what was in Matthew and Paul, and He knows what is in each of us.[1] If we will be humble and trusting, He can fashion us into "a teacher come from God" (John 3:2).

President James E. Faust spoke to this point: "The Lord has a great work for each of us to do. You may wonder how this can be. You may feel that there is nothing special or superior about you or your ability. . . . The Lord can do remarkable miracles with a person of ordinary ability who is humble, faithful, and diligent in serving the Lord and seeks to improve himself. This is because God is the ultimate source of power."[2]

Even great men and women have felt inadequate when the Lord's callings have come. Moses felt weighed down by a glaring weakness in his life. He was called as a prophet but nonetheless agonized, "O my Lord, I am not eloquent . . . : but I am slow of speech, and of a slow tongue" (Ex. 4:10). Enoch felt similarly: "Why is it that I have found favor in thy sight, and am but a lad, and all the people hate me; for I am slow of speech; wherefore am I thy servant?" (Moses 6:31). Nephi was no different: "O wretched man that I am! . . . My soul grieveth because of mine iniquities" (2 Ne. 4:17).

And Moroni lamented his weakness in writing, but as he did so, he was given these comforting words by the Lord: "I give unto men weakness that they may be humble; . . . for if they humble themselves before me, and have faith in me, then will I make weak things become strong unto them" (Ether 12:27). What a comforting and encouraging promise. Our weaknesses can become strengths with the Lord's help. He can chip away and polish and refine us until we become master teachers.

THE LORD QUALIFIES US

On one occasion Elder L. Tom Perry asked President Boyd K. Packer: "What counsel would you give recent converts prior to their first calling as a teacher?" President Packer responded, "I would tell them they can do it. Everybody can teach." He then added, "I would counsel them to pray for the gift of teaching. . . . I found out from the scriptures that you have to ask for it—ask and ye shall receive—so I would tell them to keep asking and seeking, 'and ye shall find' (see Matt. 7:7; 3 Ne. 27:29) and that the gift has to be earned, but it can come."[3]

Whether or not we want to be a teacher, there is no escaping its grasp—leaders are teachers, parents are teachers, counselors are teachers, and formal teachers are, of course, teachers. Our conversations, our expressions, and our actions are but various forms of teaching—even our silence can teach.

To those who say, "I know so little about the Church" or "I'm a new convert" or "I'm too shy" or "I've never taught before," Elder Neal A. Maxwell has given an appropriate response: "God does not begin by asking us about our ability, but only about our availability, and if we then prove our dependability, he will increase our capability!"[4] That promise from a prophet of God should erase all excuses we might otherwise put forth. With God's call and our acceptance, we are entitled to His inspiration. With His call, we can succeed. Following are some of the God-given resources we have to help us magnify our calling.

WE HAVE THE ASSISTANCE OF THE HOLY GHOST

After baptism we are given "the unspeakable gift of the Holy Ghost" (D&C 121:26). It is this gift that will "give unto you knowledge" (D&C 121:26), that will "teach you all things, and bring all things to your remembrance" (John 14:26), and that "will guide you into all truth" (John 16:13). This gift will whisper the truth to "you in your mind and in your heart" (D&C 8:2–3). If we desire and live worthily, the Holy Ghost will be our companion—in essence, our team teacher. He can stimulate our creativity and help us make connections between doctrine and real-life experiences. He can assist us in acquiring Christlike teaching techniques and attributes so we can magnify our callings. The Lord can fill us with His Spirit so we can teach with power and authority from God.

WE HAVE THE RIGHT TO RECEIVE REVELATION

Years ago Tad was released as the stake president in the Glendale, California, stake. Elder John H. Groberg was the assigned General Authority and invited Tad to join in setting apart the new stake president. Hands were laid on the new stake president's head, and then Elder Groberg said something unforgettable: "There are many revelations waiting for you." Somewhat surprised, Tad thought, "Did I leave some revelations on the table?" Then a more comforting thought came: "The genius of this church is that everyone is entitled to revelation in connection with his or her calling. God never gives us an assignment without making available

AN OVERVIEW OF TEACHING

His will and mind on the matter." In other words, for every teacher there are many revelations waiting. That is part of the divine deal. Brigham Young once said: "There is no doubt, if a person lives according to the revelations given to God's people he may have the Spirit of the Lord to signify to him His will, and to guide him and to direct him in the discharge of his duties, in his temporal as well as spiritual exercises. *I am satisfied, however, that in this respect, we live far beneath our privileges.*"[5]

As called and set-apart teachers, we are entitled to revelation to help us in this divine work. If we do not seek revelation often, then as Brigham Young counseled, "we [will] live far beneath our privileges." On the other hand, if we inquire, the Lord will fulfill His promise: "If thou shalt ask, thou shalt receive revelation upon revelation, knowledge upon knowledge" (D&C 42:61). What a magnificent promise!

In addition, the Lord gave this comforting reminder to Oliver Cowdery: "As often as thou hast inquired thou hast received instruction of my Spirit" (D&C 6:14).[6] We too can receive frequent instruction from the Lord. In that spirit, President Russell M. Nelson counseled, "My dear brothers and sisters, I plead with you to increase your spiritual capacity to receive revelation."[7] Why such an injunction? Because he knew revelation was a reality within our grasp.

WE HAVE THE SCRIPTURES

Nephi taught us to "feast upon the words of Christ; for behold, the words of Christ will tell you all things what ye should do" (2 Ne. 32:3). Perhaps you have wondered, as we have, how the scriptures can tell us all things we should do. Can they tell us the name of the person we should marry? Or the career we should pursue? Or where we should live? In addition, we might ask, "Can the scriptures teach us what we should know and do as a teacher?" The answer to the foregoing questions is yes. But how is that possible? Because the scriptures teach us the correct principles of life, including the correct principles of teaching, and invite the Spirit so we can apply those principles in ways that address any problems we may have, including our teaching concerns. Again and again in the scriptures, we find those doctrinal principles, stories, sermons, conversations, and questions that will help us to know how to teach and what to teach.

WE HAVE THE CAPACITY TO DRAW UPON OUR OWN EXPERIENCES AND THOSE OF OTHERS

Nephi explained that he "did liken all scriptures unto us, that it might be for our profit and learning" (1 Ne. 19:23). Just like the Savior, Nephi drew upon his own experiences as well as the experiences of others to help those he taught have a better understanding of the gospel. In like manner, Elder Dieter F. Uchtdorf has taught many spiritual truths that relate to his aviation experiences. President Russell M. Nelson has reflected upon his career as a heart surgeon in order to teach doctrinal insights. Others draw on their experiences with careers, hobbies, sports, or cultural arts or as a spouse, parent, or single adult. Everyone has meaningful experiences to share, even those from the seemingly common and routine events of life, if they will look for them. Our lives and the lives of our class members constitute a mighty reservoir of spiritual experiences and insights from which to draw.

WE ALL HAVE A GIFT OF THE SPIRIT AND CAN ACQUIRE MORE GIFTS

We all have one or more gifts from God: "to every man is given a gift by the Spirit of God" (D&C 46:11). One may have the gift of love; another, the gift of patience or wisdom or sociality. We can draw upon our particular gift to assist us in teaching while also seeking other gifts of the Spirit, particularly the gift to "teach the word of wisdom" and "the word of knowledge" (Moro. 10:9–10). The Lord is so anxious that we seek additional gifts that will refine us and help us magnify our callings as teachers and in other capacities that He has invited us, even commanded us, to "covet earnestly the best gifts" (1 Cor. 12:31), to "seek . . . earnestly the best gifts" (D&C 46:8), and to "lay hold upon every good gift" (Moro. 10:30). Hugh Nibley made this salient observation about those who do not receive the gifts of the Spirit: "How often do we ask for them [the gifts of the Spirit]? How earnestly do we seek them? We could have them if we did ask, but we don't. Well, who denies them? Anyone who doesn't ask for them."[8] Accordingly, the gift of teaching may be ours if we ask for it and work for it.

WE HAVE THE POWER OF OUR TESTIMONY

Nephi testified boldly to a group of disbelievers, "For it were not possible that they could disbelieve his words, for so great was his faith on the Lord Jesus Christ" (3 Ne. 7:18). What a profound statement—his testimony was so powerful that even his detractors could not challenge or discredit it. Likewise, our testimonies are powerful witnesses of the spiritual impressions we have received concerning the divinity of Jesus Christ, the reality of the Restoration, the truthfulness of the Book of Mormon, and other gospel principles. No mortal argument, no critic, and no apostate can successfully rival a testimony borne of the Spirit. Why is that? Because the Holy Ghost leaves an indelible impression upon our souls that is undeniable. When all is said and done, our testimonies of the Savior and His doctrine may be the most powerful teaching tools we have to break down defenses, penetrate hearts, and consequently deepen conversion.

CONCLUSION

We all have the capacity and necessary resources to become "a teacher come from God" (John 3:2), an instrument in His hands. If there remains any doubt, the Lord gave this glorious promise to each of us: "Fear thou not; for I am with thee: be not dismayed; for I am thy God: I will strengthen thee; yea, I will help thee; yea, I will uphold thee with the right hand of my righteousness" (Isa. 41:10). Such are the definitive promises for all those teachers who will turn themselves over to God and trust in Him.

TEACH BY THE SPIRIT

CHAPTER 5

Prepare and Teach by the Spirit

THE POWER OF THE SPIRIT

The Lord has spoken in no uncertain terms about our responsibility to teach by the Spirit: "and if ye receive not the Spirit ye shall not teach" (D&C 42:14).[1] Amulek understood this principle. On one occasion Zeezrom asked Amulek, "Will ye answer me a few questions?" Amulek replied: "Yea, if it be according to the Spirit of the Lord, which is in me; for I shall say nothing which is contrary to the Spirit of the Lord" (Alma 11:21–22). Perhaps those who teach without the Spirit are, as Peter described, "wells without water" (2 Pet. 2:17). Brigham Young was so concerned about the role of the Spirit in our teaching that he cautioned Karl G. Maeser, the president of Brigham Young Academy: "I want you to remember that you ought not to teach even the alphabet or the multiplication tables without the Spirit of God."[2]

As talented as one might be as a teacher, no other talent can compensate for lack of the Spirit because it is the Spirit that builds faith; it is the Spirit that softens hearts; it is the Spirit that enlightens minds; and it is the Spirit that brings about conversion. No doubt that is why the Lord said, "Teach the children of men the things which I have put into your hands by the power of my Spirit; and ye are to be taught from on high" (D&C 43:15–16).[3] And if we do preach by the Spirit, the Lord has promised that we will declare *"[His] word like unto angels of God"* (D&C 42:6; emphasis added). What a remarkable promise—we can teach like angels of God when we teach by the Spirit.

President Joseph Fielding Smith addressed the converting power of the Spirit: "The Spirit of God speaking to the spirit of man has power to impart truth with greater effect and understanding than the truth can be imparted by personal contact even with heavenly beings. Through the Holy Ghost the truth is woven into the very fiber and sinews of the body so that it cannot be forgotten."[4] So powerful is the Spirit that Luke records of Stephen's critics, "They were not able to resist the wisdom and the spirit by which he spake" (Acts 6:10). In like manner, Nephi and his brother Lehi spoke with such "great power . . . that they did confound many . . . dissenters" (Hel. 5:17).

WE PREPARE BY THE SPIRIT SO WE CAN TEACH BY THE SPIRIT

It is difficult, if not impossible, to teach by the Spirit if one has not first prepared by the Spirit. Thus, the goal of every teacher is to prepare by the Spirit so that he or she might teach by the Spirit. When all is said and done, the Spirit is the teacher's best friend. In fact, if we fail to teach by the Spirit, then nothing else we do really matters.

The gift of teaching by the Spirit, however, does not come easily or lightly. One does not casually request its endowment. Receiving this blessing requires study and meditation and constant prayer on our part. It does not lend itself to last-minute preparation. It does not come if our goal is to entertain rather than to inspire. It remains aloof and distant if we do not humble ourselves and acknowledge the absolute need of the Lord to guide us in our efforts. None of us is smart enough or competent enough or able enough to effectively teach the gospel without diligent preparation and total dependence on the Lord. He is our ultimate and only source of power and inspiration.

The Lord makes a significant promise to the teachers of His gospel. He promises, *"My grace shall attend you*, that you may be instructed more perfectly in theory, in principle, in doctrine, in the law of the gospel, in all things that pertain unto the kingdom of God, that are expedient for you to understand." Yet, as one might expect, there is a condition. Before that promise becomes operative in our homes and classrooms, the Lord gave this precondition: "Teach ye *diligently*" (D&C 88:78; emphasis added). In other words, we must *diligently* strive to live saintly lives, *diligently* pray for God's help, *diligently* prepare and organize our lessons, and *diligently* deliver them with all the humility and spirit we can muster. And if we do so, then the promised blessings of God's grace are ours.

It is relatively easy to display a picture, read a lesson, tell a story, or show a video. Yet, in and of themselves, these can be mechanical acts that make no lasting difference. The difficult part—the part with the real reward—is wrestling and struggling for the Spirit so testimonies can be built in the lives of those we teach. The great question thus becomes: How do we prepare ourselves to teach with the Spirit? The simple answer is that we must do those things that invite the Spirit.

First, Strive to Live a More Christlike Life

Perhaps the first question we should ask as teachers is not "What should I teach?" or "How should I teach?" but rather "What can I do to become more like the Savior?" Then the rest will naturally follow.

TEACH BY THE SPIRIT

When the Savior taught the Sermon on the Mount, He delivered the greatest sermon of all time. When He concluded, no doubt, a hush or silence settled on the crowd. Perhaps no one moved—perhaps even nature itself was momentarily stilled. There was something different in His voice, in His inflection, and more importantly, in the feelings that were transmitted directly to the hearts of His followers. The scriptures read, "The people were astonished at his doctrine: for he taught them as one having authority, and not as the scribes" (Matt. 7:28–29). It was as though a spiritual missile had struck them in the very center of their souls. Nephi spoke of this power: "when a man speaketh by the power of the Holy Ghost the power of the Holy Ghost carrieth it unto the hearts of the children of men" (2 Ne. 33:1).

The Savior is the Master Teacher because He is the Master Exemplar—His life was in perfect accord with His words. There was no gap between the two; His life matched His message. Our best preparation to receive the Spirit comes when we are striving to live in harmony with the Savior's teachings. In essence, the best way to *teach* more like the Savior is to *live* more like the Savior. No doubt that is why Alma said, "Trust no one to be your teacher nor your minister, except he be a man of God, walking in his ways and keeping his commandments" (Mosiah 23:14). President Gordon B. Hinckley echoed this thought: "The most persuasive gospel tract is the exemplary life of a faithful Latter-day Saint."[5]

In the novel *Don Quixote* there are some wonderfully incisive lines that read, "He teaches well that lives well. That is all the divinity I understand."[6] This seems consistent with an old saying: "What you are speaks so loudly I cannot hear what you say." Teachers must live what they teach. Their example is their most persuasive force—their most potent "weapon." With every advance we make towards a more godly life, however small it may be, comes increased power to lift those we teach to higher ground. Arthur Guiterman wrote a poem entitled "Education." The following lines are self-explanatory:

> *No printed page nor spoken plea*
> *May teach young hearts what man should be—*
> *Not all the books on all the shelves,*
> *But what the teachers are themselves.*[7]

Elder Neal A. Maxwell observed: "Each of you realizes . . . that you teach what you are. . . . Your traits will be more remembered, compositely, than a particular truth in a particular lesson."[8] President Gordon B. Hinckley noted: "Your students desire more than your knowledge. They deserve and hunger for your inspiration. . . . This has always been the hallmark of a great teacher."[9] And that inspiration springs from a Christlike life.

Second, Pray with Frequency and Fervor

The Savior set the example. When He needed spirituality and guidance, He sought His Father in prayer. The scriptures record that "he went up into a mountain apart to pray" (Matt. 14:23).[10] Luke describes that He knelt in the Garden of Gethsemane (see Luke 22:41)[11] and "prayed more earnestly" (Luke 22:44). Even the resurrected, glorified Christ demonstrated the need for prayer when He knelt with the Nephites and "prayed unto the Father" (3 Ne. 17:15).

The sons of Mosiah "fasted much and prayed much that the Lord would grant unto them a portion of his Spirit" (Alma 17:9). And, oh, how He responded to those pleadings. The Lord has made remarkable promises to those who sincerely and regularly pray: "Pray always, and I will pour out my Spirit upon you" (D&C 19:38).[12] What a magnificent promise, to know that if we pray frequently and fervently, the Spirit will be our constant companion as we prepare and teach.

Third, Read and Ponder the Scriptures before Other Resources

In the Doctrine and Covenants we read: "Seek not to declare my word, but first seek to obtain my word, and then shall your tongue be loosed; then, if you desire, you shall have my Spirit and my word, yea, the power of God unto the convincing of men" (D&C 11:21). Perhaps one way "to obtain [His] word" is to read the assigned scripture block *before* reading the lesson material or other resources and to write down any impressions we have, including doctrinal insights, questions we might ask, and invitations we might extend. By exercising such spiritual self-reliance, we maximize our ability to receive guidance from the Spirit. In essence we eliminate or mitigate the possibility of developing preconceived notions from the lesson materials that may hamper our ability to receive revelation.

We have found that when we have a question about the scripture passages we are reading, there is often the temptation to immediately go to commentaries for the answer. But if we refrain from doing so initially and instead wrestle with the issue, usually some personal inspiration will come. Sometimes the answer we find is the same as the one in the commentaries, but now the answer is ours, not theirs. Other times we have gained an insight that was customized for us and is different than what is presented in other resources. If we had first gone to commentaries, however, we might have lost that insight. Similarly, if we first go to the lesson material or other resources before personally studying and pondering the scriptures, we may lose some personal revelation designed especially for us.

President Marion G. Romney, not in an effort to deprecate commentaries but to put them in perspective, made this candid observation: "When I drink from a spring I like to get the water where it comes out of the ground, not down the stream after the cattle have waded in it. . . . I appreciate other people's interpretation, but when it comes to the gospel we ought to be acquainted with what the Lord says."[13] Certainly the lesson material is worthwhile and inspired, but it does not take precedence over personal revelation or the scriptures, which the Lord has said "shall be given, even as they are in mine own bosom" (D&C 35:20). After we have sought our own individual revelation, then we should review the lesson material to further refine and perfect our lesson plan. In other words, the lesson materials are not a replacement for the scriptures and our individual revelation, but a wonderful supplement to them.

If the scriptures and the words of the living prophets become our daily diet and the prime sources for our teaching, and if we look to them first for guidance, then we will receive the revelation that can help us customize our lessons to best meet the needs of those we teach. Alma and the sons of Mosiah were able to teach "with power and authority" because they fasted and prayed and "searched the scriptures diligently" (Alma 17:2–3). As we prepare like they prepared, we can teach as they did, with power and authority from God.

Fourth, Ponder the Lesson Well in Advance

Preparing spiritually is not just setting aside a fixed block of time—for example from 1:00 to 3:00 p.m. on a Saturday afternoon. Rather, it is constant pondering and reflecting—while traveling to work, in idle moments at home, while talking with family and friends. Imagine a family sitting at the dinner table and the mother says, "Next Sunday I am giving a lesson to the Relief Society sisters on faith, but I need some help. What ideas can you give me?" Her ten-year-old son may say, "When I am nice to others, it makes me feel good and closer to God, and when that happens, my faith increases." Or her teenage daughter may say, "In our Young Women class we had a lesson on gratitude, and since then I've found that when I think about the many ways the Lord has blessed me, it increases my faith in Him and love for Him." And then her teenage son may say, "Mom, will you pass the potatoes?" Even with the sudden jolt back to reality, some seeds of a lesson have been planted.

No doubt the Lord is pleased when we demonstrate sufficient humility to seek input from others concerning our lessons. Inspiration often comes from those conversations. We have seen this work in our own family as we seek input from each other and from our children and as they in turn seek input from us.

In seeking inspiration for our lessons, we must realize that revelation cannot be compressed into a predesignated block of time. It does not work that way. Revelation usually comes line upon line, precept upon precept, or as Elder David A. Bednar explained, like "the light from the rising sun . . . gradually and steadily" until "the darkness of night [is] replaced by the radiance of morning."[14] Furthermore, revelation comes at such times as the Lord desires, some of which are inconvenient and some of which are not on Saturday afternoon. Therefore, we need to be pondering our lesson well in advance so we can be prepared to receive revelation when the Lord desires to so bless us. In this regard, the Lord taught: "Treasure these things [the doctrine] up in your hearts, and let the solemnities of eternity rest upon your minds" (D&C 43:34).

The Lord is a good compensator of time. He can work within our time constraints. He knows that some are working two jobs, some are working long hours at one job, and single parents are exhausted after working and trying to raise a family. If we do all we can do, if we use our time wisely, if we strive to study our lessons well in advance, then the needed inspiration will come, sometimes in bulk, most often in increments—but it will come.

Tad learned this lesson on multiple occasions when he was assigned to reorganize stake presidencies. Usually the new stake president had ten to twenty minutes to select his counselors, but the time limitation never seemed to restrain revelation. Why? Because the

Lord knew that was all the time the new stake president had. On the other hand, when a bishop is called, the stake president may invite him to take a day or two to reflect and fast over his counselors, even attend the temple, and the Lord may expect him to do so because he has the available time. But in both cases, the necessary revelation comes. The Lord knows our time constraints and can work within them, provided, of course, that our time constraints are not caused by our own procrastination or lack of diligence.

Fifth, Record and Organize Spiritual Impressions

Before we left to supervise the Canada Toronto Mission, Elder Richard G. Scott invited us, as he had done many others, to take the time to record every spiritual impression we received. He taught: "Knowledge carefully recorded is knowledge available in time of need. . . . [That] practice enhances the likelihood of your receiving further light."[15]

One night Tad kept getting out of bed. Finally Kathy asked: "Why do you keep popping in and out of bed?" Tad replied, "Because I had several impressions and felt the need to write them down." On occasions prior to our mission, we had had impressions while in bed and simply thought, "We will write them down in the morning when it is more convenient." But you know what happens when you do that—you often forget the exact impression or the power of the message is lost.[16]

The Lord taught this principle to Joseph Smith and Sidney Rigdon as they were receiving the marvelous vision on the three kingdoms of glory. They were thrice commanded to write "while [they] were yet in the Spirit" (D&C 76:28, 80, 113). After Alma received revelation, the scriptures record, "When Alma had heard these words he wrote them down that he might have them" (Mosiah 26:33).

As we contemplate our lessons, we ought to record the spiritual impressions that do come—however small they may be and however inconvenient the time. We do this for at least four reasons: (1) it allows us to preserve the knowledge exactly as given; (2) it allows us to preserve the spiritual feelings of the moment; (3) like small acorns, those thoughts may grow into spiritual oak trees as we nurture and ponder them; and (4) if we show the Lord we truly treasure and savor His word, we are likely to receive many more revelations.

Suppose for a moment a mother is speaking to her teenage son and at one point he says, "Mom, this is really good counsel." He then takes out a notebook and starts to record the insights and impressions he received from their conversation. Once the mother has recovered from the shock, would she not want to give him more counsel in the future? So it must be with our Father in Heaven. In a sense we are all spiritual teenagers, and the question becomes "What do we do when God gives us counsel via a divine impression?" Do we roll our eyes or turn up the music or go back to sleep? Or do we welcome it and embrace it and immediately record this treasured jewel? President Russell M. Nelson has shared that he has a pad of paper by his bed so he can record the impressions that come to him in the night.

We often wondered how Nephi and his brother Lehi could receive "many revelations daily" (Hel. 11:23).[17] This seemed impossible to us, but we no longer feel that way. As we record and reverence and savor each spiritual impression given, we too can receive multiple spiritual promptings, sometimes even daily.

We have personally found it helpful to create files with titles such as *faith, baptism, love, families,* and the *Savior's Atonement*. As we receive impressions, recognize inspired thoughts at church or while reading the scriptures or other books, or discover a good idea from a newspaper article, we record the impression or copy the source. This may be done either physically or electronically. These files have been an immense resource and help to us in writing books, giving talks, teaching lessons, and preparing for family scriptural discussions and for our general edification. We should preserve and treasure a constant flow of ideas and revelation.

The Holy Ghost can "bring all things to [our] remembrance" (John 14:26), but first we must have stored these things in our minds and hearts so there is a reservoir from which to draw. An organized system of files, electronic or otherwise, can help us accomplish that objective and, in addition, recall at the needed times the spiritual impressions we have previously received. In this spirit King Benjamin expressed gratitude for the plates of brass, noting that "it were not possible that our father, Lehi, could have remembered all these things [the commandments] . . . except it were for the help of these plates" (Mosiah 1:4).

Sixth, Prepare a Written Plan

There is something about putting our thoughts in a written teaching plan that helps us crystallize and articulate them in a logical sequence. Then we are able to teach the gospel truths in a more concise and coherent manner. Otherwise, the chances that we will deliver a rambling, circuitous presentation are greatly heightened.

To seek inspiration without diligent preparation is a form of spiritual mockery; it is like trying to reap without sowing. President Nelson taught, "Good inspiration is based upon good information."[18] President Harold B. Lee taught similarly, "If you want to get revelation, do your homework."[19] As part of our homework, it is helpful to create a written plan that has built-in flexibility to accommodate classroom discussion and promptings of the Spirit. We owe it to the Lord, to our students, and to ourselves to prepare such a plan. More on this is discussed in the next chapter.

Seventh, Be Humble

The Lord said, "Be thou humble; and the Lord thy God shall lead thee by the hand, and give thee answer to thy prayers" (D&C 112:10). All teachers striving to be Christlike are teachable; they are prime examples of that foremost attribute they want their students to have. They have no misgivings about who the real teacher is—the Holy Ghost.

We have many excellent teachers at home and church, but no matter how many years of experience we have or how many degrees we hold or how well loved we are by those we teach, we can all improve and become more like the Master Teacher, provided we are humble. Perhaps the foundational quality of Christlike teachers is to be teachable. Such humility both invites the Spirit and whets our appetite to improve our teaching skills.

While we were serving as mission leaders one of our outstanding mission assistants came to Tad one day and said, "What can I do to be a better missionary?" Tad was taken aback and responded, "You are one of the best missionaries we have ever had—you are doing great." Not to be deterred, the young elder asked again, "What can I do to be a better missionary?" Recognizing the sincerity and intensity of his desire, Tad reflected on his request and a thought came to his mind, which he related. Sometime later this experience was shared with the rest of the mission. We had no idea the impact it would have. Subsequently, other missionaries came to their interviews and sincerely asked, "President, what can I do to be a better missionary?" The example of one teachable missionary greatly influenced an entire mission. Likewise, the example of one teachable teacher can have a powerful impact on an entire class, even fellow teachers.

Our Father in Heaven is anxious to help us as teachers, if we will be humble and give Him a chance. Sometimes we are so caught up with time pressures or our own wisdom or creative ideas that we forget or neglect to give the Lord a chance—to draw upon His Spirit and His ideas, which in the end will determine whether or not our lessons are successful.

CONCLUSION

No doubt every teacher wants to honor his or her calling, every teacher wants to speak by the Spirit, and every teacher wants to build faith and bring about conversion. There is no better way to do so than to live worthily and seek the Spirit daily. It is this Spirit that gives life and breath and substance to our lessons. For those who spiritually prepare, the Lord has promised, "The Holy Ghost shall teach you in the same hour what ye ought to say" (Luke 12:12).[20] If we have the Spirit, then it matters not whether we have a solitary student or a large class, for the Lord promises, "Where two or three are gathered together in my name, there am I in the midst of them" (Matt. 18:20).

Elder Jeffrey R. Holland observed: "Most people don't come to church looking merely for a few new gospel facts or to see old friends, though all of this is important. They come seeking a spiritual experience."[21] When we teach by the Spirit, we teach with power and thus make those spiritual experiences possible.

As teachers we can and should constantly plead for the Spirit, knowing that the real teacher is the Holy Ghost. We can say the words, we can preach the message, and we can lead the discussion, but only the Holy Ghost has the power to transport its impact into the minds and hearts of those we teach. It is only through His power that we can build faith in Jesus Christ, strengthen conversion, and provide spiritual experiences—the ultimate goals of every teacher.

CHAPTER 6

Create a Lesson Plan

The Lord has instructed us, "Organize yourselves; prepare every needful thing" (D&C 88:119). To assist in teaching by the Spirit, we need to do our homework and organize our thoughts by creating a lesson plan. Usually a lesson plan is most effective when it is recorded because writing "forces" us to be more precise—to articulate and crystalize our thoughts; it helps us to recognize and then eliminate the gaps in our reasoning, to shore up the soft spots, to determine a logical order to present doctrinal truths, to hone in on specific scriptures and resources that will support the doctrine being taught, and to prioritize.

The Savior addressed this issue in a parable: "Which of you, intending to build a tower, *sitteth not down first, and counteth the cost*, whether he have sufficient to finish it" (Luke 14:28; emphasis added). But how could anyone count the cost unless he or she first made plans for the tower: How high would it be? How large the diameter? How thick the walls? And what type of stone would be used? In

Create a Lesson Plan

a similar manner one needs to plan a lesson carefully, identifying what doctrinal principles will be taught, what supporting scriptures and words from living prophets will be used, what questions will be asked, and what resources (e.g., videos, analogies, stories, object lessons, etc.) will be selected to strengthen the doctrinal points. Teachers may not cover all the lesson plan in their classes because they should be flexible enough to yield to inspired classroom discussions and spiritual promptings that may lead the class in another direction, but they should always be ready with a full lesson plan.

Some people feel a lesson plan may be too prescriptive, and it could be, if the teacher allows it to take precedence over inspired classroom discussions and the Spirit. But such is not an excuse or a reason for failing to have a lesson plan. Why? Because it is possible to have the best of both worlds—to have an inspired plan and to make adjustments in class as the Spirit directs. In fact, the former promotes the latter. Spiritual preparation precedes spiritual teaching.

There is no one and only way to develop a lesson plan, but there are universal principles that are helpful. For example, suppose we were teaching 2 Nephi 2 on the Fall of Adam and Eve and the Savior's Atonement. Some of the universal principles to consider might be as follows:

DOCTRINAL PRINCIPLES

As we read the scripture block, we should first list the doctrinal truths and record the spiritual impressions we receive that will best meet the needs of our family or class members. Then, as we read the lesson material, we should refine and adjust our notes as necessary. For example, after our personal reading of the scriptures, we might feel impressed to emphasize that the Fall was a positive step forward, not backward as taught by much of Christianity. We might also want to emphasize that this is only possible because the

Savior's Atonement provided the means to overcome the negative consequences of the Fall.

SCRIPTURES AND WORDS OF THE LIVING PROPHETS

Once we have chosen the doctrinal truths to focus on, we might then select from the scriptural block any pertinent verses on the topic and appropriate scriptural cross-references. For example, 2 Ne. 2:22–26 teaches that if there had been no Atonement of the Savior, then Adam and Eve "would have remained in a state of innocence, having no joy, for they knew no misery; doing no good, for they knew no sin." In addition, we may reference Moroni 10:32–33, which helps us know that the Savior's Atonement redeemed us from the Fall, making it possible to not only return to God's presence but also become like Him: "Yea, come unto Christ, and be perfected in him . . . ; and if ye shall deny yourselves of all ungodliness, and love God with all your might, mind and strength, then is his grace [the enabling powers of Christ's Atonement] sufficient for you, that by his grace ye may be perfect in Christ." We could also use the Topical Guide or Guide to the Scriptures to find additional scriptures and research conference talks that give further insight and support to these doctrinal truths.

QUESTIONS

In developing our lesson plan, we should ponder and construct questions that will build faith and strengthen conversion. Some of these questions might help us better understand the doctrine being taught; others might be directed more toward behavior. Both types of questions are important. For example, we might ask, "Why can someone not progress in a state of innocence?" Or "How does the Savior's Atonement overcome the effects of the Fall?" These are doctrinally oriented questions. Other questions, of a more behavioral nature, might be "Why is the Fall, coupled with the Atonement, such a great blessing in my personal life?" Or "How can I best express my appreciation to the Savior for His Atonement?" In addition to your own questions, the Church's lesson materials give suggested thoughts (see chapter 18 for more on asking inspired questions).

OTHER RESOURCES

There are many resources that can support the doctrinal truths we teach. For example, how might we help a class understand the restricting nature of Adam and Eve's state of innocence in the Garden of Eden? We have found it helpful to use analogies, such as the following: Suppose we invited you to drive to our home in Utah, but we asked you to drive there in neutral. You might respond, "That's impossible. I can't." We might then reply, "Just push the pedal to the metal." Frustrated, you might answer, "But I can't get there unless I put my car in drive." In like manner, while Adam and Eve were in the Garden, they were in a state of spiritual neutral; they could not progress until they were removed from the Garden and their lives put into a state of "spiritual drive." Thus the need for the Fall.

We might use a painting of Adam and Eve holding hands as they journey into a fallen world. This might trigger a question on what new challenges they would face, but also what new opportunities would be available. If someone were teaching in an English-speaking area, they might couple this picture with these poetic lines from John Milton:

> *The World was all before them, where to choose*
> *Their place of rest, and Providence their guide:*
> *They, hand in hand, with wandering steps and slow,*
> *Through Eden took their solitary way.*[1]

These poetic lines might lead to a question such as "How do you think they felt as they entered a fallen world?" Some songs from the hymnbook might also invite the Spirit and reinforce these doctrinal truths, such as "Adam-ondi-Ahman" or "I Know that My Redeemer Lives."[2] Likewise, we might use a picture of the Savior in the Garden of Gethsemane and ask, "What price did the Savior have to pay in the Garden and on the Cross in order to make it possible for us to return to God and become like Him?"

ORGANIZING A LESSON PLAN

After commencing with meaningful prayer, there are many ways a lesson plan might be constructed. Below is only one of those ways that may prove helpful. It is an outline that incorporates some of the principles and resources discussed above, with the primary focus being the doctrine:

DOCTRINAL PRINCIPLE	SUPPORTING SCRIPTURES	QUESTIONS	SUPPORTING RESOURCES
The Fall of Adam and Eve necessitated the Savior's Atonement.	Genesis 2:17 2 Ne. 2:22–26 D&C 29:41–42	What negative conditions of the Fall needed to be corrected?	Analogy: Compare innocence to driving in neutral.
The Savior's Atonement overcame: • death, by resurrection. • sin, by repentance. • afflictions, by giving strength and comfort. • weaknesses, by providing perfecting powers.	1 Cor. 15:20–21 Hel. 14:15–18 Alma 7:11–12 Moro. 10:32–33	Why will even the wicked be resurrected? How does the Savior's Atonement perfect us as well as cleanse us?	• Picture of the Savior in the Garden • Hymn: "I Know that My Redeemer Lives"

CONCLUSION

As the Gods sat in council to plan the creation of the earth, they declared "that their plan was good" (Abr. 4:21). With the Lord's help, our lesson plans can also be "good" and thus lay the foundation for a lesson that builds faith and inspires us to become more like the Savior. The more we do our homework in creating a plan, the greater the opportunity and right we have to call upon the Holy Spirit to assist us in our teaching effort.

TEACH THE DOCTRINE

CHAPTER 7

The Power of the Doctrine

DOCTRINE CHANGES LIVES

The Lord gives specific counsel to the laborers of this dispensation: "I give unto you a commandment that you shall *teach one another the doctrine of the kingdom*" (D&C 88:77; emphasis added).[1] The message is clear: we are to teach the pure, undiluted doctrine of the Church, not our own social theories, "warm and fuzzy" ideas, or gospel hobbies. The doctrine of the gospel constitutes eternal truths and ordinances that, if understood and embraced, lead to exaltation.

The simple truths of the gospel have a powerful effect for good. That is the genius of the missionary lessons. They are not complicated or tricky or sophisticated; yet those simple truths carry a potent, persuasive power to inspire people to be more like Christ. Doctrine has an innate rationality that appeals to both mind and heart (see D&C 8:2–3).

Who can hear the plan of salvation in its entirety and not say, "That is beautiful, that is fair, that is just, and that is right"? When we taught our teenage son Nathan the plan of salvation from the scriptures, he responded, "That is so clear. Why doesn't everyone believe it?" Recently in our sacrament meeting, two of the speakers, who were converts to the Church, said that the most significant doctrine to them in their conversion was the plan of salvation. They said it gave them a plan and a purpose to life. In addition, our friend Lynda, when she was first taught this plan by the missionaries, exclaimed, "What? There's a plan?!"

Kathy witnessed the converting power of doctrine while she and Tad were serving a mission in Toronto, Canada. A wonderful woman, Amanda Kearns (a pseudonym), a widow and single mother of three teenagers, was being taught the missionary lessons by Elder Barnes and Elder Jones (pseudonyms), who were excellent missionaries. Like the sons of Mosiah, they learned the doctrine and studied the scriptures with intensity. And they taught with the Spirit. One evening they asked Kathy to go with them to teach Amanda and her family. Kathy went to the lesson and participated, but when she got home, she said to Tad, "I don't think that she will be baptized." Amanda was very polite but seemed reluctant to have the missionaries in her home. She just did not seem responsive. Later she admitted that she had even tried to hide from the missionaries.

However, when the elders taught Amanda about the plan of salvation and eternal marriage, she said she felt the Spirit witness to her for the first time that the gospel was true. She dearly loved her husband, who had passed away four years previously, and she said, "*If there is a way I can be with him again, then I will do it.*"

One year after her baptism, Elder Barnes (who had since been released and gone home) flew back to Toronto with his family and had the blessing of being present in the temple when Sister Kearns received her endowments. Not only was Elder Barnes *there* but he stood in as proxy for Sister Kearns's dear husband during the sealing. We were able to be there also, just one day before the end of our mission. What joy Elder Barnes felt, what joy we felt, and what joy Sister Kearns felt. This scripture exemplifies the feelings we had in the temple that beautiful day: "And if it so be that you should labor all your days in crying repentance unto this people, and bring, save it be one soul unto me, how great shall be your joy with him in the kingdom of my Father!" (D&C 18:15).

Alma taught of the converting power of doctrine. As chief judge, he held the greatest political power in the Nephite nation. No doubt he knew this power could compel action, but it could not compel a change of heart. For this reason he stepped down as chief judge so "*he might preach the word of God unto them* [the Nephites], *to stir them up in remembrance of their duty*, . . . seeing no way that he might reclaim them save it were in bearing down in pure testimony against them" (Alma 4:19; emphasis added). So Alma "began to deliver the word of God" (Alma 5:1) from city to city. Partway through his mission, he reflected upon the consequences of teaching the doctrine: "And now, as the preaching of the word had a great tendency to lead the people to do that which was just—*yea, it had had more powerful effect upon the minds of the people than the sword, or anything else, which had happened unto them*—therefore Alma thought it was expedient that they should try the virtue of the word of God" (Alma 31:5; emphasis added).

After the people of King Benjamin heard his message, they testified: "Yea, we believe all the words which thou hast spoken unto us; and also, we know of their surety and truth, because of the Spirit of the Lord Omnipotent, which has wrought a mighty change in us, or in our hearts, *that we have no more disposition to do evil, but to do good continually*" (Mosiah 5:2; emphasis added).

There is an inherent power in doctrine that motivates one to both accept the doctrine and live it. No wonder Ammon and his missionary companions spoke of "the power of his word . . . in us" (Alma 26:13). Accordingly, the doctrine, when taught in purity and power,[2] is a divine catalyst that spurs the soul to Christlike action. Jarom wrote of the gospel teachers who preached to the people and "did prick their hearts with the word, *continually stirring* them up unto repentance" (Jarom 1:12; emphasis added). The sons of Mosiah preached the doctrine with such effectiveness that "by the power of their words many were brought before the altar of God" (Alma 17:4).

The prophet Jeremiah was a living witness of this truth. As he taught the word of God, he was rejected, mocked, and reviled on a daily basis. He was discouraged and ready to give up, to abandon his teaching responsibilities. Then he spoke of the power of the doctrine in his life: "But his word was in mine heart as a burning fire shut up in my bones, and I was weary with forbearing, and I could not stay" (Jer. 20:9). The word of God was so compelling, so persuasive, that it drove him on in spite of powerful opposing forces.

DOCTRINE INVITES THE HOLY GHOST

President Henry B. Eyring taught: "If you teach the doctrinal principles, the Holy Ghost will come."[3] Why? Because when we teach the doctrine we make it possible for the Holy Ghost to fulfill one of His chief purposes—namely, to bear witness of doctrinal truths.[4] In essence, the doctrine is a spiritual magnet that invites and draws upon the enlightening and confirming powers of the Holy Ghost.

DOCTRINE COUNTERS FALSEHOODS

Alma taught that the scriptures "convinced many of the error of their ways, and brought them to the knowledge of their God unto the salvation of their souls" (Alma 37:8). Paul made it clear that

The Power of the Doctrine

our study of the doctrine is imperative so that we can confront and counter those who "will not endure sound doctrine" (2 Tim. 4:3). Paul further addressed this point: "Holding fast the faithful word as he hath been taught, that he may be able by sound doctrine both to exhort and to convince the gainsayers [those who deny or oppose the truth]" (Titus 1:9).

This ability to know and exhort correct doctrine must have been critical to the New Testament Saints, because Peter counseled in a similar manner: "Be ready always to give an answer to every man that asketh you a reason of the hope that is in you with meekness and fear" (1 Pet. 3:15). The doctrine is both sword[5] and shield.[6] It both attacks and defends against the false philosophies of the evil one.[7] The Lord gave this promise to those who feast upon His doctrine: "And whoso treasureth up my word, shall not be deceived" (JS—M 1:37).

A missionary once came to Toronto, where we were serving as mission leaders. After a short time there, he called Tad and said he needed to go home. He then explained why: "Well, President, I met a man on the street and he showed me in the scriptures that God is a spirit (see John 4:24) and that Christ and the Father are one being (see John 10:30). I had never seen those scriptures before and had no answer for him. I don't think I have the necessary testimony to stay." After discussing these concerns, Tad said, "Go work with your companion to understand what those scriptures mean. Find every scripture in the Bible you can that speaks of God having a body of flesh and bones (in addition to His spirit) and that God the Father and His Son, Jesus Christ, are two separate beings. Then my wife and I will come next Tuesday to your companionship study, and you teach us the truth."

Tuesday came, and we knocked on his apartment door. The elder had a bright smile and a paper in his hand filled with scriptures on both sides. As we sat down with his companion and him, he started to share with us scripture after scripture supporting the Church's stand on the doctrine of the Godhead. Finally we said, "That's wonderful, Elder. You've got it, but now we need to go to another appointment."

"Oh, no," he said. "I've got a lot more scriptures to share." We stayed a while longer while he taught us with enthusiasm and confidence. Finally, we had to leave. While we have probably forgotten the exact phrasing, we will never forget the spirit of his parting words: "I want to go find that guy on the street and teach him what the Bible really says." An in-depth study of the scriptures had helped him counter doctrinal falsehoods, and in addition, strengthen his own testimony.

DOCTRINE COMFORTS

Doctrine provides truths that can comfort us and sustain us in our difficult times. Jacob wrote that the word "healeth the wounded soul" (Jacob 2:8). What a beautiful and descriptive way to define this divine power. Paul added: "we through patience and comfort of the scriptures might have hope" (Rom. 15:4). When Moroni learned the truth that his weakness could be made a strength by the grace of God, he declared, "And I, Moroni, having heard these words, was comforted" (Ether 12:29). After writing of the Lord's Second Coming, Paul told the Saints of Thessalonica: "Wherefore comfort one another with these words" (1 Thes. 4:18). The scriptures give us an eternal perspective and thus comfort and hope that in the eternal scheme of things, there will be perfect mercy and justice.

Tad was fourteen when his fifteen-year-old sister suddenly died from a kidney disease. It all occurred within a week, and it was difficult for him to understand. He remembers seeing his father weeping, stretched out on the bedroom floor. Tad had faith but wondered why his sister, who was so good, had not survived after receiving a positive blessing from a worthy priesthood bearer. It was one of those questions that periodically gnawed at him.

Then one day, somewhere in his teenage years, Tad either read or was made aware of Doctrine and Covenants 42:44, 46, 48, which reads: "And the elders of the church, two or more, shall be called, and shall pray for and lay their hands upon them in my name; and if they die they shall die unto me, and if they live they shall live unto me. . . . And it shall come to pass that those that die in me shall not taste of death, for it shall be sweet unto them. . . . And again, it shall come to pass that he that hath faith in me to be healed, *and is not appointed unto death*, shall be healed" (emphasis added). That scripture was sufficient for Tad. The Spirit helped him know that his sister's death was not due to lack of faith or some medical neglect but because she was "appointed unto death," and furthermore, because of her pure and righteous life, death was "sweet unto" her.

How many thousands who have lost a spouse or child have been consoled as they read the doctrine of the eternal nature of the family? No doubt countless others have been comforted by the scriptures as they reflected on experiences of parents, even prophets of God, who struggled to bring back children wrestling with their testimonies. How many of us, after we have sinned, have been comforted, even in our moments of greatest despair, when we read in the scriptures of the Savior's expansive healing powers—the power to heal "the most lost of all mankind" (Alma 24:11), to cleanse those who are "the very vilest of sinners" (Mosiah 28:4), and to give unto us "beauty for ashes" (Isa. 61:3)? God's doctrine, His plan of happiness, and the Savior's Atonement can comfort and sustain us—yes, even heal us and help us endure in our times of greatest need.

DOCTRINE SAVES US AND PERFECTS US

One of the virtues of doctrine is that it intrinsically bears witness of its own divine nature and saving power. Paul taught: "Take heed unto thyself, and unto the doctrine; continue in them: for in doing this *thou shalt both save thyself, and them that hear thee*" (1 Tim. 4:16; emphasis added). It would be difficult, if not impossible, to honestly study true doctrine, to reflect upon it, to ponder it, and then simultaneously to think or do evil. Nephi taught this truth: "Whoso would hearken unto the word of God, and would hold fast unto it, they would never perish; neither could the temptations and the fiery darts of the adversary overpower them" (1 Ne. 15:24).

So powerful is the word of God that Helaman taught that it "convinced many of the error of their ways, and brought them to the knowledge of their God unto the salvation of their souls" (Alma 37:8). What more could we hope for the word of God to do?

In that course of saving us, the doctrine has the power to simultaneously refine and perfect us. As Paul said, "The doctrine . . . is according to godliness" (1 Tim. 6:3), meaning that the doctrine both teaches and inspires us to be godly.

DIFFERENT TEACHING LEVELS

While many teach at celestial heights, some fail to heed the Lord's counsel to focus on the doctrine and thus teach at more terrestrial realms. Following are various categories of instruction into which many teachers may fall.

The Survival Level

At this level the teacher figuratively, perhaps literally, provides Cheerios and toys to help pass the time away. The clock is this teacher's worst enemy. He or she is on survival mode until the final bell rings. Of course, for certain young ages, food and toys may appropriately occupy a part of the lesson time, but somewhere there must be a focus on one or more doctrinal points, however simple they may be.

The Entertainment Level

This is the teacher who provides games, jokes, drama, and charisma but uses them as an ends, not a means. Instead of these resources supporting the doctrine, they replace it.

The Informational Level

Many of the academic teachers of the world fall into this trap. Their focus becomes names and dates and places. Such information is often taught in a vacuum, without the foundation of character and morals to guide its use. These teachers produce *Trivial Pursuit* champions rather than disciples of Christ. Unfortunately, these instructors are preoccupied more with the facts of the story than its morals, and more with the side issues than the key doctrinal principles. They hone in on the quartz when the diamond is visibly waiting to be discovered and disclosed.

The Philosophical Level

A particular trap for the would-be intellectual is to focus on the philosophies or reasonings of the world. Paul warned against such teachers on multiple occasions. When speaking to the people at Corinth, he said: "We speak, not in the words which man's wisdom teacheth, but which the Holy Ghost teacheth" (1 Cor. 2:13). To the Colossians he added, "Beware lest any man spoil you through philosophy and vain deceit, after the tradition of men, after the rudiments of the world, and not after Christ" (Col. 2:8). Elder Jeffrey R. Holland made this astute observation: "When crises come in our lives—and they will—the philosophies of men interlaced with a few scriptures and poems just won't do. Are we really nurturing our youth and our new members in a way that will sustain them when the stresses of life appear? Or are we giving them a kind of theological Twinkie—spiritually empty calories? President John Taylor once called such teaching 'fried froth,' the kind of thing you could eat all day and yet finish feeling totally unsatisfied."[8] The doctrine of men is fleeting and faltering; the doctrine of God is enduring and exalting.

The Motivational Level

These teachers are able to motivate someone to temporarily participate in a service project or read the scriptures. However, their method is often a one-shot approach. The instruction may cause a temporary change in behavior, and that is good, but it has not quite reached the level that brings about a permanent change of heart.

The Inspirational Level

These teachers are able to teach the doctrine with such clarity and power that their words, transmitted by the power of the Holy Ghost, can permanently change hearts. Alma the Younger spoke of such a miracle in his father's life and in the lives of those to whom his father preached the gospel: "And behold, he [Alma the Elder] preached the word unto your fathers, and a mighty change was also wrought in their hearts. . . . And behold, they were faithful until the end; therefore they were saved" (Alma 5:13). Likewise those Lamanites who believed in the words of Ammon and his brethren "never did fall away" (Alma 23:6).

King Benjamin witnessed a similar miracle as he taught the doctrine of the Atonement of Jesus Christ to his people: "And they all cried with one voice, saying: Yea, we believe all the words which thou hast spoken unto us; and also, we know of their surety and truth, because of the Spirit of the Lord Omnipotent, which has wrought a mighty change in us, or in our hearts, that we have no more disposition to do evil, but to do good continually" (Mosiah 5:2).

The gospel is not neutral. Parents and gospel teachers are not neutral. We preach the doctrine with power and authority. Some may say, "Children and students need to see and hear both sides of the picture." And they surely do. Unfortunately—from a thousand classrooms, textbooks, news shows, movies, and websites—they are already learning the other side. Our job is to preach the Lord's side with purity and conviction. Great teachers are passionate about teaching the doctrine with the Spirit.

TEACHING WHAT MATTERS MOST

Each of the doctrinal principles of the kingdom is important, but all are not equal in importance. The Savior acknowledged the payment of tithes by the Pharisees as a correct doctrinal practice but then scolded them for omitting "*the weightier matters of the law, judgment, mercy, and faith*" (Matt. 23:23; emphasis added). Alma taught this same truth: "I say unto you there be many things to come; and behold, *there is one thing which is of more importance than they all*—for behold, the time is not far distant that the Redeemer liveth and cometh among his people" (Alma 7:7; emphasis added).

The Atonement of Jesus Christ is the center and foundation of our doctrine. President Boyd K. Packer taught that the Savior's Atonement "is the very root of Christian doctrine. You may know much about the gospel as it branches out from there, but if you only know the branches and those branches do not touch that root, if they have been cut free from that truth, there will be no life nor substance nor redemption in them."[9]

Perhaps the most masterful discourse on the Atonement of Jesus Christ in the revealed scriptures is the one delivered by King Benjamin (see Mosiah 2–5). As directed by an angel, he declared, "I have spoken plainly unto you that ye might understand" (Mosiah 2:40). With clarity and conciseness, he proceeded line by line and verse by verse with compelling logic and an uncompromising testimony that cannot honestly be refuted by the mind or heart. The spiritually attuned received the wondrous atoning truths in undiluted fashion, akin to a spiritual transfusion of pure doctrine. There was no need for outside collaborating sources or historical evidences. None of that was necessary because these spiritually mature Saints were ready and eager to receive the atoning doctrine in its fullest dose. And so they did. It can be likewise in our homes and classes.

There is nothing we can ever teach that is more important, more far reaching, and more persuasive for good than the doctrine of the Atonement of Jesus Christ. It must be at the heart and core and center of all our teachings. It must be referenced again and again in our lessons and in our homes. It is this doctrine that solidifies testimonies, gives hope, purifies us, and even perfects us. It is this doctrine that makes salvation possible. It is this doctrine that is the spiritual glue that links all other gospel principles in a unified whole. It deserves our most diligent studying, our deepest pondering, our most passionate expressions of love and gratitude, and our most fervent testimonies. We teach and treat this doctrine in reverential awe and with profound respect.

Our students must come to know that the Savior's Atonement is the single most important thing in our lives and in their lives—the greatest evidence of God's love we possess—that nothing is its equal or even comparable. This event stands alone throughout eternity—unsurpassed, unequaled, unmatched by any other. To a large extent, our success as teachers will be measured by the degree to which our children and students come to know, love, and appreciate this sublime doctrine. Of all we teach—this is what matters most, the doctrine of the Atonement of Jesus Christ.

CHAPTER 8

How Can I Best Teach the Doctrine?

Once one realizes the importance of teaching the doctrine, the next question becomes, "How do I teach the doctrine most effectively?" We do not propose to be experts on how to achieve this objective, but we have observed others who are. Accordingly, we share the following ideas.

LET THE SCRIPTURES BE THE PRIMARY SOURCE TO TEACH THE DOCTRINE

The doctrine is found in the canonized scriptures and in the words of the living prophets (see D&C 68:4). Referring to the scriptures, the Lord counseled, "Rely upon the things which are written; for in them are all things written concerning the foundation of my church, my gospel, and my rock" (D&C 18:3–4).

The Savior repeatedly used the scriptures to teach doctrine. He was and is our Master Exemplar. When Satan tempted Him on three occasions, He responded each time with, "It is written" (Matt. 4:4,

7, 10) and then followed up with a scriptural quote. As He walked the road to Emmaus with two disciples by His side, "he expounded unto them in all the scriptures the things concerning himself" (Luke 24:27). It was no different when the Savior came to the Nephites, to whom He "expounded all the scriptures" (3 Ne. 23:6).[1]

The Savior and the prophets use the scriptures as their primary source to teach doctrine. President Ezra Taft Benson wrote: "Always remember, there is no satisfactory substitute for the scriptures and the words of the living prophets. These should be your original sources."[2]

Paul taught of the connection between the scriptures and doctrine: "All scripture is given by inspiration of God, and *is profitable for doctrine*, for reproof, for correction, for instruction in righteousness" (2 Tim. 3:16; emphasis added). The scriptures are the focus and foundation of any doctrinal discussion. They define the parameters of what we may legitimately explore and the depths to which we may plumb. The scriptures are the principal reservoir from which we should drink and teach.

The scriptures and doctrine go hand in hand. We cannot teach the doctrine effectively without the scriptures as our primary tool, and we cannot honestly and sincerely read the scriptures without learning doctrine. Paul, one of the greatest missionaries of all time, "reasoned with them [the Jews] out of the scriptures" (Acts 17:2). Orson Hyde was called as a missionary with the instruction that he should be "reasoning with and expounding all scriptures" (D&C 68:1). The scriptures are our foundation for doctrinal understanding. No wonder Alma observed, "Their souls were illuminated by the light of the everlasting word" (Alma 5:7).

Introducing Scriptures

How we introduce the scriptures often assists others in understanding the doctrine to be taught. For example, if we merely ask someone to read Ephesians 2:19–20 without providing any context or focus, the verses may be difficult to understand. Many people, especially youth and those who are learning about the gospel for the first time, are often unfamiliar with scriptural language. It is foreign to them and, consequently, often difficult to comprehend. They may be happy just to "get through" reading the scripture aloud without making mistakes, let alone understanding what it means.

Rather than calling on people to mechanically read verses of scripture, how can we introduce them in a way that fosters meaningful insights? Before inviting someone to read Ephesians 2:19–20, the teacher might provide some context by saying: "Paul is writing to new converts of the Church in Ephesus. He then explains who constitutes the foundation of the church to which they now belong." After giving this context, the teacher might ask a question: "As you read these verses, ask yourself, 'Who does Paul say composes the foundation of Christ's Church?' and 'What is Paul's point in making this comparison?'" This might lead to a discussion on why apostles and prophets are essential in Christ's Church today, why they are evidence of the true Church, and why the comparison to a foundation helps us understand that apostles and prophets are the ones who receive the revelation on which the Church stands. Teachers can set the stage for an inspired discussion by serving up the scriptures on a silver platter rather than a paper plate.

Scripture Chains

Another way to teach the doctrine effectively is to create scripture chains. Scripture chains are not just a series of related scriptures or cross-references. They are much more. They are scriptures cited in a sequential order that allows the doctrine to be taught line upon line, precept upon precept. In essence, each scripture builds upon the preceding one. For example, suppose the question is asked, "How do we know that God is not just a spirit but also has a glorified body of flesh and bones?" The following scripture chain might be used:

You could begin with **Luke 24:36–43**, which states that Jesus was resurrected with a body of "flesh and bones." This scripture also reveals that He did "eat [fish and honeycomb] before them," further evidence of His corporeal nature. Suppose, however, someone asserts—as some Christians do—that Jesus shed His resurrected body of flesh and bones when He ascended into heaven, and thus He is a spirit in heaven today. You might then go to **Romans 6:9–10**. This scripture states that after Christ was resurrected, He "dieth no more; death hath no more dominion over Him," meaning Christ could never die again after His Resurrection. This is important because death is defined as the separation of body and spirit (see **James 2:26**). Therefore, Christ could not shed His body after His Resurrection or He would suffer a second death (i.e., separation of body and spirit). This was an event that Paul said could not happen. Accordingly, Christ must have a body of flesh and bones in heaven today.

Another scripture chain could address the question, How could Joseph Smith have seen God, since the scriptures declare, "No man hath seen God at any time; the only begotten Son, which is in the bosom of the Father, he hath declared Him" (**John 1:18**)?[3] If we turn, however, to **John 6:46**, we will realize that John made an exception to that declaration. In this scripture he states that men which are "of God" can see God. John later defines who a man "of God" is. In **3 John 1:11**, he states: "He that doeth good is *of God*" (emphasis added). In other words, good, righteous people are "of God" and therefore can see God. Further, **Acts 7:55–56** gives a concrete example of a good man, Stephen the martyr, who in fact saw God.

Scripture chains can help teach the doctrine in a logical order

How Can I Best Teach the Doctrine?

and answer many questions that might otherwise arise, particularly when someone has mistakenly declared doctrinal certainty based on a solitary scripture.

LOOK FOR PATTERNS

Elder David A. Bednar taught: "*Searching* in the revelations for connections, patterns, and themes builds upon and adds to our spiritual knowledge . . . ; it broadens our perspective and understanding of the plan of salvation."[4] One such pattern is exemplified in the raising of Lazarus from the dead. The Savior approached the grave or cave where Lazarus had lain for four days. He instructed those who were nearby to remove the stone cover. Then in a loud voice He cried out, "Lazarus, come forth" (John 11:43), and the scriptures record that "he that was dead came forth, bound hand and foot with graveclothes: and his face was bound about with a napkin" (John 11:44). At that point Jesus commanded the onlookers to unbind him.

One might ask, "Why didn't Jesus remove the stone with a show of power? Why didn't Jesus unwrap the revived corpse?" Why didn't He perform a turnkey miracle? Perhaps He was teaching those present the divine law of economy, namely, that we must do all we can, and when we have reached our limits—when we have asserted all our mental, mortal, and spiritual energies; when we have exercised our agency to its maximum—then the powers of heaven will intervene. Mortals could remove the stone and unwrap the corpse, so they must do so for their own spiritual growth, but only the power of God could call the dead to life.

That same pattern was followed when Jesus raised the daughter of Jairus from the dead. Once the Savior performed that remarkable feat, He "commanded that something should be given her to eat" (Mark 5:43). Why didn't the Lord take away her hunger at the same time He healed her or miraculously provide her food? No doubt, because mortals who were present had access to food and could provide this necessity of life.

The experience of the brother of Jared and the sixteen stones is yet another example of the Lord expecting us to contribute our share to the solution. In each instance the pattern was established that mortals must do all they can, and when their powers are exhausted, the powers of heaven will intervene.[5] In other words, we must exercise our fullest powers of agency to reap the fullest possible spiritual growth. These patterns and truths discovered in the scriptures and as taught in the home and classroom can help us know how to govern our own lives.

LIST YOUR QUESTIONS ABOUT THE DOCTRINE

Before we begin preparing a lesson or writing a book, we often list all the questions we have on a particular doctrinal topic. We then try to prioritize them in order of their natural development. At this point, we try to answer each question the best we can; then we read the scriptures and words of the living prophets on the topic. Afterward, we refer to secondary sources. For example, if we were giving a lesson on the Holy Ghost, we might pose some preliminary questions, such as:

- Who is the Holy Ghost?
- How does He differ from the Light of Christ?
- What is the difference between the *power* of the Holy Ghost and the *gift* of the Holy Ghost?
- What functions does the Holy Ghost serve?
- How do I know when the Holy Ghost is speaking to me?
- How do the gifts of the Spirit relate to the gift of the Holy Ghost?

How Can I Best Teach the Doctrine?

In the course of this process, we would go to the "Holy Ghost" entry in the Topical Guide or Guide to the Scriptures and read many of the scriptures referenced. In addition, we would read the Bible Dictionary sections on the Holy Ghost and Light of Christ. In fact, we should refer to the Bible Dictionary at every opportunity we get. It may not be canonized scripture, but it is certainly informative and inspired. For example, the section on the Holy Ghost explains: "The Holy Ghost is manifested to men on the earth both as the *power* of the Holy Ghost and as the *gift* of the Holy Ghost. The power can come upon one before baptism, and is the convincing witness that the gospel is true. It gives one a testimony of Jesus Christ. . . . The gift can come only after proper and authorized baptism, and is conferred by the laying on of hands. . . . The gift of the Holy Ghost is the right to have, whenever one is worthy, the companionship of the Holy Ghost" (emphasis in original). This passage answers the question about the difference between the power of the Holy Ghost and the gift of the Holy Ghost.

Asking questions in advance makes us more alert to the answers the scriptures and secondary sources may offer. Otherwise, we may pass by such insights unnoticed.

TEACH THE DOCTRINE WITHOUT DILUTION

President J. Reuben Clark Jr. spoke of the need to teach the doctrine in a straightforward, undiluted way: "The youth of the Church are hungry for things of the Spirit; they are eager to learn the gospel, and they want it straight, undiluted. . . . You do not have to sneak up behind this spiritually experienced youth and whisper religion in his ears; you can come right out, face to face, and talk with him. You do not need to disguise religious truths with a cloak of worldly things; you can bring these truths to him openly."[6]

The doctrine is powerful and persuasive when it comes directly from the scriptures or the mouths of modern-day prophets. We do not need a spoonful of sugar to wash the doctrine down. As recorded in Psalms: "How sweet are thy words unto my taste! yea, sweeter than honey to my mouth!" (Ps. 119:103).

TEACH THE DOCTRINE CLEARLY AND SIMPLY

Paul taught, "Except ye utter by the tongue words easy to be understood, how shall it be known what is spoken? for ye shall speak into the air" (1 Cor. 14:9). Nephi explained why simplicity is so critical: "My soul delighteth in plainness unto my people, *that they may learn*" (2 Ne. 25:4; emphasis added). John Taylor likewise emphasized this point: "It is true intelligence for a man to take a subject that is mysterious and great in itself and to unfold and simplify it so that a child can understand it."[7]

A man who hired Tad to lecture on legal matters said: "Tad, if you can't teach it to a ten-year-old, you don't know it well enough to teach it." Similarly, while serving as a stake president, Tad and his counselors adopted the following strategy for stake priesthood meetings—address their messages to the twelve-year-old deacons, and if they enjoy it and understand it, the high priests will most likely enjoy it and understand it. The Doctrine and Covenants addresses this very issue: "The Lord sent forth the fulness of his gospel, his everlasting covenant, *reasoning in plainness and simplicity*" (D&C 133:57; emphasis added).

Some years ago, we conducted a mission tour in the Pacific. The mission president asked if we would teach the missionaries about the Savior's Atonement. As we contemplated this assignment, we invited the mission president to have each of the missionaries, in advance of the meeting, teach the Atonement to a child about ten years of age, assess the child's level of understanding, and then record the experience. The missionaries discovered that teaching a ten-year-old requires a lot of thought, preparation, and simplicity—the way the gospel was meant to be taught.

Part of simplicity is developing a line of reasoning that builds one step upon another. The Lord spoke of the importance of reasoning: "let us reason together, that ye may understand" (D&C 50:10). Reasoning takes thought and effort. Lesson plans are an important tool in achieving simplicity because they help us prioritize the doctrinal principles we will teach, refine our reasoning, and focus on those questions and supplementary resources that will best assist us in teaching the doctrine.[8]

The clearer we teach the doctrine, the easier we make it for the Holy Ghost to bear witness of its truthfulness. Elder B. H. Roberts taught, "To be known, the truth must be stated and the clearer and more complete the statement is, the better opportunity will the Holy Spirit have for testifying to the souls of men that the work is true."[9]

Some of our missionaries taught with such clarity that the Holy Ghost naturally or readily confirmed every word and thought they spoke. On a few occasions, however, we observed a lesson in which it was very difficult to follow the line of reasoning presented by the missionary. Even though he or she may have been an obedient missionary, we believe the Holy Ghost could not, or at least would not, bear witness of a truth that had not been clearly taught. The prime role of the Holy Ghost is not to compensate for lack of doctrine, or to clarify that which is confusing, but to bear witness of doctrine that has been succinctly declared. Thus, in order to maximize the Spirit, we as teachers must be not only worthy but also able to teach gospel truths logically, clearly, and concisely.

MEMORIZE SCRIPTURES

Unfortunately, memorization has become a lost art for many students. Tad's mission president was an ardent advocate of this learning technique. He expected his missionaries to memorize a scripture a day and recite it to their companion during study time. How grateful Tad was for this encouragement and expectation. We tried to carry on this tradition while serving as mission leaders—we invited our missionaries to memorize a scripture a day. It was not easy for some, but we learned it was possible to do some memorization daily.

One elder, from a small town in Arizona, was assigned to our mission. He was just off the farm and said, "I can't do it, President. I can't memorize." Tad replied, "Just work on one sentence at a time." Being obedient, he did his best. In his final interview, Tad said to him, "I understand you have now memorized over fifty scriptures." The missionary responded with a smile, "No, President. Over seventy scriptures."

Memorizing a scripture helps it become embedded in the depths of our soul, never to be lost. Additionally, the scripture will be readily available to draw upon when the Holy Ghost wants to bring it to our attention. Memorizing scripture also seems to lead to a more active and retentive mind. Speaking of memorization, Elder Richard G. Scott taught: "Great power can come from memorizing scriptures. To memorize a scripture is to forge a new friendship. It is like discovering a new individual who can help in time of need, give inspiration and comfort, and be a source of motivation for needed change."[10] He also shared this insight: "When scriptures are used as the Lord has caused them to be recorded, they have intrinsic power that is not communicated when paraphrased."[11]

Tad's father used to take the bus to work so he could memorize scriptures and passages by Shakespeare. He did it consistently day after day. On one occasion, he was representing a defendant who had been convicted of a crime. He was pleading for leniency in the sentencing phase of the trial. "Your honor," he said, "remember Portia's plea before the court, 'the quality of mercy is not strained.'"[12]

The judge replied: "I tell you what, Mr. Callister, if you can quote that entire passage by memory, I'll let your client go on probation."

Tad's father replied, "That's a deal." To the astonishment of the judge, he quoted it all by memory.

The judge then said, "A deal's a deal." His client was given probation.

While this story is a secular example, memorized scriptures can likewise be readily brought to our attention to assist us in moments when their spiritual truth and impact are needed.

We can particularly teach our children and youth to memorize the Articles of Faith, scriptures, and uplifting poetry. We have found in our later years that the scriptures we memorized when we were young have readily stayed with us, while we struggle to retain the ones we learned later in life.

CONCLUSION

The ideal teachers follow the Spirit and teach the doctrine even when their own intellect and passion may lead them in another direction. They build faith, not skepticism. Their ultimate weapon is the doctrine as taught by the scriptures and the Spirit, coupled with their testimony.

Teaching the doctrine is both a privilege and a responsibility that deserves and requires our most rapt attention, our most profound efforts, and our deepest spirituality. If we are humble and teachable, God can take us and mold us and shape us so we can teach His doctrine with a precision and power that no one can honestly refute. Even more importantly, it will resonate in the hearts and minds of our family and class members in such a way that it will become woven into the very fabric of their souls. And then, in times of doubt or struggle or needed reassurance, the Spirit will whisper to their souls and give them a reminding witness of the doctrinal truths stored in their spiritual bank. The Lord must love those who teach the doctrine, for Paul wrote, "Let the elders that rule well be counted worthy of double honour, especially they who labour in the word and doctrine" (1 Tim. 5:17).

Sister Virginia Pearce Cowley, a former counselor in the Young Women General Presidency, observed: "The skilled teacher does not want students who leave the class talking about how magnificent and unusual the teacher is. This teacher wants students who leave talking about how magnificent the gospel is!"[13]

The gospel and the doctrine should be our focus, and when it is, our students will realize how pertinent it is in their lives, how mind-stretching it can be, how logical it is, how appealing it is to the passions of their hearts, and how intrinsically converting it is—yes, how truly magnificent the doctrine is in every way.

CHAPTER 9

Focus on Doctrinal Principles, Not Rules

GOD FOCUSES ON PRINCIPLES

Joseph Smith taught: "I teach [the people] correct principles and they govern themselves."[1] What does the word *principle* mean? It generally connotes a general or basic law. The Lord used this word multiple times in giving instructions on how to teach:

- "The elders, priests and teachers of this church shall teach the *principles* of my gospel, which are in the Bible and the Book of Mormon" (D&C 42:12; emphasis added).
- "Teach ye diligently and my grace shall attend you, that you may be instructed more perfectly in theory, *in principle*, in doctrine, in the law of the gospel" (D&C 88:78; emphasis added).[2]
- "And Zion cannot be built up unless it is by the *principles* of the law of the celestial kingdom" (D&C 105:5; emphasis added).
- "The powers of heaven cannot be controlled nor handled only

upon the *principles* of righteousness" (D&C 121:36; emphasis added).

In each of the foregoing scriptures, the emphasis is on principles, not rules.

WHY PRINCIPLES ARE MORE PRODUCTIVE THAN RULES

Why is it usually more effective to teach principles than rules? First, rules often apply to only one or a few specific situations, while principles generally have much broader application. Elder Richard G. Scott taught, "Principles are concentrated truth, packaged for application to a wide variety of circumstances."[3] Second, principles create an environment where agency can be maximized and thus flourish, while rules tend to minimize agency by restricting, sometimes even dictating, our choices. And third, principles often contain the reasoning for a desired action, and with this increased understanding comes an increased desire to change our nature. For example, as we live the principle of repentance, we learn that it leads to a remission of our sins (see Alma 12:34), which then heightens our desire to repent.

The law of Moses, known as the lesser law, traditionally contained a set of 613 rules. It was given to the Israelites because of their unworthiness to abide by the greater law, composed of principles, higher ordinances, and the Melchizedek Priesthood. When the Savior came in the meridian of time, He replaced the lesser law of Moses with the higher law of Christ. The former was rule-driven; the latter was principle-driven. The Lord usually gives us all the rope we can handle.

In the early days of the Church, the Lord taught the principle known as the law of consecration, wherein the Saints gave everything they had to the Church and received back what was required for their needs and wants. Unfortunately, the members of the Church were unprepared for this divine principle, so the Lord backtracked a little and gave a law that was partly rule-driven and partly principle-driven—the law of tithing.

EXAMPLES OF TEACHING PRINCIPLES

One can quickly see the value of teaching principles over rules by analyzing the following exchange: A teenage son says to his father, "Dad, can I watch TV on Sunday?" The father replies, "No, son. You know the rules—no TV on Sunday." The son replies, "But, Dad, I wanted to watch general conference." Quickly, the father does an about-face. "Oh, there is an exception for that." What if the son wanted to watch a special Church devotional? Is there another exception for that? Or what if he wanted to see a special series on the lives of the great Reformers? How many rules does it take to govern TV watching on Sunday?

Rules and more rules were at the center of the Mosaic law. But in the Old Testament, the Savior teaches a very simple principle concerning the Sabbath day and how to honor it: "Remember the sabbath day, to keep it holy" (Ex. 20:8). Why is that principle important? Because as we keep the Sabbath holy, it will simultaneously make us holy. In contrast, the Jewish leaders created a mechanical list of rules to apply on the Sabbath, many of which were in conflict with this underlying principle.

One such conflict arose when the Savior entered a synagogue. He saw a man with a withered hand. The Jewish leaders were ready to accuse the Savior if He broke their rule of no healing on the Sabbath. But the Savior was not to be caught in their intended trap. He addressed the unspoken but burning question of the moment—could a man heal someone on the Sabbath day even if it violated a rule of the Mosaic law? The Savior gave the answer by stating a principle in the form of a question: "Is it lawful to do good on the sabbath days, or to do evil?" (Mark 3:4).[4] The Savior had no list of rules, no list of dos and don'ts for Sabbath activity. It came down to two principles—keep the Sabbath day holy and do good on that day.

These are the types of principles we can teach our children and students. For example, if our children ask if they can watch a certain movie or engage in certain activities on the Sabbath, we might review with them the principles enunciated by the Savior and then ask, "Will that movie or that activity help you keep the Sabbath day holy (meaning make you holy)—will it help you do good?" If instead, we merely give yes or no answers to our children's questions, we will shift their agency and accountability from them to us. But if we teach the correct principles that govern their choices and let them answer their own questions, then we give them a chance to exercise their own agency and, in the process, accelerate their spiritual growth. In addition, it will help them understand how to act in future situations of a similar nature.

But what if a child does not make the right choice and he or she chooses to watch an inappropriate movie? Then, like the Lord did with the law of consecration and the law of tithing, we may need to back up a step and implement some rules until the time of spiritual maturity is attained. In other words, we use principles whenever we can so as to maximize the agency and growth of our children, but if they cannot "handle" principles, then we implement the fewest rules necessary until they become more spiritually mature.

President Russell M. Nelson gave this wise counsel: "Don't answer a behavioral question with a behavioral answer. It is much better to give an answer based upon a principle, or even better, with a doctrinal answer, if you can. Then your teaching will endure even to subsequent generations."[5] He also observed, "Correct principles

Focus on Doctrinal Principles, Not Rules

are derived from an understanding of divine doctrine."[6] Rules tend to be fleeting in nature; on the other hand, principles and related doctrine tend to be eternal.

On occasion, our missionaries would ask if they could engage in a certain activity on their preparation day that was not specifically referred to in the missionary handbook. Usually we would respond with a principle: "If this activity prepares you physically, mentally, and spiritually to teach the gospel for the rest of the week and it is safe, then do it. If not, then don't do it. We trust you to make the right decision." Or they might ask, "Can I listen to this certain musical selection?" We would reply: "You don't need to ask us that question; if the music is not only entertaining but also uplifting and inviting of the Spirit, then go ahead. If not, don't listen to it." If missionaries could live by principles, they would not need long lists of rules for preparation-day activities, appropriate music, use of cameras, computers, etc. Instead, a few correct principles could replace those many rules with a higher law.

While serving as stake president, Tad met with a young man who wanted to turn his life around and serve a mission. He appeared at their interview with an earring in each ear. At one point, Tad asked the young man to read from 1 Corinthians 8. This scripture talks about meat that was offered to certain idols. Some people felt it was appropriate to eat such meat, but others did not. Then Paul taught a profound principle: "But meat commendeth us not to God: *for neither, if we eat, are we the better, neither, if we eat not, are we the worse.*" In other words, there is no moral good or evil in eating such meat, just as there is no moral good or evil in wearing earrings. But then Paul made his point: "But take heed by any means this liberty of yours (i.e., your decision to eat meat offered to idols) become a stumbling block to them that are weak." In other words, what happens if someone refuses to hear your message because they think eating meat offered to idols is incompatible with a servant of God? And then Paul concludes: "Wherefore if meat (i.e., earrings) make my brother to offend, I will eat no flesh (i.e., not wear earrings) while the world standeth, lest I make my brother to offend" (1 Cor. 8:8–9, 13; emphasis added). After reading this together, the young man responded, "I understand." At the next interview, there were no earrings. Soon thereafter, he left for his mission and served honorably. The young man could have been told the rule—no earrings in the mission field—but Paul taught the correct principle in such a way that the young man now understood the underlying rationale that could help govern his decisions in this as well as in many other similar situations.[7]

CONCLUSION

Principles are compatible with the higher law; rules, with the lesser law. Our constant focus should be to teach doctrinal principles whenever possible. Why? Because principles have the greatest capacity to lift us to celestial heights, and in the end, principles—not rules—will govern us in the celestial kingdom (see D&C 105:5).

CHAPTER 10

Putting Together the "Gospel Puzzle": Doctrinal Relationships

We often teach doctrinal principles in isolation, and that methodology certainly has its place and time. Sometimes, however, it is instructive to teach the relationships among doctrinal principles since they all have the same underlying goal—namely, to help us obtain eternal life. In this pursuit, doctrinal principles tend to supplement, complement, overlap, and reinforce each other. Understanding the correlation among doctrinal principles can give us a new and broader perspective—somewhat like looking at a completed puzzle rather than each piece individually. For example, some might ask how the following three doctrinal principles relate to each other or if they act independently of one other:

The plan of salvation
The Savior's Atonement
The doctrine of Christ

As we gain an understanding of these doctrinal relationships, we realize that each doctrinal principle is an essential component of the same "gospel puzzle" rather than each serving as its own "gospel puzzle." In fact, each doctrinal principle of the gospel is dependent upon the others for its ultimate success. One principle, absent the others, cannot fully accomplish the goal for which it is intended.

THE PLAN OF SALVATION

The plan of salvation is the divine program that sets out the way to return to God's presence and become like Him so we might live "in a state of never-ending happiness" (Mosiah 2:41) and, like God, have a fulness of joy. Hence this plan is also known as the "plan of happiness" (Alma 42:16). The author of this plan—its originator so to speak—is God the Father. In one sense this plan might be compared to a map or GPS system that shows us the only possible way to return to God and become like Him. In and of itself, however, this plan cannot get us to the desired destination. It can show the way, but it is not the means by which we reach our goal; hence the need for the Savior's Atonement.

THE SAVIOR'S ATONEMENT

The goal of the Savior's Atonement is to make it possible for us to return to God's presence and become like Him so we might have a fulness of joy. It is the means by which the plan of salvation accomplishes its prime purpose. In order to fulfill this purpose, the Savior performed His Atonement, which generated the necessary powers to overcome the following four obstacles that hinder us in our quest:

> Physical death
> Sin and its consequences
> Common afflictions, temptations, and infirmities of life
> Weaknesses and imperfections

The first two obstacles can be overcome by the *redemptive* powers of Christ's Atonement, since He redeemed us from death by His Resurrection (see 1 Cor. 15:20–22) and from the stain of our sins by making available repentance—which is only made possible because He suffered and descended beneath all things (see Isa. 53:3–5).[1] The last two obstacles mentioned above can be overcome by the *enabling* powers of Christ's Atonement; His suffering endowed Him with the power to strengthen us in our afflictions and temptations (see Alma 7:11) and the power to overcome our weaknesses so we can become godlike (see Moro. 10:32–33).

The author of the Atonement is, of course, Jesus Christ. In one sense, His Atonement can be compared to a spiritual vehicle that has the power to transport us along the divine path designated by the plan of salvation. But this vehicle, in and of itself, cannot get us to the desired destination. We need a driver; hence the need for the doctrine of Christ.

THE DOCTRINE OF CHRIST

This doctrine commands us to have faith in Jesus Christ, repent, be baptized, receive the gift of the Holy Ghost, feast upon the words of Christ, and endure to the end (see Acts 2:37–41; 2 Ne. 31:15–21). As we individually apply this doctrine and participate in these ordinances, we become the spiritual driver and can draw upon the full powers of Christ made possible through His Atonement (the spiritual vehicle that makes our progress possible). This enables us to return to God's presence and become more like Him. As Sunday School General President Mark L. Pace noted: "As we live the doctrine of Christ, we exercise our agency and invite the Atonement of Christ to be effective in our lives."[2] In this way, the doctrine of Christ becomes the key that unlocks the powers of the Savior's Atonement so the plan of salvation can become a reality in our lives, not just an idealistic dream.

SUMMARY OF RELATIONSHIPS AMONG DOCTRINAL PRINCIPLES

The interrelationship among these three doctrinal principles might be summarized as follows:

DOCTRINAL PRINCIPLE	AUTHOR OR CONTRIBUTOR	COMPARISON
The plan of salvation	Heavenly Father	Map
The Savior's Atonement	Jesus Christ	Vehicle
The doctrine of Christ	Each of us	Driver

None of these doctrinal principles working alone can save us, but when they work in harmony with each other, the goal of salvation, even exaltation, is possible. That is why it is so important to teach not only the individual doctrinal principles of the gospel but also how they relate to each other. By doing so, we gain an increased vision of the entire "gospel puzzle." And with that increased vision comes increased motivation to walk the path to eternal life.

CONCLUSION

The principle of doctrinal interdependency has many applications. For example, one might contemplate the relationship between faith, repentance, baptism, and the gift of the Holy Ghost and the reason for this sequential order. In essence, each principle and ordinance builds upon the former. One might discuss how and why this is the case. Likewise, one might discuss the interrelationship between fasting and prayer and why they are often combined. Or

Putting Together the "Gospel Puzzle": Doctrinal Relationships

why the doctrine of the premortal existence is critical to understanding and accepting the Church's stance against abortion. When one understands the former, one will better understand the latter.

Putting together a puzzle always seems easier if we can first see the entire picture as set out on the cover of the box. This overview allows us to see how each piece fits into the total picture. It gives us a sense of purpose and vision and direction as we proceed. So it is with the gospel. If we can teach how a particular doctrine fits in with the plan of salvation, the Savior's Atonement, or the doctrine of Christ, then we can usually enlarge one's understanding of the particular gospel principle being taught. For example, suppose we are teaching the law of tithing. If we can emphasize that this principle is not really about money, but faith, then we have tied it back to the first principle espoused in the doctrine of Christ. If we can teach that becoming like God is not some new, unorthodox principle, but the end goal of the plan of salvation, then we have again enlarged our perspective.

Perhaps this is, in part, what Paul was speaking of when he said, "That in the dispensation of the fulness of times he [Christ] might gather together in one all things in Christ" (Eph. 1:10). All things certainly include the doctrinal principles and ordinances of the gospel. As we better understand their interrelationships, we help "gather together in one all things in Christ."

CHAPTER 11

How Should We Interpret the Scriptures?

Teaching the doctrine requires us to both read the scriptures and interpret them. At first blush this may seem an easy task, but history has proved the contrary. Have you ever wondered why we have one Bible but hundreds of different Christian churches? Because they all interpret the Bible differently; if they interpreted it the same, they would be the same church.

How then does the Lord want us to interpret the scriptures so that we can do as Paul said: "keep the unity" and come to "one Lord, *one faith*, one baptism"? (Eph. 4:3, 5; emphasis added). In other words, what are the operative divine principles of interpreting the scriptures that will help us teach the doctrine in its pure and undiluted form?

There are many methods of interpreting the scriptures. Some are man-made and hence have led to the establishment of hundreds of different Christian churches. Such man-made interpretations were the cause of Joseph Smith's frustration as he sought the truth: "The teachers of religion of the different sects *understood the same passages of scripture so differently* as to destroy all confidence in settling the question by an appeal to the Bible" (JS—H 1:12; emphasis added). Fortunately, God has endorsed certain methods of interpreting the scriptures. When these methods are utilized, they lead to a united belief in Christ's true doctrine.

Following are various methods of interpreting the scriptures, the first of which are man-made and the latter of which are God-given.

MAN-MADE METHODS OF INTERPRETATION

First: The Priority Method

This method was utilized on at least one occasion by Martin Luther. He read Romans 3:28, which says, "A man is justified by faith without the deeds of the law," and James 2:24, which reads, "By works a man is justified, and not by faith only." He concluded that these two scriptures were in opposition. As a consequence he unilaterally determined that Paul should trump or take priority over James. He even went so far as to suggest that the book of James should be cast out of the Bible. His exact words were "Many sweat to reconcile St. Paul and St. James . . . but in vain. 'Faith justifies' and 'faith does not justify' contradict each other flatly. If any one can harmonize them I will give him my doctor's hood and let him call me a fool." Luther went on to say, "Let us banish this epistle [of James] from the university, for it is worthless."[1] The obvious weakness in such a method of interpretation is that it pits one Apostle against another, thus promoting chaos and conflict rather than harmony and order, as should be the case in Christ's Church. C. S. Lewis also warned against this method of interpretation: "We must not use an apostle's teaching to contradict that of Our Lord"[2] or, we might add with similar logic, to contradict that of another Apostle.

Second: The Tunnel-Vision Method

Under this method, some view a few scriptures on a subject and exclude all others on the same subject and thus limit their vision of the total truth. They see part of the way ahead but have no peripheral vision and thus are blind to everything on their right and left. In essence, they have self-inflicted vision problems. This often occurs when some place their sole reliance for salvation on a few selected scriptures. For example, Ephesians 2:8–9 reads: "For by grace are ye saved through faith; and that not of yourselves: it is the gift of God: not of works, lest any man should boast." Some people interpret this scripture to mean that we are saved by grace (which is true)[3] but also advocate that we are eligible for that saving grace *solely* by believing in Christ (which is untrue).

Faith is an important step in the salvation process, but it is not the only step. James posed the question, "What doth it profit, my brethren, though a man say he hath faith [i.e., belief only], and have not works? *can faith save him*?" (James 2:14; emphasis added). In other words, can belief alone save a man? Lest there be any question, James, "a servant of God" (James 1:1), said "no" to that question five different times (see James 2:17–26).

If you wanted to know how to obtain salvation, would you read only a portion of the scriptures on salvation, or would you read *all* of the scriptures on the subject? Of course the honest searcher of truth would read them all. While serving as mission leaders, we would invite missionaries who had questions about Ephesians 2:8–9 to read *all* the scriptures referring to salvation in the Bible and then compare them with similar scriptures in the Book of Mormon. In so doing, we asked them to discover for themselves if God requires only faith to be eligible for His grace and salvation or if He also requires something more, and if so, what.

These missionaries *always* returned with the same answer—"Faith in Jesus Christ," they would say, "is one critical component to be eligible for God's saving grace, but it is *not the only component*." Their study taught them that someone must also keep God's commandments, which include (1) repentance, (2) baptism, (3) receiving the gift of the Holy Ghost, and (4) enduring to the end. That is what Peter the Apostle taught. Peter had spoken to a group of people about the divine Sonship of Jesus Christ. They believed what he told them was true, and then they asked: "What shall we *do?*" In essence they were saying, "We have faith in Jesus Christ; now what else must we do to be saved?" (see Acts 2:40). Peter responded: "Repent, and be baptized *every one of you* in the name of Jesus Christ for the remission of sins, and ye shall receive the gift of the Holy Ghost" (Acts 2:37–38; emphasis added). Peter taught them that belief can become true faith only when accompanied by obedience to God's commandments. The tunnel-vision method of interpretation presents a portion of the truth, but when someone presents it as the whole truth (e.g., we are saved by faith alone), it becomes an untruth.

Third: The Single-Witness Method

On occasion people will quote John 4:24 ("God is a Spirit") and say, "The Bible clearly states that God is a spirit; therefore, God cannot have a glorified body of flesh and bones." To one such person we responded, "Is there another scripture in the Bible to support your proposition that God is only a spirit? There are over one thousand pages to choose from." He looked somewhat bewildered and, unable to think of any others, responded, "This is God's word—I only need one scripture." But that is an incorrect conclusion. One scripture is *not* God's standard for interpreting His word. On multiple occasions He has declared, "In the mouth of *two or three* witnesses shall every word be established" (2 Cor. 13:1; emphasis added).[4]

In the real estate field, there is a common phrase used to dispel false notions about the existence of a seemingly valid market:

"One sale does not a market make." In the religious field a similar principle applies: "One scripture does not a doctrine determine." One scripture is not sufficient to comply with God's law of multiple witnesses.

Fourth: The Square-Peg-in-the-Round-Hole Method

Imagine for a moment a child with a toy tool set trying to hit a square peg into a round hole. It might be amusing to watch, but the child's efforts would be futile. Unfortunately, that is the method used by many when interpreting 1 Corinthians 15:29, which discusses proxy baptism for the dead. Other supporting scriptures of this ordinance might be found in Hebrews 11:40 and Doctrine and Covenants 124:29–41; 127:5–8; and 128:1–18. We once read a book by a Christian author attempting to explain 1 Corinthians 15:29. He said there were over forty different interpretations of this "difficult" scripture.[5] Another author offered the interpretation that the word *martyrdom* should be substituted for *baptism*.[6] There was no contextual basis to support his conclusion, no Greek translation that yielded such a result, and no independent early Christian writing to give credence to his theory. It was no more than a square peg in a round hole. It was as though these authors wanted any interpretation but the plain, literal interpretation—that the ancient Church practiced baptisms for the dead. The Book of Mormon prophet Jacob described those who despised plainness and thus were always "looking beyond the mark" (Jacob 4:14).

The problem with this method of interpretation is that it is driven by a predetermined agenda to reach a given conclusion—usually in accord with someone's existing belief structure—rather than an honest desire to know the truth. Such an attitude is reminiscent of the friend of Galileo who refused to look through Galileo's telescope "because he really did not want to see that which he had so firmly denied."[7]

How Should We Interpret the Scriptures?

Fifth: The Majority-Wins Method

This method is driven by the philosophy that the one with the most scriptures on his or her side wins. It is often used by those who quote scriptures on faith versus those who quote scriptures on works. It occurs to a lesser degree on other subjects, such as determining the real Sabbath day—Saturday or Sunday. There are scriptures that seemingly support both positions. But such an approach is based on two false premises: First, that, independent of the Spirit, the majority is right. That has never been God's standard for the truth. For centuries, the majority believed the world was flat, and they were wrong. For centuries the majority believed the sun revolved around the earth, and they were wrong. John Milton spoke to this issue: "How few sometimes may know, when thousands err."[8] Numbers can be a helpful start, but alone they do not determine truth. And secondly, as discussed below, this method assumes that these scriptures are in opposition to one another, when they can usually be read in harmony.

GOD'S METHODS OF INTERPRETATION

So that we do not become confused in understanding the scriptures, God has endorsed certain methods of interpretation that lead us to a unity of faith.

First: The Multiple-Witnesses Method

As stated above, God requires multiple witnesses to determine the truth: "In the mouth of two or three witnesses shall every word be established" (2 Cor. 13:1). The Savior confirmed this: "It is also written in your law, that the testimony of two men is true" (John 8:17). For example, while there seems to be only one scripture to support the claim that God is a spirit, there are multiple scriptural witnesses and underlying logic to support that the Father and Son have glorified bodies of flesh and bones.[9]

Second: The Common-Sense Method

The gospel of Jesus Christ is not exempt from common sense and reason. The Lord said through Isaiah, "Come now, and let us reason together" (Isa. 1:18).[10] Paul went to the synagogues and "reasoned with them out of the scriptures" (Acts 17:2).[11] Peter declared that every Saint ought to be able to explain "a reason of the hope that is in [them]" (1 Pet. 3:15). For a moment let us apply the principles of reason and common sense to the following doctrinal issues. Which of the following statements makes more sense?

- God is a mysterious, undefined, unseen spirit without body, parts, and passions? Or, God has a glorified body of flesh and bones, in whose image we are literally created (see Gen. 1:26–27)? Which doctrine would lead one to a better understanding of God, to a more familial relationship with Him, and to a greater appreciation for our own bodies?
- Good people who never heard the gospel of Jesus Christ while in mortality are condemned to hell? Or, all people, either on this earth or in the spirit world after they die, will have a full opportunity to hear the gospel of Jesus Christ before the Final Judgment? Which doctrine seems more just? Which doctrine is more representative of God's love and desire to save all humankind? Which harmonizes with Peter's account of the Savior preaching the gospel to the dead?[12]

When faced with a doctrinal conflict, one might appropriately ask questions of reason and common sense, such as, Which is consistent with the way Jesus did it? Which will be consistent with the symbolism of the ordinance? And which will produce a more godlike people? Answering those questions will go a long way toward helping us understand how the Lord would have us interpret His scriptures.

Third: The Harmony Method

This method recognizes that a scriptural passage, when read in isolation, may have two or more reasonable interpretations but that the correct interpretation is the one that is in harmony with other scriptures on the same subject. For example, John 10:30 ("I and my Father are one") may have two reasonable interpretations when read in isolation: first, that the Father and Son are one essence or being—as taught by the Nicene Creed—or, second, that they are separate beings but one in purpose and will. If the first interpretation is chosen, then it will be in conflict with the myriad of other scriptures indicating that the Father and Son are separate individuals. If the second interpretation is selected, then it will be in harmony with the other scriptures on the subject—namely, that the Father and Son are two separate beings but nonetheless one in purpose and will.

Some years ago we attended a Christmas musical concert. The choir sang beautifully. One number featured a trumpeter. He played the first verse of a Christmas song. It was sweet and melodious. The choir joined in for the next verse, but something went wrong—the harmony with the trumpeter was nothing short of a discordant disaster. We felt sorry for the musicians; people were hanging their heads in embarrassment, hoping it would abruptly end. Finally, the conductor, unable to endure it any longer stopped midsong and said, "Folks, I am sorry—after the choir practiced this song with the trumpeter, we changed keys, but we forgot to tell him." She then invited the trumpeter to change keys, which, with great skill, he did. They then joined forces in a melodious and harmonious conclusion.

The trumpeter could be likened to the person who reads John 10:30 and interprets it to read that the Father and Son are one being. When played (i.e., read) in isolation, it sounds good, but when the choir joined in (i.e., the other scriptures on the subject sang their tune), the end result was a terrible discordance. The only way the trumpeter could be in harmony was to change his key (i.e., his interpretation of John 10:30), and when he did so (i.e., he now understood that the Father and Son are two beings who are one in purpose and will), then harmony prevailed.

Harmony is a fundamental principle of Christ's gospel and thus a fundamental principle in interpreting the scriptures. C. S. Lewis understood this and so wrote: "I take it as a first principle that we must not interpret any one part of Scripture so that it contradicts other parts."[13]

Fourth: Confirmation by the Holy Ghost

This method assumes that He who gave the scriptural word is in the best position to interpret the word. This is why Peter said, "No prophecy of the scripture is of any private interpretation. For the prophecy came not in old time by the will of man: but holy men of God spake as they were moved by the Holy Ghost" (2 Pet. 1:20–21). That is the key. Scriptures come by the Holy Ghost: "And whatsoever they shall speak when moved upon by the Holy Ghost shall be scripture" (D&C 68:4). Accordingly the Lord declared, "The things of God knoweth no man, but the Spirit of God" (1 Cor. 2:11–16).[14]

As great as our powers of reason may be, they will never be a substitute for the Spirit of God. Interpreting the scriptures is like learning a foreign language—a spiritual language that the natural man cannot understand without the aid of a translator. And there is only one perfect translator, and that is the Holy Ghost.

During our mission in Toronto, Canada, we had twenty-four Mandarin-speaking missionaries assigned to our area because of the large contingent of Chinese people living there. One evening we held a devotional for the Chinese Latter-day Saints and their friends. The speaker was an Area Seventy from China. He spoke

How Should We Interpret the Scriptures?

in Mandarin. Because we did not speak the language, we needed a translator, and one of the newer missionaries volunteered. The speaker discoursed for well over an hour, and on a subject light-years beyond the translating capacity of this well-intentioned but inexperienced elder. There would be long moments of silence, sometimes intervals of two to three minutes, then we would hear something like this come over our earphones: "He is saying something about the Resurrection and science; I just can't quite understand it all." It went on like this for the entire meeting. At the conclusion of the devotional, we heard some of the Chinese members say: "Oh, that was one of the best talks I've ever heard!" Something, however, got lost in the translation. Likewise, if we do not have the Holy Ghost as our translator, then much will get lost in our understanding of the scriptures. No matter how good our intentions may be or how high our IQs may register, without the Holy Ghost, we simply lack the capacity to fully understand the spiritual language of God.

Joseph Smith learned this great truth immediately after he was baptized and received the Holy Ghost: "We were filled with the Holy Ghost, and rejoiced in the God of our salvation. Our minds being now enlightened, *we began to have the scriptures laid open to our understandings, and the true meaning and intention of their most mysterious passages revealed unto us in a manner which we never could attain to previously, nor ever before had thought of*" (JS—H 1:74; emphasis added).

Although the confirmation of the Holy Ghost is the conclusive test for truth, in most cases the Holy Ghost will not give us His full confirming witness until we have applied the former tests—until we have pondered, treasured up, feasted, reasoned, and studied the very best we can—until we have done all within our power to understand God's message and will. Then comes the witness of the Holy Ghost that speaks the certain truth.

CONCLUSION

The Lord has given us safeguards for interpreting His scriptures so that we might learn the truth as He would have it taught—so we might all come to "one Lord, *one faith*, one baptism" (Eph. 4:5; emphasis added).

TEACHING SKILLS THAT SUPPORT THE DOCTRINE

CHAPTER 12

The Power of Repetition

THE LORD TEACHES WITH REPETITION

The Lord uses repetition as an effective teaching technique. Moroni, a messenger of God, appeared to Joseph Smith three times during the course of a night and then again the next morning. With each appearance, Moroni repeated the things he had previously taught and then built upon them (see JS—H 1:30–49). The Savior, on three successive occasions, asked Peter if he loved Him and then told Peter three times to feed His sheep or lambs (see John 21:15–17). Peter was shown on three occasions the vision that would lead to the preaching of the gospel to the Gentiles (see Acts 10:5–16). And in one sermon the Savior repeated five times what the kingdom of heaven is like, but each time He used a different parable to teach the point (see Matt. 13). What can we learn from these examples? The Master Teacher uses repetition to teach gospel truths.[1]

When reading the Doctrine and Covenants, one may notice that once the Lord introduces a principle, He often repeats it in quick succession thereafter until no doubt He is satisfied that the principle has been both understood and applied. For example, in July 1830, the Lord instructed each missionary to "open his mouth" (D&C 24:12). He then repeated this command twice in September 1830 (see D&C 28:16; D&C 30:5). Again in October 1830, He commanded, "Open your mouths" in three successive verses (D&C 33:8–10). In the following month, the injunction was again mentioned: "Lift up your voice and spare not" (D&C 34:10). There could be no doubt, no uncertainty in the minds of those early missionaries, that God wanted them to open their mouths.

In August 1831, the Lord taught another very important principle—that we should make many decisions on our own without always waiting for divine direction: "Verily I say, men should be anxiously engaged in a good cause, and do many things of their own free will, and bring to pass much righteousness; for the power is in them, wherein they are agents unto themselves" (D&C 58:27–28). The Lord thereafter taught this principle on multiple occasions and in multiple ways. In the same revelation He gave an example of this principle when He directed that the details of a financial transaction be left to the discretion of the bishop, "as seemeth him good" (D&C 58:51).

In the same month, a question arose as to whether the elders should make or buy a boat for their journey down the river. The Lord simply told them to do "as seemeth you good, it mattereth not unto me" (D&C 60:5). In other words, do not expect to be directed by me in everything; use your own good judgment to the fullest extent possible. Four days later, this principle was reinforced as the Lord told His missionaries, "It mattereth not unto me . . . whether they go by water or by land" and "Let them journey together, or two by two, as seemeth them good" (D&C 61:22, 35). Later the Lord told another missionary, "Go ye and preach my gospel, whether to the north or to the south, to the east or to the west, it mattereth not, for ye cannot go amiss" (D&C 80:3). The Lord emphasized the principle that we need to exercise our own judgment, wherever and whenever possible, by His repeatedly teaching the principle and by giving multiple concrete examples of how we might do so.

THE PROPHETS SPEAK WITH REPETITION

The prophets also teach with repetition. President Lorenzo Snow repeatedly taught the doctrine of tithing. Why? Because it was necessary for the spirituality of the Saints and financial solvency of the Church. President Heber J. Grant spoke so frequently on the Word of Wisdom that he received numerous letters asking him to stop. In the October 1935 general conference, he said: "I have been requested time and time again—principally by anonymous letters—'For heaven's sake find a new subject, and quit preaching so much on the Word of Wisdom.'"[2] President David O. McKay repeatedly preached missionary work, President Ezra Taft Benson spoke again and again on the Book of Mormon, President Thomas S. Monson spoke repeatedly on rescuing the lost, and President Russell M. Nelson has spoken frequently on our need to increase our capacity to hear and receive revelation. In fact, it seems that each prophet has highlighted certain themes in his ministry and has focused on them again and again. It is this repetition that brings about conviction and eventually leads to action.

WHAT CAN WE LEARN FROM THE SAVIOR AND HIS PROPHETS?

When we teach a gospel principle, we too should refer to it on multiple occasions throughout the lesson and give concrete examples of how and when to apply it, just as the Savior and His prophets have done. The principle of repetition seems to operate best when two guidelines are employed: (1) subsequent references build upon a prior explanation, as Moroni did with Joseph Smith, and (2) the principle is repeated using different examples.[3] When the Savior explained what the kingdom of heaven was like (see Matt. 13), He gave one parable to help the farmer understand (like unto a grain of mustard seed), another for the businessman (like unto a pearl of great price), another for the fisherman (like unto a net cast into the sea), and yet another for the housekeeper (like unto leaven). The doctrine was repeated in such a variety of ways that listeners from all walks of life could receive it in a way that was meaningful and understandable to them.

But how, as a parent or teacher, can we apply these principles of repetition in our teaching style? How can we do so without being boring or tedious? A teacher can commence class by reviewing one or two key principles from the prior week or by providing a summary at the end of class. Parents and teachers can use stories, analogies, object lessons, videos, and the like to both support and repeat doctrines previously taught. In addition, class members can be invited to share how they applied doctrinal principles taught in the prior week's lesson.

While serving as mission leaders in Canada, we learned it was very difficult for nonmembers of the Church to comprehend the Apostasy. This concept was foreign to most of them. This difficulty would, with some frequency, manifest itself when a missionary issued the baptismal invitation. The person being taught would then reply, "But I have already been baptized." The missionary, somewhat frustrated, would think, "But I told you about the Apostasy and loss of priesthood authority and the need for a restoration." Regardless of what they had taught, the recipient simply did not "get it." In fact, we found most hearers of the gospel message needed to hear about the Apostasy multiple times, in multiple ways, before fully understanding this doctrine. Therefore, in addition to teaching various scriptures on the Apostasy, we also tried to use various analogies and object lessons that would reinforce the doctrine.

For example, one such analogy was this: Suppose you had a spacious garden that was replete with beautiful flowers. It was maintained by twelve conscientious, expert gardeners, who watered and nurtured and weeded with meticulous care. Then one by one these gardeners died, with no replacements. What would eventually happen to the garden? Who would win—the weeds or flowers? The person being taught might respond: "Soon the weeds would sprout and quickly choke out the remaining flowers. The flowers could not survive without the loving and tender care of its gardeners." The missionaries might then add: "Likewise, when the Apostles were alive, the various doctrinal principles of the kingdom were pure and beautiful in every way. As a weed or false doctrine sprouted, the twelve Apostles quickly removed it with a correcting epistle or sermon. But when the Apostles died, the pure doctrinal principles (i.e., flowers) could not withstand the emergence of false doctrines (i.e., weeds) that crept into the Church, and the Apostasy, or loss of Christ's Church, became a historical fact."

We would also teach the Apostasy using this analogy: Suppose you entered a room with twelve lights and no windows. What would happen if, one by one, you turned off each light? The person being taught might respond with something like, "Well, the room would get darker and darker each time." The missionary would then say, "What would happen when all the lights were out?" The hearer might respond, "You would have total darkness." The missionary would then explain that the twelve lights are like Christ's original twelve Apostles. As each one died, the light in Christ's Church became dimmer and dimmer until the light was totally gone and the Church was lost from the earth. In order for the twelve lights to be operative again, the Lord had to restore twelve Apostles to the earth to lead His Church. This is called the Restoration. Many could relate to these analogies.

Other analogies and object lessons were used in this repetition process. In the course of doing so, the hearer's level of understanding often increased from 50 percent to 65 to 85 and then to nearly 100 percent, until they could say, "Now I get it. Now I understand why there had to be a restoration and why I need to be rebaptized."

THE NEED FOR REPETITION

President Dallin H. Oaks taught about the benefit of focusing on a few principles, rather than many, and then teaching them repeatedly. He illustrated this principle by sharing the following: "I'm told somewhere in Florida there is what is called the river of grass. It is a mile wide and about an inch deep, and the passage of the water makes no mark on the landscape. However, if that quantity of water were concentrated in a narrow channel, it would make a mark on the landscape just like many streambeds we have seen. Concentrate your teaching on a few principles, rather than trying to emphasize everything. Don't be a mile wide and an inch deep."[4] In other words, if the principles we teach are so broad and so numerous (wide) with little repetition (depth), it is likely that there will be "no mark" after some time has lapsed. But if we teach a few principles well and constantly repeat them, there may be a substantial mark to evidence our efforts.

Elder L. Aldin Porter, a former member of the Presidency of the Seventy, shared this experience that helped him understand the need for repetition. "Years ago," he said, "I had a small insurance agency up in Idaho. A successful, retired businessman moved to the Boise valley to settle down. After he was bored from playing golf and afternoons of fishing, I asked him to visit my operation

The Power of Repetition

and give me some business advice. The man accepted the invitation and spent two or three days talking to employees, watching, and listening. Finally, we went to lunch to discuss his findings." The retired businessman told Elder Porter: "You make one major mistake. When you tell people something, you think they hear you, and they don't. The first time we teach a concept or a principle, nobody hears us. The second time we teach a concept or a principle, people say, 'I've heard that somewhere before.' The third time we teach a concept or a principle, people say, 'That's a good idea, but I would have to change. I don't want to change.'" And then this gentleman said to him, "Now that's as far as we generally go. We say, 'Well, I've already told him three times. What do you want?' The fourth time you teach a concept or a principle, people say, 'That is a good idea. Someday I may try it.' The fifth time you teach a concept or a principle, people say, 'That is a good idea. I'll try it today.'" Then this gentleman leaned over his lunch and said to Elder Porter, "Now, those are the geniuses, the rest of them take longer."[5]

The need for repetition was reinforced for Tad while he was serving as a stake president. The stake leaders had decided to teach the law of morality, not as a single lesson, but in a series of repetitive lessons. The first week Tad spoke to the youth, the second week the bishop spoke to them, and then the third week the youth leaders led a discussion on what moral principles had been taught. Youth came forward to make needed confessions, but for some who had broken God's moral laws, it took two or three weeks before they completely understood the significance of these laws or until they got the courage to come forward or until their conscience was sufficiently pricked. Repetition allows the Spirit to bore deeper and deeper until it finally penetrates the core of one's soul.

REPETITION BLESSES BOTH LEARNER AND TEACHER

The need for repetition is not just for the learner—it is also for the teacher. We had a friend who always had a joke to tell. "How do you remember all these jokes?" we asked. He replied, "When I hear a good joke, I immediately tell it three times, and then I have it." We think we must have been some of his regular "victims," but in truth that is not a bad principle for mastering spiritual truths. When we receive a spiritual impression or a good thought, we might share it multiple times until we "have it."

CONCLUSION

Participation in temple ordinances and the weekly partaking of the sacrament are reminders that repetition is a divine teaching tool.[6] This principle was recently further confirmed for us when we read a scripture in the Doctrine and Covenants and noticed it begin with the words, "*And again*, verily I say unto you" (D&C 67:10; emphasis added). We wondered how many times the Lord or His servants used the phrase "and again" in the scriptures. To our surprise, it appears on numerous occasions. There is no question that the heavens use repetition to teach the gospel. We as teachers can likewise use it as a powerful tool to build God's kingdom.

CHAPTER 13

The Power of Discourse, Stories, Parables, and Object Lessons

DISCOURSE

Meaningful discussion is a critical factor in building faith and testimony. But it does not, nor should it exclude, powerful discourse and instruction. The teacher is not just a facilitator of gospel discussion but also an instrument who, under the direction of the Holy Ghost, can teach great doctrinal truths; bear powerful testimony; share stories, art, and music that support the doctrine; and extend inspired invitations. The ideal teacher is always seeking that perfect balance between discussion and discourse. Unfortunately, the discourse method often gets a bad name, not because it has no role in the teaching process, but because teachers sometimes overuse it at the expense of meaningful discussion. As a result, the pendulum occasionally swings too far and teachers abandon any discourse for the sake of discussion.

In 2018 the First Presidency gave the following instructions on this regard:

TEACHING SKILLS THAT SUPPORT THE DOCTRINE

The goal of every teacher is to teach the pure doctrine of the gospel. Teaching may include leading inspired discussions; however, it also includes many other teaching responsibilities that are not expressed in a term like *discussion leader*. The sacred responsibilities of a teacher are found in *Teaching in the Savior's Way*. For this reason, we invite leaders and members to use the term *teacher* (and not *discussion leader*, *facilitator*, or *moderator*) when referring to those who have been called and set apart to teach in the priesthood and auxiliary organizations of the Church.[1]

The Savior is the Master Teacher, whom we all want to emulate, but we can also learn divine teaching principles from angels. For example, an angel instructed Nephi about the tree of life. At first, the angel's teaching was in the form of a discussion. The angel constantly asked questions of Nephi in order to allow him the agency to respond and furthermore to assess his level of understanding. As the discussion continued, the angel built upon each answer Nephi gave. However, when we arrive at 1 Nephi 11:24 and continue through 1 Nephi 14, the prime method of teaching changes from discussion to discourse. For more than one hundred verses the angel teaches by instruction and through a vision of what the future holds. In that entire interchange, only one question requires Nephi to give more than a yes or no answer. This is clearly not a discussion—it is a discourse—a spiritual download of doctrinal and prophetic insights. The angel teaches us an important lesson—both discussion and discourse have their roles. To rely solely on one method at the expense of the other may be discounting the most effective way to teach a given doctrine at a given time. The Spirit must direct not only the doctrine we teach but also the method in which it is delivered.

The Power of Discourse, Stories, Parables, and Object Lessons

STORIES

A story is a powerful means to teach a gospel principle and evoke a thoughtful discussion. Stories teach truths in a simple way to which we can often relate. Stories are easily remembered, and they have a powerful motivating force when they refer to someone who has demonstrated the faith or courage we would like to emulate. Who among us does not remember the stories of David and Goliath or of Daniel in the lion's den or of Shadrach, Meshach, and Abed-nego in the fiery furnace or of the two thousand sons of Helaman, who did not doubt because of their mothers' faith? How many sermons would it take for us to remember and live the principles taught in those simple stories? The scriptures are filled with stories that appeal to children and adults alike.

Years ago, Kathy attended a stake conference in Hawaii where a young mother was one of the speakers. The young mother said that she had been reading stories from the scriptures to her three-year-old son but had become somewhat discouraged. Her son always wanted the same story, over and over again—the story of Abinadi in front of King Noah. While that young boy loved that story, it seemed as though he was not listening. He would run around the room or jump up and down on the bed while she was trying to tell the story. One day she walked into the family room and was horrified to see him standing on the top of one of the high bookshelves! Not knowing what to do to prevent him from falling, and not wanting to frighten him, she walked carefully into the room. When he saw her, he said, "Touch me not, for God shall smite you if ye lay your hands upon me" (Mosiah 13:3).

Children often listen more than we realize, and they usually learn when we teach them from the scriptures. When we do so, then their heroes become righteous men and women, like Nephi, Moroni, Eve, and Mary, rather than the secular idols of the world.

TEACHING SKILLS THAT SUPPORT THE DOCTRINE

Our lessons should frequently contain faith-promoting stories—not as stand-alone activities but as support for the doctrine we are teaching. Elder Bruce R. McConkie, who understood the power of doctrinal discourse, also understood the power of a faith-promoting story:

> There is, of course, nothing wrong with telling a modern faith-promoting story. . . . Indeed, this should be encouraged to the full. We should make every effort to show that the same things are happening in the lives of the Saints today as transpired among the faithful of old. . . . Perhaps the perfect pattern in presenting faith-promoting stories is to teach what is found in the scriptures and then to put a seal of living reality upon it by telling a similar and equivalent thing that has happened in our dispensation and to our people and—most ideally—to us as individuals.[2]

In this spirit, class members can be invited to share personal stories that support the doctrinal principle being taught.

At general conference in October 1974, President Boyd K. Packer told a touching story that had a powerful effect upon us and increased our love and appreciation for the Savior and His tender mercies. Elder Packer told of one of the handcart companies "struggling to reach the Great Salt Lake Valley":

> Archer Walters, an English convert who was with the company, recorded in his diary under July 2, 1856, this sentence: "Brother Parker's little boy, age six, was lost, and the father went back to hunt him."
>
> The boy, Arthur, was next youngest of four children of Robert and Ann Parker. Three days earlier the company had hurriedly made camp in the face of a sudden thunderstorm.

The Power of Discourse, Stories, Parables, and Object Lessons

It was then the boy was missed. The parents had thought him to be playing along the way with the other children.

Someone remembered earlier in the day, when they had stopped, that they had seen the little boy settle down to rest under the shade of some brush. Now most of you have little children and you know how quickly a tired little six-year-old could fall asleep on a sultry summer day and how soundly he could sleep, so that even the noise of the camp moving on might not awaken him.

For two days the company remained, and all of the men searched for him. Then on July 2, with no alternative, the company was ordered west.

Robert Parker, as the diary records, went back alone to search once more for his little son. As he was leaving camp, his wife pinned a bright red shawl about his shoulders with words such as these: "If you find him dead, wrap him in the shawl and bury him. If you find him alive, you could use this as a flag to signal us."

She, with the other little children, took the handcart and struggled along with the company. Out on the trail each night Ann Parker kept watch. At sundown on July 5, as they were watching, they saw a figure approaching from the east! Then, in the rays of the setting sun, she saw the glimmer of the bright red shawl.

One of the diaries records: "Ann Parker fell in a pitiful heap upon the sand, and that night, for the first time in six nights, she slept."

Under July 5, Brother Walters recorded: "Brother Parker came into camp with a little boy that had been lost. Great joy came through the camp. The mother's joy I cannot describe."

TEACHING SKILLS THAT SUPPORT THE DOCTRINE

We do not know all of the details. A nameless woodsman found the little boy and described him as being sick with illness and with terror, and he cared for him until his father found him.

So here a story, commonplace in its day, ends—except for a question. How would you, in Ann Parker's place, feel toward the nameless woodsman who had saved your little son? Would there be any end to your gratitude?[3]

In a sense, the story of Ann and Robert Parker's son is every person's story. And who did the nameless woodsman symbolize but Jesus Christ, the Savior of us all, who is willing to save each one of us who may be lost at one time or another on the trail of life.

PARABLES

Certainly the Savior used parables effectively as a teaching tool. Fortunately, many of those parables are used today in a similar manner, such as the parable of the good Samaritan or the parable of the lost sheep. But parables did not end with the New Testament. Even if we find it difficult to create our own parables, we have leaders and teachers who have created parables that may be used by us today. Elder James E. Talmage wrote at least eleven parables, all of which are included in a book entitled *The Parables of James E. Talmage*.[4] We seldom hear them used today, but they are filled with rich doctrinal insights.

President Boyd K. Packer was a master at using parables. One is known as the parable of the pearl and the box: "A merchant man seeking precious jewels found at last the perfect pearl. He had the finest craftsman carve a superb jewel box and line it with blue velvet. He put his pearl of great price on display so others could share his treasure. He watched as people came to see it. Soon he turned away in sorrow. It was the box they admired, not the pearl."[5]

The Power of Discourse, Stories, Parables, and Object Lessons

This parable has many applications. Is it the beautiful conference center in Salt Lake City we admire or the teachings that emanate from it? A person's physical beauty or inner character? The cover of a book or its contents? The programs of the Church or its doctrine?

There is something about a parable that not only reinforces the doctrinal principle being taught but also has an inherent capacity to help transition the doctrine from the theoretical to the practical.

OBJECT LESSONS

The Savior used object lessons to teach doctrinal truths. When asked if it was "lawful to give tribute unto Caesar, or not," He requested they bring Him some tribute money. "And they brought unto him a penny. And he saith unto them, Whose is this image and superscription? They say unto him, Caesar's." Then came the lesson and the reason the use of the coin was so powerful: "Then saith he unto them, Render therefore unto Caesar the things which are Caesar's; and unto God the things that are God's" (Matt. 22:17–21). There was something about the image of Caesar on the coin that helped teach the concept that Caesar had his kingdom, namely, the temporal world, and that God has His—the spiritual world. The coin helped highlight this distinction.

On one occasion the disciples asked, "Who is the greatest in the kingdom of heaven?" The Savior then "called a little child unto him, and set him in the midst of them." The lesson then followed: "Except ye be converted, and become as little children, ye shall not enter into the kingdom of heaven. Whosoever therefore shall humble himself as this little child, the same is greatest in the kingdom of heaven" (Matt. 18:1–4). No more needed to be said. Seeing the child in front of them was the exclamation point to the principle taught.

TEACHING SKILLS THAT SUPPORT THE DOCTRINE

Object lessons can help us remember a principle long after the lesson is over.

We too can use object lessons as part of our rich and varied teaching styles. We once tried to teach our missionaries the importance of having daily contact with their investigators (see Alma 21:23). Kathy taught an object lesson to help teach this principle:

An elder was called to the front. Kathy would invite him to clasp his hands and then would pour water into them with the instruction not to let any water drip through his fingers. She then went on with her lesson as he stood there. As hard as the missionary tried to retain the water in his hands, it would leak out drop by drop. The other missionaries would watch with some amusement. After several minutes she would check to see how the missionary in front was doing. There was usually little if any water left in his hands. Kathy then asked the missionaries what this had to do with daily contacting. After some discussion, they recognized that the water represented the Spirit, and the clasped hands represented the people they were teaching, and even though they as missionaries would fill these peoples' lives with the Spirit on each visit, as soon as they left, the Spirit often slowly departed. It reminded the missionaries of the need to emphasize with those they were teaching that daily prayer and scripture study would help keep their lives filled with the Spirit. In addition, daily contact by the missionaries would provide for a renewal of the Spirit.

Ideas for object lessons are available in many of the Church's curriculum materials. Family and friends can also share ideas of effective object lessons they have witnessed. Object lessons, of course, are a means, not an end. If they provide entertainment alone, we have missed the mark. All teaching should focus on the doctrine and a desire to live it.

The Power of Discourse, Stories, Parables, and Object Lessons

CREATIVITY

It is not illegal to be creative. Our lessons can be spiritually entertaining and refreshing, provided they are also dignified and faith promoting. The Lord is creative. He did not create just one type of animal or one flower or one tree or one parable or one object lesson. He expressed these living forms and gospel principles in myriad ways. We should also strive to be creative. Creativity gives a richness and breadth and depth to the subject we are teaching. It makes learning more joyful. Imagine if you were teaching a lesson on beauty and the difference between merely defining what a flower is versus displaying several different types of flowers and letting people see them and smell them and touch them. Or imagine a teacher trying to teach in the abstract that the gospel "tastes" good, versus the teacher who invites a class member forward to eat a freshly baked chocolate chip cookie and then asks that class member to relate how the satisfying taste of the cookie can be compared to the satisfying taste of good doctrine.

Our lessons do not have to be dull to be spiritual. On the other hand they need to be a lot more than whipped cream; there needs to be spiritual substance, some real substance underneath. Hopefully our lessons will be sprinkled with stories, analogies, art, music, videos, and object lessons that give some life and joy to motivate the learner—but always with the purpose to support the doctrine. Some might say, "But I am not creative. I can't think of those things." The Holy Ghost can help inspire us in this regard. Joseph Smith observed: "A person may profit by noticing the first intimation of the spirit of revelation; . . . it may give you sudden strokes of ideas."[6] In addition, you have Church resources, leaders, the power of prayer, the Holy Ghost, and friends to help.

CONCLUSION

The resources and teaching techniques described here can make our family and Church discussions rich and varied. They were utilized and demonstrated by the Savior. As we likewise incorporate them into our lesson plans and teaching at home, we will more fully emulate the Savior's way of teaching.

CHAPTER 14

The "Like Unto" Principle

THE SAVIOR USED THE "LIKE UNTO" PRINCIPLE

Nephi spoke of a key teaching principle: "I did *liken all scriptures unto us,* that it might be for our profit and learning" (1 Ne. 19:23; emphasis added). Perhaps no teaching principle or technique was used more frequently by the Savior than this one. It is a masterful way to relate to people and teach them at a level they can understand. Often the Savior's phraseology included the words "like unto," or similar language, demonstrating a comparison.

The Savior had the remarkable ability to take a gospel principle or doctrine and compare it to a common object or life experience in such a way that people could say, "Oh, now I understand that principle or doctrine—it has been compared to an object or experience to which I can relate." In essence, the Savior converted what might have been an abstract thought to a practical reality. He took a secular object or event and transformed it to the spiritual realm. This may have been His most powerful teaching technique. Of course, it did not supersede the Spirit, but it did become an ideal vehicle through which the Spirit could operate.

This teaching technique of comparing, or "likening unto," was used by the Savior to (1) teach a divine principle or doctrine, (2) invite others to action, (3) teach the worth or unique characteristics of an individual, and (4) teach His own divine Sonship. Following are some examples.

Teaching a Divine Principle or Doctrine

The Savior taught the divine principle that salvation is not just a matter of confessing Christ; it also requires one to do the will of the Lord: "Not every one that saith unto me, Lord, Lord, shall enter into the kingdom of heaven; but he that doeth the will of my Father which is in heaven" (Matt. 7:21). The Savior could have left His teaching at this, but He did not. So there would be no misunderstanding, no ambiguity about the doctrine, He gave a comparison so that people could relate this doctrinal principle to their personal lives.

The Savior *likened* those who do the will of the Lord "unto a wise man, which built his house upon a rock," and when "the floods came, and the winds blew, and beat upon that house, . . . it fell not: for it was founded upon a rock." On the other hand, the Savior *likened* those who hear but do not do the word of the Lord "unto a foolish man, which built his house upon the sand," and when the floods and wind "beat upon that house, . . . it fell: and great was the fall of it" (Matt. 7:24–27). How could anyone teach the false doctrine that belief alone brings salvation after hearing the foregoing principle taught and supported by those "like unto" examples?

The Lord used many other "like unto" comparisons to explain other gospel principles and doctrines. For example, He likened the divine principle that one should do good on the Sabbath to the man who rescued his sheep that had fallen into a pit on the Sabbath.

The "Like Unto" Principle

Then came the spiritual truth—He asked if the healing of a man or woman on the Sabbath is not more important than tending to the needs of a sheep (see Matt. 12:11–13). On another occasion He likened His future three days in the tomb to Jonas's three days "in the whale's belly" (Matt. 12:40). He likened the signs of the last days, which signal Christ's Second Coming, to the fig tree putting forth its leaves, signaling the forthcoming summer (see Matt. 24:32–35; Mark 13:28–31; Luke 21:29–33). He likened His love for the people of Jerusalem and His desire to gather them to a hen who gathers "her chickens under her wings" to protect them (Matt. 23:37). The list of "like unto" examples continues on and on.

On at least eleven occasions, the Savior used the "like unto" principle to describe and explain the doctrine pertaining to the kingdom of heaven. Two of these examples are listed below:

THE KINGDOM OF HEAVEN IS LIKE UNTO:	DOCTRINAL PRINCIPLE
1. "a grain of mustard seed" (Matt. 13:31–32; Luke 13:18–19).	Just as the mustard seed "is the least of all seeds" but has great growth, so the Church will start small but have great increase.
2. "a merchant man, seeking goodly pearls: who, when he [finds] one pearl of great price," sells all he has and buys it (Matt. 13:45–46).	When people search for the true church and find it (the pearl of great price), they should give up all they have to acquire it.

The Savior taught us by example that we can be more effective teachers if we regularly use the "like unto" principle when teaching doctrinal truths.

One Sunday we had a family study class via the internet with our children and grandchildren. Our son was giving the lesson on

King Benjamin's sermon and focusing on the transformation from the natural man to the spiritual man—in essence, becoming a new creature in Christ. To illustrate this transformation, he showed a picture of a caterpillar and asked the young children what it was. They all knew. He then showed a picture of a butterfly that evolved from the caterpillar and asked if they were the same creature. This led to a discussion that though they had similar DNA and origins, they were nonetheless different creatures. The analogy made was that the natural and spiritual man may have the same DNA and origins, but the spiritual man is indeed a new creature in Christ—"like unto" a butterfly that can experience freedoms it has never known before. This "like unto" example gave additional perspective to the meaning of becoming a new creature in Christ.

Inviting Others to Action

On occasion the Savior would use a comparison to invite someone to action. As the Savior walked by the Sea of Galilee, He saw Peter and Andrew fishing. He then drew upon their secular profession to invite them to participate in a new, spiritual profession: "Follow me, and I will make you fishers of men" (Matt. 4:19). No doubt this comparison between their current secular profession and their future spiritual one helped these disciples capture a vision of their future missionary work and served as an incentive for that mission.

Teaching the Unique Characteristics and Worth of an Individual

The Savior compared His disciples to "the salt of the earth" (Matt. 5:13), to "the light of the world" (Matt. 5:14), and to a "branch" that abides in the "vine" (John 15:4). By likening us to these earthly elements and the positive qualities they represent, the Lord elevates our feelings of self-worth.

The "Like Unto" Principle

Teaching His Divine Sonship and Mission

The Savior declared His divine Sonship and mission on multiple occasions. In doing so, He often compared His Sonship to some object or event to which His listeners could readily relate. To the woman at the well, He declared that He was the living water: "But whosoever drinketh of the water that I shall give him shall never thirst" (John 4:14). To those who witnessed the miracle of the loaves and fishes, He stated, "I am the bread of life" (John 6:35). After giving sight to a blind man, He spoke of an even greater light: "I am the light of the world" (John 8:12). To those who tended flocks, He declared, "I am the good shepherd" (John 10:14); to one who would soon witness the raising of Lazarus from the dead, "I am the resurrection and the life" (John 11:25); and to those who worked in the vineyards, "I am the vine, ye are the branches" (John 15:5). He repeatedly declared His Messiahship by utilizing the "like unto" principle.

A RECCURRING PRINCIPLE

These many examples help us understand the prominence of this "like unto" principle in the Savior's teaching. He used it again and again and again. It was not some fringe concept, some occasionally used technique; it was at the center and forefront of His teaching.

We learn from the Savior's example that people are better able to comprehend and retain doctrinal principles that are likened unto something temporal with which they are familiar. Many of the prophets have adopted this technique. People often smile when Elder Dieter F. Uchtdorf (formerly a commercial pilot) begins one of his aviation analogies, because they know they are going to both enjoy it and learn from it. One such analogy is as follows:

> Suppose you were to take off from an airport at the equator, intending to circumnavigate the globe, but your

course was off by just one degree. By the time you returned to the same longitude, how far off course would you be? A few miles? A hundred miles? The answer might surprise you. An error of only one degree would put you almost 500 miles (800 km) off course, or one hour of flight for a jet. No one wants his life to end in tragedy. But all too often, *like* the pilots and passengers . . . we set out on what we hope will be an exciting journey only to realize too late that an error of a few degrees has set us on a course for spiritual disaster.[1]

President Boyd K. Packer was a master at this technique. His cake analogy shows how the gospel should not be delivered and, conversely, how it should be delivered. Once seen, the demonstration is never to be forgotten. Kathy has used it with great effectiveness in many teaching situations. President Packer tells of this "like unto" demonstration in his own words:

> We scheduled zone conferences. For each one, Sister Packer baked a three-tiered cake, which she and Sister Bateman decorated beautifully—thick, colorful layers of frosting, trimmed beautifully, and with "The Gospel" inscribed across the top. When the missionaries were assembled, with some ceremony we brought the cake in. It was something to behold.
>
> As we pointed out that the cake represented the gospel, we asked, "Who would like to have some?" There was always a hungry elder who eagerly volunteered. We called him forward and said, "We will serve you first." I then sank my fingers into the top of the cake and tore out a large piece. I was careful to clench my fist after tearing it out so that the frosting would ooze through my fingers, and then as the elders sat in total disbelief, I threw the piece of cake to the

elder, spattering some frosting down the front of his suit. "Would anyone else like some cake?" I inquired. For some reason, there were no takers.

Then we produced a crystal dish, a silver fork, a linen napkin, and a beautiful silver serving knife. With great dignity I carefully cut a slice of the cake from the other side, gently set it on the crystal dish, and asked, "Would anyone like a piece of cake?"

The lesson was obvious. It was the same cake in both cases, the same flavor, the same nourishment. The manner of serving either made it inviting, even enticing, or uninviting, even revolting. The cake, we reminded the missionaries, represented the gospel. How were they serving it?

After the demonstration we had no difficulty—in fact, there was some considerable enthusiasm—in inspiring the missionaries to improve their teaching.[2]

OTHER "LIKE UNTO" EXAMPLES

We have found it most helpful to use "like unto" examples when teaching various gospel principles. For example, what is the relationship among justice, mercy, and repentance? In the following example the law of justice is *likened* unto the law of gravity, mercy is *likened* unto a parachute, and repentance is *likened* unto a rip cord.

Suppose for a moment a man riding in a small plane sees a lush, green valley below, and contemplating an exhilarating free fall, makes a rash decision. He spontaneously jumps from the plane. After doing so, he quickly realizes the foolishness of his action. He wants to land safely, but there is an obstacle—the law of gravity. He moves his arms with astounding speed, hoping to fly, but to no avail. He positions his body to float or glide so as to slow the descent, but the law of gravity is unrelenting and unmerciful. He tries to reason with this basic law of nature: "It was a mistake. I will never do it again. I have learned my lesson." But his pleas and petitions fall on deaf ears. The law of gravity, *like* the law of justice, has no passion; it knows no mercy; it has no forgiveness, and it knows no exceptions. Fortuitously though, he suddenly feels something on his back. His friend in the plane, sensing the moment of foolishness, had placed a parachute there just before the jump. He finds the rip cord and pulls it. Relieved, he floats safely to the ground. Now we might ask: "Was the law of gravity violated or compromised in any way? Or rather, was another law invoked that was compatible, yet merciful?"

When we sin, we are *like* the foolish man who jumped from the plane. No matter what we do on our own, only a crash landing awaits us. We have no power to reverse the course. We are subject to the law of justice, which *like* the law of gravity, is exacting and unforgiving. We can be saved only because the Lord provides us with a spiritual parachute. This is *like unto* the Savior's Atonement. If we have faith in Jesus Christ and repent (*like unto* pulling the rip cord), then the protective and saving powers of the Atonement are unleashed on our behalf and we can land unharmed. Without this spiritual parachute, there is no hope, but with it, there is every hope of salvation.

Another "like unto" example might be comparing the commandments to the painted lines on a highway. Keeping within the lanes marked by the lines will help us get to our destination safely. If we do not, we put our life at risk. Likewise if we keep (live) within the commandments, they will help us get to our eternal destination spiritually unharmed.

CONCLUSION

Some might ask: "But what if I cannot think of good analogies or 'like unto' examples? How can I avail myself of them?" First,

The "Like Unto" Principle

the scriptures and lesson materials have many excellent examples. Second, if we take time to think about the subject we are teaching and wrestle with it and pray about it and do not give up easily, then examples will often come. And third, we have family and class members who can aid us by sharing their insights and creativity. As an example of this, President Packer once likened repentance unto soap and then invited those he was teaching "to put their minds to work on the subject of teaching repentance" and share other examples they could think of. "In an hour of discussion we produced a dozen or more life situations that might be used."[3]

Tad ministers to a great family who has a daughter named Emily Clark. She was seventeen years old at the time of one of his visits. With her parents' consent, he invited her to give a missionary lesson on any subject she chose; the rest of the family would play the role of nonmembers. The next time Tad returned, he was in for a most pleasant surprise. Her lesson was on why the Lord waited so long to restore His Church to the earth after the Apostasy had taken place. She commenced with an analogy, a "like unto" example, which she developed completely on her own. She asked her younger sister, Rachael, how to make a cake. A discussion then ensued about the necessary ingredients—flour, eggs, oil, salt, and so on. She asked, "Once you have these ingredients, do you just mix them in any proportions and then stick them in the oven and a cake comes out?" They then discussed the need to mix them in the right proportions and the need to preheat the oven to the right temperature.

She then made her brilliant "like unto" example: "Preparing for the Restoration," she said, "is *like* baking a cake; you must have all the necessary ingredients in the right proportions for the Restoration to occur." She then led a discussion about those necessary ingredients—a people who were free from the superstitions of the medieval world, a people who had freedom of speech and religion, a place free from the religious intolerance of Western Europe. She then discussed the events that were necessary to make those ingredients available—the Magna Carta, movable type, the Reformers, the founding of America, the pilgrims, and the Revolutionary War—all evidences of "preheating" the oven for the cake (the Restoration). She then explained that once those ingredients were available and the oven preheated, the Lord could bring about the Restoration (i.e., bake the cake). We all understood. Periodically, her parents would look at each other with amazement, as if to say, "How in the world did she come up with this analogy?" It was so brilliant—perhaps because it was so simple and so easy to relate to. She is living proof that with some thought and prayer, we can develop "like unto" analogies.

In developing this teaching technique, we may draw upon experiences from our careers or hobbies, from sports or culture, from being a spouse, parent, or single adult. Everyone has meaningful experiences, even in the seemingly routine events of life. From these we may make "like unto" parallels that have spiritual implications and that can help others build faith. We too can use this teaching technique, so frequently and effectively used by the Savior.

CHAPTER 15

Responding to Difficult Questions

THE NEED TO ADDRESS DIFFICULT QUESTIONS

President M. Russell Ballard spoke to Church Educational System employees about the great need for their students to master the doctrine and the related historical context so they can respond "to questions and challenges they hear and see every day among their peers and on social media." Lest there be any question about this timely need, he said: "Gone are the days when a student asked an honest question and a teacher responded: 'Don't worry about it!' Gone are the days when a student raised a sincere concern and a teacher bore his or her testimony as a response intended to avoid the issue. Gone are the days when students were protected from the people who attacked the church." President Ballard then explained the reason this knowledge was so critical in the students' lives: "so they can experience a mature and lasting conversion to the gospel and a lifelong commitment to Jesus Christ."

President Ballard then made this comparison: "We give medical inoculations to our precious missionaries before sending them into the mission field so they will be protected against diseases that can harm or even kill them. In a similar fashion, please, before you send them into the world, inoculate your students by providing faithful, thoughtful and accurate interpretation of gospel doctrine, the scriptures, our history, and those topics that are sometimes misunderstood."

President Ballard then made the following promise: "As you teachers pay the price to better understand our history, doctrine and practices—better than you do now—you will be prepared to provide thoughtful, careful and inspired answers to your students' questions."[1]

As important as it is for teachers to prepare themselves and respond with knowledge and the Spirit, it is even more important for parents to be prepared to respond to such questions. One Church study showed that youth sought answers to difficult questions from their parents before going to the internet. Fortunately, parents are the first line of defense.

PRINCIPLES THAT GOVERN ANSWERS TO QUESTIONS

Below are some principles that may help us respond to questions that may be of concern to family members and others.

Expect Some Questions to Go Unanswered

Every parent and teacher will receive difficult gospel questions from time to time. We ought to be prepared to answer every question we possibly can in the spirit of Peter's injunction to the Saints: "Sanctify the Lord God in your hearts: and be ready always to give an answer to every man that *asketh you a reason of the hope that is in you with meekness and fear*" (1 Pet. 3:15; emphasis added).

While we can answer many questions, sometimes the appropriate answer is "I don't know." We should expect some questions to go unanswered, at least at the current time, for the following reasons:

One, God requires us to have faith. As a test of our faith, He chooses not to reveal certain truths. Mormon was about to record some "greater things," when he said, "But the Lord forbade it, saying: I will try the faith of my people" (3 Ne. 26:10–11). Nephi did not know the reason for creating a second set of plates. He simply observed: "Wherefore, the Lord hath commanded me to make these plates for a wise purpose in him, *which purpose I know not*" (1 Ne. 9:5; emphasis added). Even the Savior did not have the answer to every question during His mortal ministry. While stretched out upon the cross, He cried out, "My God, my God, why hast thou forsaken me?" (Matt. 27:46). There was no immediate answer; nonetheless, His faith in the Father did not wane.

Faith, by its very nature, means we will not have all the answers. Unfortunately, some people demand the underlying rationale for every command and perfection in every Church leader—in essence they want a religion without faith, and they can't have it—because no such thing exists.

Two, our minds are finite, and accordingly, there are questions for which we could not understand the answer, even if it were given to us. For example, a baby cannot comprehend calculus, even though it is truth. The Lord highlighted this divine principle when He said: "As the heavens are higher than the earth, so are my ways higher than your ways, and my thoughts than your thoughts" (Isa. 55:9).[2] King Benjamin expressed a similar sentiment: "Man doth not comprehend all the things which the Lord can comprehend" (Mosiah 4:9).

Three, God withholds certain truths because their release would be premature in His divine timetable. The Savior made this observation to His disciples: "I have yet many things to say unto you, but ye cannot bear them now" (John 16:12).³ Our lack of spiritual maturity and readiness may delay the timetable for our receipt of certain answers.

Four, historic and scientific truths often come in installments, and therefore in the interim, there may exist a seeming conflict between history or science on one hand and religion on the other, but in the end they will be in perfect accord. We see this, for example, with regard to archaeological discoveries. There may initially be a gap between the truths of the Book of Mormon and what archaeology has to offer. But time is a great friend to truth. For years critics claimed that cement and barley did not exist in Book of Mormon times—they were anachronisms that "proved" the Book of Mormon a fraud. Then, after the passage of many years, archaeology revealed its truth—cement and barley were discovered to have existed in Book of Mormon times. The question that had raised doubt in the skeptic became one more confirmation for the man and woman of faith.

We should not be surprised or taken aback when we have an unanswered question; rather, *we should expect some unanswered questions*. Even prophets have unanswered questions. When Adam was asked by an angel why he offered sacrifices, he could only reply, "*I know not*, save the Lord commanded me" (Moses 5:6; emphasis added). When Nephi was asked by an angel if he understood "the condescension of God," he replied, "I know that he loveth his children; *nevertheless, I do not know the meaning of all things*" (1 Ne. 11:16–17; emphasis added).⁴ Not having all the answers to all of our questions is part of God's plan, but in the interim we should seek all the truth we can with unwavering faith in God.

Alexis de Tocqueville was the brilliant social scientist who wrote the incomparable two-volume series titled *Democracy in America*. To his credit he submitted his intellect and will to God's. "I am unacquainted with [God's] designs," he said, meaning he didn't understand all of His purposes, "but, I shall not cease to believe in them because I cannot fathom them, and *I had rather mistrust my own capacity than his justice.*"[5] What a humble, faith-filled declaration!

Faith acknowledges the reality of an intellect and morality higher and more superior than one's own—namely, that of God's. Accordingly, faith strikes at the core of pride and nourishes the virtues of humility and divine trust. This, in turn, enhances our capacity to learn, enlarges our eternal perspective, gives added hope, and deepens our commitment to be obedient. In essence, faith, which of necessity results in some unanswered questions, has an inherent capacity to accelerate our spiritual progress—which in the end is the prime purpose of the plan of salvation.

Do Not Attempt to Prove Spiritual Truths with Secular Means

One may determine the height of a room with a tape measure or the weight of a rock with scales, but one cannot determine the height or size of one's faith or the truth of a divine doctrine with secular instruments. The Lord has provided secular tools to discover secular truths, and divine tools to determine divine truths. As a result, neither archeology nor geography nor linguistics nor DNA can prove or disprove Joseph Smith's First Vision or the doctrinal truths of the Book of Mormon—that can be done only by employing spiritual tools, such as the test used by Joseph Smith (see James 1:5–6) or the test put forth by Moroni (see Moro. 10:4–5).[6]

Seek for a Spiritual Witness

If someone has received a spiritual witness of the divinity of the Book of Mormon or the plan of salvation or the Prophet Joseph Smith, that will always trump intellectual questions or doubts a person may have. Why is that? Because the Spirit is the only certain and infallible test of spiritual truth. As the Savior said, "The Spirit of truth . . . will guide you into all truth" (John 16:13). In other words, we should not lose faith in the many things we do know, because of a few things we do not know.

Elder Jeffrey R. Holland spoke powerfully to this point:

> In the moments of fear or doubt or troubling times, hold the ground you have already won, even if that ground is limited. . . . The size of your faith or degree of your knowledge is not the issue—it is the integrity you demonstrate toward the faith you do have and the truth you already know. . . . I am not asking you to pretend to have faith you do not have. I am asking you to be true to the faith you do have. Sometimes we act as if an honest declaration of doubt is a higher manifestation of moral courage than is an honest declaration of faith. It is not![7]

Use the Wisdom and Testimonies of Church-Sponsored Materials and Those around You

The Church now publishes articles online to help answer controversial questions concerning doctrine, social issues, and historical events.[8] We all know it is much easier to answer difficult questions after careful thought than in the heat of a spontaneous discussion. We would all do well to study the answers to these questions in advance.

One teacher employed some helpful principles in responding to a difficult question. A man asked the following question: "My parents were sealed in the temple, later divorced, and then had a cancellation of their sealing. Whom am I sealed to in the next life?" The teacher, instead of having a meltdown, did something extremely wise. He said to the man: "That is a very good question. No doubt you have given it some considerable thought. Would you please share any insights you have gained on the matter?" The man seemed pleased to respond and did so. The teacher then invited others to share their thoughts. It was obvious the teacher wanted to benefit from the collective wisdom of those present. As a result the teacher neither panicked nor dominated the response. The question was not completely answered, but as the teacher focused on doctrinal principles shared by class members, insights developed that helped lay the foundation for a more complete answer in the future.

FOCUS ON THE BOOK OF MORMON— THE KEYSTONE OF OUR RELIGION

Once we know that Christ suffered for our sins in the Garden of Gethsemane so we might repent, and also that He died on the cross so we might be resurrected, then we can accept the natural conclusion of that knowledge—namely, that He is our Redeemer and Savior. We may not understand why He chose Judas to be an Apostle—who later proved to be a thief and traitor. We may not understand why He selected Peter to be His chief Apostle—who in a fit of anger cut off the ear of the high priest's servant. And we may not understand why He initially commanded His Apostles not to preach the gospel to the Gentiles (see Matt. 10:5), but we do know there must be a reasonable answer to each of those questions. Why? Because we have now crossed the bridge of doubt and accepted Jesus as our Redeemer and Savior, and therefore know He is the perfect embodiment of all truth.

In like manner, once we know the Book of Mormon is the word of God, then we can accept the natural conclusion of that knowledge—namely, that Joseph Smith must have been a prophet of God and that through his instrumentality, the true Church of Jesus Christ was restored to the earth. We may not understand all the ramifications of polygamy. We may not completely understand the translation methodology of the Book of Abraham. And we may not fully understand the reason for variations in the multiple accounts of the First Vision. But we do know there must be a reasonable answer to each of those questions. Why? Because we have now crossed the bridge of doubt and accepted the Book of Mormon as the word of God and therefore the divine implications that flow from that truth.

The Book of Mormon is a powerful, dynamic, even compelling witness of the prophetic calling of Joseph Smith and the truth of this Church. As mentioned, archaeology has already proved that time is on the side of this divine book (with the discovery of metal plates, cement, and barley dated to Book of Mormon times—all claimed by the critics in earlier days to be anachronisms). Messages such as "Men are, that they might have joy" (2 Ne. 2:25) and "When ye are in the service of your fellow beings ye are only in the service of your God" (Mosiah 2:17) and scores of other profound insights have a divine ring and majesty to them. Any parent would be proud to have two or three such statements remembered by his or her posterity. How then could Joseph Smith, a young newlywed and on his own, generate scores of such memorable phrases?

The doctrine contained in the Book of Mormon is not only enlightening, but stunning, such as the doctrinal revelation that Jesus can not only cleanse us but also perfect us (see Moro. 10:32–33). The witnesses to the Book of Mormon are a brick wall to the critics—critics who have a small handful of dubious quotes stacked against an avalanche of undeniable testimonies by those men who repeatedly put their lives and reputations on the line in defense of this book. And most of all, the Spirit bears witness to every person, who with a sincere heart and real intent, seeks to know of the Book of Mormon's truthfulness (see Moro. 10:4–5).

The Book of Mormon is the rock foundation for the spiritual

Responding to Difficult Questions

truth-seeker. All the other issues raised by the critics are peripheral—diversions from the key question at hand—is the Book of Mormon the word of God? If it is the word of God (and surely it is), then all the peripheral issues will resolve themselves in due time.

If we have doubts because we are looking beyond the Book of Mormon, then we are looking beyond the mark. The Book of Mormon should be the focus of our truth-seeking. Either Joseph Smith personally wrote the book and it is a fraud, or he translated it by the gift and power of God and it is divinely inspired.

On occasion, friends who are struggling with their testimonies ask us about a specific question that has raised doubts in their minds. Sometimes we have a satisfactory answer, and sometimes we do not. In the latter case we often reply, "We do not currently know the answer to that question, but we would like to ask you a question. Do you think that Joseph Smith, at age twenty-three, with a limited education, who could not write a coherent letter, as attested to by his wife, wrote the entire Book of Mormon without any notes, in a single dictation draft in approximately sixty-five days—that he invented the multitude of inspiring stories in that book—that he authored the incredible doctrine found within its pages, much of which was contrary to the religious teachings of his day—that he created the legion of thought-provoking statements that hang on peoples' walls and refrigerator doors, or that he was such a lucky guesser that archaeology keeps proving him right after the critics have derided his claims as false? Or alternatively, do you believe he translated that book by the gift and power of God? If the latter, then Joseph was a prophet and the Church is absolutely true, and for the time being we can live with a few unanswered questions.

The central question for our dispensation has and always will be "Is the Book of Mormon the word of God?" Once we have answered that question, then the sum of all other questions pales in comparison. That is why Joseph Smith referred to the Book of Mormon as the keystone of our religion—because it is also the keystone of our testimonies. It is God's intellectual, emotional, and spiritual gift to all truth-seekers. That is why we, as parents and teachers, should repeatedly read, study, and bear testimony of this book and its witness of Christ so that it might become the rock foundation of our children's testimonies—"a sure foundation, a foundation whereon if men build they cannot fall" (Hel. 5:12).

WHAT ABOUT THOSE WHO LOSE FAITH BECAUSE OF UNANSWERED QUESTIONS?

President Boyd K. Packer once wondered about those who criticized and even apostatized from the Church. He wrote: "I had an impression, as revelations are. It was strong and it was clear, because lingering in my mind was: 'Why? Why—when we need so much to be united?' And there came the answer: 'It is permitted to be so now that the sifting might take place, and it will have negligible effect upon the church.'"9

What happens when people leave this Church because of some unanswered questions? It is our observation that they have nowhere to turn because they know too much. Simply said, this Church has ruined them for any other. What other church teaches the doctrine of the premortal existence, the gospel being preached to the dead, the three kingdoms of glory, and eternal marriage? What other church claims to have the Aaronic and Melchizedek Priesthood or has temples, twelve Apostles, or modern-day revelation? There is no other church that has all of this, so where do the disenchanted go? In most cases, having no other satisfactory church to join, they either become a religion unto themselves or they walk the path towards agnosticism. Fortunately, in a few cases, like the prodigal son, when they have eaten the husks of pride and man-made doctrines long enough, they repent and return, finally realizing they traded their 24-karat gold for fool's gold. And like the father of the prodigal son, our Heavenly Father rejoices and embraces them in the cloak of His gospel and welcomes them back to their spiritual home.

CONCLUSION

The historical concerns, the alleged scientific inconsistencies—these are the sideshow. The center stage is the teachings, doctrine, priesthood power, and other fruits of the Church. We can live with some human imperfections, even among prophets of God—those are to be expected. We can live with some alleged scientific findings contrary to the Book of Mormon—time will correct those. We can live with some seeming historical anomalies—they are minor in the total landscape of truth. But we cannot live without the doctrinal truths and ordinances restored by Joseph Smith; we cannot live without the priesthood of God to bless our family; and we cannot live without knowing we are sealed to each other and our children for eternity. That is the choice we face—a few unanswered questions on one hand versus a host of doctrinal certainties and the power of God on the other. For us, the choice is an easy one, a rational one, and a heartfelt one. Hopefully, it will be the same for our children and those in our classes as we teach them the truths of the gospel with power and conviction.

CHAPTER 16

A Testimony Seals the Truth of the Doctrine

THE RELATIONSHIP BETWEEN DOCTRINE AND TESTIMONY

President J. Rueben Clark talked about the role that testimony can play in the teaching experience: "The first requisite of a teacher for teaching these [gospel] principles is a personal testimony of their truth. No amount of learning, no amount of study, and no amount of scholastic degrees can take the place of this testimony, which is the *sine qua non* [a necessary condition] of the teacher in our church school system."[1]

A teacher's testimony coupled with doctrine is the supreme spiritual food we can offer to students who come hungering for the truth. Testimony and doctrine are like the blades in a pair of scissors. They are most effective when they work in tandem.

President Joseph F. Smith gave this wise counsel concerning the relationship between testimony and doctrine: "The [teacher] is sent into the [classroom] to preach the gospel . . . expounding the truths

A Testimony Seals the Truth of the Doctrine

embodied in the first principles of the gospel; then if he bears his testimony under divine inspiration, such a testimony is a seal attesting the genuineness of the truths he has declared." Then he added this caution: "But the voicing of one's testimony, however eloquently phrased or beautifully expressed, is no fit or acceptable substitution for the needed discourse of instruction."[2] In other words, testimony in a vacuum is not a replacement for doctrine, but it is most productive when it seals the truth of the doctrine that has been previously taught.

Alma was a prime example of this principle put into action. He preached one of the most powerful sermons found in the scriptures on how our hearts might be changed. His insights and related questions resulted in a doctrinal masterpiece (see Alma 5). But this was not the conclusion of the matter. The capstone would be his testimony:

> And this is not all. Do ye not suppose that I know of these things myself? Behold, I testify unto you that I do know that these things whereof I have spoken are true. And how do ye suppose that I know of their surety?
>
> Behold, I say unto you they are made known unto me by the Holy Spirit of God. Behold, I have fasted and prayed many days that I might know these things of myself. And now I do know of myself that they are true; for the Lord God hath made them manifest unto me by his Holy Spirit; and this is the spirit of revelation which is in me. (Alma 5:45–46)

Elder Bruce R. McConkie also spoke of the relationship between testimony and doctrine: "The inspired teacher, the one who teaches by the power of the Spirit, is expected to bear testimony that the doctrine he teaches is true. . . . This is the crowning seal placed on gospel teaching—the personal witness of the teacher that the doctrine he has taught is true! Who can argue with a testimony? Unbelievers may contend about our doctrine. They may wrest the scriptures to their destruction. They may explain away this or that from a purely intellectual standpoint, but they cannot overpower a testimony."[3]

OUR SPIRITUAL EXCLAMATION POINT

The story is told of the company accountant who was called to meet with the board of directors. The board was considering the acquisition of a smaller company. They wanted the accountant's opinion as to whether or not to proceed. The accountant reviewed the financial statements of the smaller company, recognized its precarious financial condition, and warned against making the acquisition. He told them that the company to be acquired had a negative cash flow and would quickly drain the resources of the larger company. Nonetheless, the board elected to go ahead and make the acquisition. Several months later it became obvious that the acquired company was indeed destroying the profitability of its parent company. The accountant was called to face the board. They told him he was being fired because he had not sufficiently warned them of the impending danger.

Shocked, he replied, "I was the one who told you not to proceed. I was the one who warned you of the future financial crises."

"Yes," the board responded, "but you didn't pound your fist on the table when you told us."

When we bear our testimony, we spiritually (not literally) pound our fist on the table, emphasizing the truth of the doctrine we have taught so there is no misunderstanding, no wondering about our conviction of its truthfulness. It is our spiritual exclamation mark to the doctrine we have taught.[4]

A Testimony Seals the Truth of the Doctrine

WHAT DIFFERENCE CAN OUR TESTIMONIES MAKE?

Mary Hales, wife of Elder Robert D. Hales, related the account of her sister who, when she was seven years old, was asked at school to list the religion of her parents. She wrote that her father was a Mormon, but she put a question mark in the space for her mother's religious affiliation. "When my sister came home from school," Sister Hales recalled, "my mother—who never raised her voice—was beside herself. She said, 'What were you thinking? We have Family Home Evening. I go to church. I hold family prayer. I teach Primary. What were you thinking?' My sister said, 'But Dad always says it [his testimony] at Family Home Evening. He says it. You don't say it. So I thought you were maybe still deciding.'"[5] Our children and students need to know that we are not "still deciding" about the doctrinal truths of the gospel. They need to hear and feel our testimonies loud and clear.

Our testimony is essential to our teaching because it invites, perhaps more than any other tool or technique we can use, the power of the Holy Ghost to witness the truth of that which we have spoken. The Apostle John spoke of its importance in overcoming the devil: "And they overcame him by the blood of the Lamb, *and by the word of their testimony*" (Rev. 12:11; emphasis added). President M. Russell Ballard spoke of the converting power of a testimony: "Testimony—real testimony, born of the Spirit and confirmed by the Holy Ghost—changes lives."[6]

Parley P. Pratt taught the gospel to John Taylor, and then unfortunately, Parley's testimony about Joseph Smith started to waiver for a season. When Parley shared his doubts with John Taylor, John responded as follows: "Now Brother Parley, it is not man that I am following, but the Lord. The principles you taught me led me to Him, and I now have the same testimony that you then rejoiced in.

If the work was true six months ago, it is true today; If Joseph Smith was then a prophet, he is now a prophet."[7] When all else is forgotten, a teacher's testimony can have lasting effects. A student may not recall the words of a lesson, but the feelings—the impressions of that moment—can be indelibly inscribed on the human heart.

BEARING TESTIMONY BLESSES US AS WELL AS OTHERS

Bearing our testimony is a witness for others. But it also does more. It strengthens our own testimony. It invites an increase of the Spirit into our own lives, confirming the truth of the doctrine to which we are testifying. President Boyd K. Packer confirmed this truth: "Oh, if I could teach you this one principle. A testimony is to be *found* in the *bearing of it*! . . . It is one thing to receive a witness from what you have read or what another has said; and that is a necessary beginning. It is quite another to have the Spirit confirm to you in your own bosom that what *you* have testified is true."[8]

We also accrue other blessings when we bear our testimony: "Ye are blessed, for the testimony which ye have borne is recorded in heaven for the angels to look upon; and they rejoice over you, and your sins are forgiven you" (D&C 62:3). What magnificent promises to those who sincerely bear their testimonies.

As critical as testimony is, Elder Bednar added this important caveat: "Knowing that the gospel is true is the essence of testimony. Consistently being true to the gospel we know is the essence of conversion."[9]

WHEN SHOULD I BEAR MY TESTIMONY?

Testimonies may be borne spontaneously as the Spirit directs. Some feel inclined to bear testimony as a doctrinal point is being taught; others prefer to bear testimony at the conclusion of the

A Testimony Seals the Truth of the Doctrine

lesson. There is no fixed formula. Perhaps this might help: Do not bear your testimony so often that it becomes routine, but often enough that there is no doubt where you stand on doctrinal issues; and certainly bear it when the Spirit prompts. In this respect Paul reminded us, "Be not thou therefore ashamed of the testimony of our Lord" (2 Tim. 1:8). Our testimony is a gift from God that He expects we will share with others.

CONCLUSION

An indispensable part of our teaching should be the bearing of testimony. King David spoke of its convincing power: "The testimony of the Lord is sure" (Ps. 19:7). And so it is.

EDIFY ONE ANOTHER

CHAPTER 17

Set High but Loving Expectations

THE SAVIOR'S EXPECTATIONS

No doubt you recall the story of Peter walking on water. As he saw the surging waves, he started to lose faith and began to sink. The Savior extended His hand and said, "O thou of little faith" (Matt. 14:31). One might wonder: "Why did He say that to Peter? How many other men have had the faith to walk on water, even for a few steps?" But the Savior was not comparing Peter to other men; He never does that. In truth, He was saying, "O ye of little faith compared to what *you* can become." Our Savior expects each of us to, step by step, eventually become like Him.

As parents and teachers we should have high but loving expectations for our children and those in our classes. To each of us the Savior enjoined: "Be ye therefore perfect, even as your Father which is in heaven is perfect" (Matt. 5:48). The Savior never lowers His standards to accommodate our shortcomings, but rather He provides the needed resources and encouragement to help us overcome those shortcomings so we can rise to His level of expectation. In addition, He exercises loving patience that gives us time to achieve that divine standard.[1]

OUR EXPECTATIONS

Parents and teachers will usually find that children and students rise to the parents' and teachers' level of expectation. Jamie Escalante had a well-paying job at a computer company until he resigned to become a high school teacher. As fate would have it, he was assigned to Garfield High, located in East Los Angeles, California, not far from our hometown. There he would teach basic math.

A movie based on his life shares a scene in which the principal meets with teachers and other school administrators. The principal reminds them that the school is on probation because of its academic failures. One of the teachers present mentions that the only way to have higher test scores is to move the school out of the slums. In other words, move the school to a place where rich kids live. Another chimes in that you can't teach logarithms to illiterates. Finally, after a moment of silence, the newest teacher, Jamie Escalante, speaks up: "The students," he says, "will rise to the level of our expectation."

One then sees him teaching in the classroom. It is obvious that he is no ordinary teacher. One sees hope being planted in the eyes of his students for the first time—maybe they can not only pass math but even master it.

At one of the subsequent administration meetings, Jamie Escalante announces that he wants to teach calculus the next year. The only way the juniors can prepare for it, however, is to take trigonometry and advanced algebra in summer school. The other teachers and administrators are shocked at such a suggestion. "That's ridiculous," says one of them. "Our kids can't handle calculus." Then he

Set High but Loving Expectations

adds, "There are some teachers in this room who can't handle calculus." But Jamie Escalante is not discouraged or derailed—he has incredible faith in the potential of these young people and a vision of what they might become. Finally, permission is granted. Upon announcing to his students that they should enroll in summer school, he hears remarks such as, "We will be seniors—it will be our year to slack off." But somehow these students know deep down that this is their chance, their opportunity to rise to heights never before achieved in their lives.

After a difficult summer of sweltering classrooms, Jamie's faithful students return for their senior year to confront the difficult subject of calculus. At one point, one of the frustrated young men says, "Everybody knows I'm the dumbest. I can't do calculus."

Jamie responds, "Do you have the desire?"

The boy says, "Yes." That was enough. He stayed on.

Finally, the moment of truth comes for these students as they take the high school Advanced Placement test. If they score a three out of five, they qualify for college credit; if they score a four, they are well qualified; and if they score a five, they score the equivalent of an A for college credit. By way of background, this calculus test is so difficult that only a small percentage of all US high school students even attempt it.

With great anxiety, eighteen students take the test and then, with equally great anxiety, wait for the results. To their great delight and amazement, all eighteen students receive college credit. It was miraculous. No other school in Southern California had so many students qualify. But then a problem arises; those who administered the test think the students must have cheated. Their scores are substantially higher than those of any other school. Surely, they think, this is impossible from students at such a school as Garfield High, located in East LA. This stigma hangs over the students until finally each agrees to retake the test, this time with as much additional supervision as the school district desires. They retake the test. Anxiously they wait for their test scores. Finally the scores are given to the principal over the phone—four, five, another five, four, three, four—all eighteen students again qualify for college credit. It was a resounding victory for vision and faith in the human spirit. It was a great reminder that the youth in the humblest barrios of East LA could rise to the same heights as those in the private and expensive schools of Beverly Hills. Why? Because they all had the same common denominator—they were all children of God with the same divine potential.

The movie concludes by putting on the screen the number of students from Garfield High who passed the Advanced Placement test in subsequent years:

1983: 31
1984: 63
1985: 77
1986: 78
1987: 87

What made the difference? The vision and expectations of one teacher and the determination of students who made no excuses along the way.[2]

One missionary who had been assigned to our mission in Toronto had greatly struggled in school. His native language was English, and he had been called to preach the gospel in Spanish. At the beginning of his mission, he approached Tad several times and asked to be transferred to an English-speaking area. Spanish, he said, was impossible for him. He was reminded that a prophet of God had called him to speak Spanish, but the repeated requests for a transfer still came. One day he was in the mission office. He started eating one of the cookies that was in a jar on a table. He was there with several other missionaries.

Tad asked him if he knew how to say cookie in Spanish. "No," he replied.

Tad said "Elder, there is a new rule for you. From this day forward you cannot eat it or wear it until you can say it in Spanish."

One of the nearby Elders remarked, "You are going to have a hungry, naked elder on your hands."

"No," Tad replied, "We are going to have an elder who learns Spanish."

He did not become the most fluent Spanish speaker in our mission, but he did learn the language sufficiently to teach many people in Spanish, to baptize in Spanish, and to become a leader of a Spanish district. He went home a new man, learning that his capabilities had far exceeded his initial expectations.

Teachers can rightfully expect that their students will be respectful in class (see D&C 88:121), listen carefully (see Acts 17:11), record impressions (see D&C 76:80, 113), and at least make an effort to participate (see D&C 88:122). If teachers make these expectations known in a loving manner and encourage students along that path, then many will rise to that level of expectation. As we reflect upon our school and Church classes, we realize that it was never the easy teacher who stimulated us or lifted us to greater heights; rather, it was the ones who challenged us and then inspired and helped us to reach those lofty goals. Like the Savior, we as teachers can have high but loving expectations.

CONCLUSION

When there are low expectations, people usually achieve less than their full potential. How many of us would strive for godhood if we did not know that God both desired and expected it of us?

Most of us would consider it an impossibility. In fact, most of the world already does.

Suppose for a moment you are a high jumper participating in a track meet, but to your surprise, when you show up to participate, there is no high jump pit, no crossbar over which to jump. Instead the official tells you: "Just go out on the field and jump as high as you can. I have a laser gun that will measure your height." Somehow you know you will not jump your highest. Instinctively you know that the crossbar somehow extracts from you every last bit of energy and strength you possess. In essence it has the power to lift you to greater heights. So it is with inspired expectations. They are like spiritual crossbars. In a loving, patient way, teachers and parents can have expectations for their children and students that will lift them to greater heights, even to godhood.

CHAPTER 18

What Makes for an Inspired Question?

THE POWER OF A GOOD QUESTION

The power of a good question is of inestimable worth. In most cases, the caliber of the question will determine the caliber of the discussion. A good question is like an alarm clock that awakens us out of our mental doldrums. It is a catalyst that jump-starts our mental engines. It causes the cerebral wheels to move and thrusts upon us a certain uneasiness, an anxiety that triggers a fixation on the subject at hand until relief comes only in the form of an answer that is satisfying to the mind and acceptable to the heart. Until that answer comes, however, one's mind is in overdrive—considering all the options, weighing, sifting, and sorting.

A tremendous difference exists between being told the answer and discovering it. It is somewhat like looking at a picture versus painting one, receiving a book compared to writing one, or listening to Rachmaninoff's Piano Concerto no. 3 versus playing it. Discovering the answer brings immense satisfaction, gives ownership, and makes a permanent deposit in our memory bank—not just some in-and-out entry.

A good question can often be the springboard for an entire sermon or class discussion. So it was for Amulek, who discerned "that the great question which is in your minds is whether the word be in the Son of God, or whether there shall be no Christ" (Alma 34:5). In response, Amulek delivered his wonderful sermon on the infinite nature of Christ's Atonement.

Good questions open the door to revelation and inspired discussions. In this regard President Henry B. Eyring said: "Some questions invite inspiration. Great teachers ask those."[1] Below are some types of questions that might help accomplish this objective.

QUESTIONS THAT ENLIGHTEN THE MIND AND PENETRATE THE HEART

Certain questions cause us to think more deeply and feel more intensely—the two mediums through which the Lord gives revelation (see D&C 8:2–3). By their nature these questions encourage us to contemplate the possible answers in our minds (see D&C 9:7–9) and ponder them in our hearts (see Moro. 10:3). For example, a teacher might ask, "Why did the Lord allow His Church to be taken from the earth?" or "Why did He wait 1,600 to 1,700 years after the Apostasy to restore it?" or "What sacrifices did Joseph Smith make to bring about the Restoration?" These questions might stimulate the mind. Then a teacher might ask a question that elicits our feelings: "How do Joseph Smith's sacrifices affect your appreciation for him as a prophet?"

A Church handbook for seminary and institute teachers makes this important observation: "Questions [that invite feelings] help bring the gospel from students' minds down into their hearts. And when they *feel* in their hearts the truthfulness and importance of a gospel doctrine or principle, they are more likely to apply it in their lives."[2]

QUESTIONS THAT ELICIT SELF-EVALUATION

Paul taught, "Examine yourselves, whether ye be in the faith" (2 Cor. 13:5). Questions can help bring about self-evaluation. During the storm on the Sea of Galilee, the Savior's disciples cried out, "Master, Master, we perish." He calmed the raging storm and then asked, "Where is your faith?" (Luke 8:24–25). It was a moment for self-examination. The resurrected Lord asked this same type of question of the Nephite disciples: "What manner of men ought ye to be?" (3 Ne. 27:27). Sometimes the Lord answered His own question, but the very asking gave the hearers pause for reflection and thus often resulted in greater self-evaluation.

The climax of Alma's sermon to the people of Zarahemla consisted of eleven consecutive, introspective questions, such as "Have ye spiritually been born of God? Have ye received his image in your countenances? Have ye experienced this mighty change in your hearts?" (Alma 5:14). A thoughtful teacher might ask similar questions that require students to evaluate their faith and worthiness: "Do you believe you can be totally cleansed of your sins because of the Savior's sacrifice? Do you have faith that His Atonement can help you overcome your weaknesses? Do you have a broken heart and a contrite spirit?" The very pondering of these questions can be a stimulus for change.

QUESTIONS THAT HEIGHTEN OUR LEVEL OF COMMITMENT

Other questions invite us to heighten our level of commitment. Three times the Savior asked Peter, "Lovest thou me?" (John 21:15–17). No doubt Peter responded each time with greater passion and an even deeper commitment to the Holy One. Teachers might ask similar questions: "Do we love the Savior enough to forgive others as He forgives us? Do we appreciate His sacrifice to the extent that we are willing to consecrate our all in furthering His cause?"

QUESTIONS THAT INSPIRE TESTIMONY

When Jesus was in Caesarea Philippi, He asked His disciples: "Whom do men say that I the Son of man am?" Various responses were given. But that was only the lead-in question. Then came the real question: "But whom say ye that I am?" That question opened the door for Peter to bear his powerful testimony: "Thou are the Christ, the Son of the living God" (Matt. 16:13–16). One can imagine the electrifying power felt at that moment, both by Peter and the other disciples present.

Later in His ministry, the Savior used the same methodology to elicit a testimony from Martha. Jesus had just declared to Martha that He was "the resurrection, and the life." He then continued, "And whosoever liveth and believeth in me shall never die." Then came His pointed question to Martha: "Believeth thou this?" He was inviting her to share her testimony, and she did not disappoint Him. She replied, "Yea, Lord: I believe that thou are the Christ, the Son of God, which should come into the world" (John 11: 25–27). No doubt the bearing of that simple but powerful testimony invited an immersion of the Spirit, which brought about a further and deeper witness of the truth she bore.

We as teachers can ask similar questions: "Who would like to tell about a time when they felt the Spirit while reading the Book of Mormon?" or "How have you been touched by the words of a living prophet?" or "How do you feel about the Savior?" or "How do you feel about the principle we have just learned?" President Henry B.

What Makes for an Inspired Question?

Erying suggested that we "invite individuals to search their memories for feelings."³

QUESTIONS THAT SERVE AS EFFECTIVE ANSWERS

Questions can also serve as effective answers. Corianton wondered why the coming of Christ "should be known so long beforehand." The answer his father, Alma, gave was in the form of a series of rhetorical questions: "Behold, I say unto you, is not a soul at this time as precious unto God as a soul will be at the time of his coming? Is it not as necessary that the plan of redemption should be made known unto this people as well as unto their children?" (Alma 39:17–18). As Corianton pondered his father's questions, he had the answer to his own question.

If someone were to ask you, "What happens to those who died but never heard the gospel?" you might similarly respond with a question: "Do you believe God loves those people as much as He loves you? Do you believe God is the same yesterday, today, and forever? Do you believe God wants to save all His children?" The obvious answers to those questions will go a long way toward answering the initial question.

QUESTIONS THAT DETERMINE LEVELS OF UNDERSTANDING

After the Savior delivered a series of parables, He paused and asked this question: "Have ye understood all these things?" (Matt. 13:51). Questions such as this give both the teacher and student an opportunity to assess levels of understanding. Ammon applied this teaching principle when preaching to King Lamoni. He asked him, "Believest thou that there is a God?" King Lamoni answered, "I do not know what that meaneth." Ammon realized that he needed to step back for a moment and begin with a simpler question to which King Lamoni could relate: "Believest thou that there is a Great Spirit?" King Lamoni responded, "Yea" (Alma 18:24–27). Ammon knew he could now take the next step and accordingly explained that this Great Spirit was in fact God. Now there was a common understanding from which to build upon and teach additional gospel truths.

While visiting our mission in Toronto, Elder M. Russell Ballard, of the Twelve Apostles, gave this wise counsel to our missionaries: "Ask questions to determine if the investigator understands. If he doesn't understand then re-teach the principle. The only way you can confirm if he understands is to ask questions. Don't be in such a hurry that you rush past his understanding."[4]

Having those we teach answer a question is worth much more than the missionary giving the answer because it both reveals their level of understanding and maximizes their agency, thus accelerating their progress. Once we recognized the importance of questions that reveal understanding, we tried to teach our missionaries how they might transform a statement into a question. For example, instead of stating that the Apostles were necessary to keep the Church doctrine unified, one might ask, "How did the Apostles keep the Church doctrine unified?" Using a question, rather than a statement, invites learners both to act and to reveal their level of understanding.

QUESTIONS THAT REVEAL THE TOTAL ICEBERG

Steven T. Linford wrote an article in which he compared the tip of an iceberg to the answer a student might give, meaning there is more beneath the surface. His analogy and related comments are as follows:

> Sometimes a student shares a thought, but the teacher senses there is more the student could share. The portion of

What Makes for an Inspired Question?

information the student initially shares might be compared to the tip of an iceberg: there is much more beneath the surface. A simple follow-up question will provide an opportunity for the student to descend from "surface-level" answers to the deeper, more meaningful thoughts and feelings. When this appropriately happens, students will disclose magnificent and monumental portions of the iceberg that can lift and edify students in the classroom.

One teacher shared an experience he had in class after he had heard the iceberg analogy. He was discussing with his students times when they had seen a source of true power. One young man, who rarely commented in class, raised his hand and said, "I have learned that the priesthood power is power from God." The teacher said he actually visualized an iceberg and then said, "Danny, it sounds like you know what you are talking about. Would you tell us more?" Danny continued, "When my little sister was born, she was born with many health complications. The doctors said she wouldn't live for even one hour." Then he added, "Then she died, and my dad blessed her, and she started to live again." Concluding, he said, "She is nine years old now."

After Danny had shared this experience, the teacher stated that a powerful feeling had entered the room. He looked at his students and asked, "Does anyone else know that priesthood power is the true power of God?" Amber raised her hand and said, "I have never had an experience like that, but when Danny was talking, I know I felt the Spirit."[5]

Follow-up questions can deepen our understanding of a doctrinal principle and build upon the Spirit that is already present. Alert teachers listen carefully to the answer given and then follow up with appropriate questions that will reveal an even greater portion of the iceberg. For example, "What did you learn from that experience?" or "How did that experience strengthen your testimony?"

QUESTIONS THAT SET THE STAGE

Sometimes the Savior asked a question, not with the intent to receive a verbal response, but to set the stage for the doctrine He wanted to teach. He knew the question would start the mental engines running. For example, on one occasion the Savior said to a man sick of palsy: "Son, be of good cheer; thy sins be forgiven thee." The Savior knew what the onlooking scribes were thinking—that His words were blasphemous. So He asked this thought-provoking question of them: "Whether is easier, to say, Thy sins be forgiven thee; or to say, Arise, and walk?" Without waiting for an answer, He said to the man: "Arise, take up thy bed, and go unto thine house. And he arose" (Matt. 9:2–7). Suffice it to say, the question raised by the Savior was answered.

The scribes accused the Savior of casting out devils "by the prince of the devils." The Savior responded with a simple question: "How can Satan cast out Satan?" He then gave His masterful answer: "If a kingdom be divided against itself, that kingdom cannot stand. . . . And if Satan rise up against himself, and be divided, he cannot stand" (Mark 3:22–26). His question set the stage for the answer.

Teachers might do similarly. For example, a teacher might ask: "If someone reads and prays about the Book of Mormon, can he truly receive a spiritual impression that will confirm its truthfulness?" The teacher might then share, or ask class members to share, a testimony of how the Spirit has confirmed the divinity of the Book of Mormon to them.

What Makes for an Inspired Question?

QUESTIONS THAT BUILD SELF-RELIANCE

The Savior often answered a question with a question that was intended to cause the inquirer to think more deeply about his or her concern. This helped the learner to develop self-reliance, to think through the issue, and to dispel the notion of a learning-entitlement culture. When a lawyer asked the Savior, "What shall I do to inherit eternal life?" the Savior pushed back a little and, instead of immediately giving the answer, replied: "What is written in the law? how readest thou?" (Luke 10:25–26).[6] In other words, "What do you think? How do you interpret the scriptures on this matter?" The Savior was building spiritual and mental self-reliance.

This same process was followed when the brother of Jared approached the Lord and announced that he had prepared the vessels for the voyage across the ocean. At that point the brother of Jared expressed a valid concern by asking the question "Behold there is no light in them. Behold, O Lord, wilt thou suffer that we shall cross this great water in darkness?" The Lord could have given the solution, but instead He replied, "What will ye that I should do that ye may have light in your vessels?" (Ether 2:22–23). That question caused the brother of Jared to think—to be self-reliant—and as a consequence he discovered a solution and reaped the growth that came by doing so.

Suppose a student were to ask, "Is the Atonement retroactive? In other words, could the people of Old Testament times have their sins removed *before* the purchase price was paid by the Savior in the garden and on the cross?" Resisting the temptation to give the instant answer, a wise teacher might respond with another question: "Do we have anything in our current society that allows us to enjoy the benefits *before* we pay the price?" The resulting discussion might reveal that a credit card achieves that result. Someone might explain how this secular principle applies to a divine principle—namely, that the Savior's credit was the equivalent of pure gold in the premortal existence because He always kept His word. Accordingly, under the laws of justice, the benefits of His Atonement could be enjoyed in Old Testament times—before the purchase price was paid—because there was no doubt He would "pay the bill" when it was presented to Him in the garden and on the cross.[7]

HOW DO I STRUCTURE A GOOD QUESTION?

Factual questions can help students acquire helpful background information. Such inquiries, however, are usually a means, not an end. As a general rule, questions that begin with the words *when* or *where* often lead to perfunctory or factual answers. For example: "When was Joseph Smith born?" or "Where is the city of Bethlehem?" These questions are helpful in setting the stage, but in and of themselves they do little to stir emotions, fire human resolve, or lead to insightful discussions.

On the other hand, questions that begin with the words *why*, *what*, or *how* often lead to more thoughtful answers. For example, consider what questions below might be most thought-provoking and inviting of the Spirit:

- When was the Savior crucified?
- Where was the Garden of Gethsemane?
- Why did the Savior enter the Garden of Gethsemane?
- What did He accomplish in this garden and on the cross?
- How has His Atonement made a difference in your life?

Good questions usually help us understand and live the doctrine more fully. In addition to the suggestions above, questions that repeatedly lead to the same answers—such as "Read the scriptures," "Pray," or "Go to church"—could be structured in a way that might produce more thoughtful answers. For example, "How have you made your prayers more meaningful?" or "What study methods

What Makes for an Inspired Question?

do you employ that help you understand the scriptures better?" or "What have you done to prepare for church that has made it a more sacred experience for you?"

CONCLUSION

Questions are vital to inviting the Spirit, but not all questions are equal in accomplishing this aim. We can all improve in the art of asking meaningful questions. We can do this by carefully reviewing the questions asked by the Savior and His prophets, by listening to and analyzing the questions asked by inspired teachers, and by diligently pondering and praying for help in asking questions that will invite revelation and prompt inspired discussions.

CHAPTER 19

How Can I Lead an Inspired Discussion?

THE ROLE OF THE TEACHER

Richard Holzapfel wrote a book about the construction and dedication of the Salt Lake Temple, titled *Every Stone a Sermon*. The implication of this title is that every stone used to build the temple had one or more significant stories it could tell from its vantage point. In like manner, we might say, "Every Saint a sermon." Every member of the Church has had personal experiences and spiritual impressions that can bless the lives of others. President Thomas S. Monson reiterated this point: "Each child in each classroom, each young man or young woman, each student in seminary or institute, each adult in [Sunday School classes], each missionary—yes, every one of us—has a story waiting to be told."[1] Part of the genius of Christlike teachers is their ability to unlock that vast reservoir of spiritual testimony and experiences. Below are some ideas on how a teacher might tap that reservoir.

How Can I Lead an Inspired Discussion?

INCREASING THE QUALITY OF CLASSROOM DISCUSSIONS

The quality of a discussion is often influenced by the quality of the lead-in question. Does the question inspire class members to think and ponder? Does it allow freedom of thought, or does it require a specific answer and thus lead class members to try and guess what the teacher wants them to say? Perhaps questions such as the following could lead to an inspired discussion on the Restoration—questions that stimulate the mind and invite feelings of the heart:

- What truths did Joseph Smith learn while he was in the grove of trees?
- How did these truths differ from what contemporary churches taught?
- What scriptures support the truths Joseph learned?
- How do these truths affect your life?

HELPING PEOPLE FEEL GOOD ABOUT THEIR CONTRIBUTIONS SO THEY WANT TO CONTRIBUTE MORE

We can help those we teach feel more confident about their ability to participate in a discussion when we respond positively to sincere comments. For example, we might say, "Thank you for your answer. That was very thoughtful" or "What a good idea! I had never thought of that before" or "That is a good example" or "Thank you for being willing to contribute."

LISTENING TO THE ANSWER

Listening intently to the answer given is an evidence of our love for and interest in the one responding. Sometimes we may be anxious to move on to the rest of the lesson material, but our patient attention will do two things: one, it will manifest to that individual and to the others in the class that we do care about what each person has to say, and two, it will help us formulate what to say next. Perhaps something that is said will trigger a question that can lead to a new insight or even greater in-depth discussion of the doctrine being taught. Elder Jeffrey R. Holland made this significant promise: "If we listen with love, we won't need to wonder what to say. It will be given to us—by the Spirit and by our friends."[2]

HANDLING AN AWKWARD SILENCE AFTER A QUESTION

Sometimes, there may be an awkward silence after a question is asked while class members are thinking. It might be appropriate to let the silence prevail and let the pondering continue. On other occasions it might be helpful to rephrase the question in a way that may be more understandable to them and allow more time for class members to think about it. Some class members feel more comfortable responding when they are given sufficient time to think about what they want to say in advance. Accordingly, we might occasionally give class members a moment to silently reflect on a question before we ask anyone to respond. For example, we might say, "I would like you to take thirty seconds or so and ponder this question before you respond: How has the Holy Ghost made a difference in your life?" Or alternately, we might write a question on the board before the class starts so that class members will have adequate time to think about it.

INVOLVING THOSE WHO ARE HESITANT TO PARTICIPATE

One way to increase participation is to invite class members to share their thoughts in small groups and then ask a few of them to share their groups' insights with the rest of the class. Often people feel more comfortable sharing ideas in smaller settings.[3]

If we notice that certain class members are not participating, we could focus the discussion on their individual strengths and interests. For example, we might say, "Sister Rodriquez, all of your children have served missions. What did you do to inspire them and prepare them?" Or we could say, "Bill, you excel at basketball. Why is teamwork and unity so important for your team, and how might these same principles apply to a family?"

Some class members respond more readily when they are asked to share their own experiences. For example, we could ask, "When have you seen the truthfulness of this principle in your life?" or "In what ways have you been blessed as you have followed the prophet?"

WHAT IF ONE PERSON DOMINATES THE CLASS DISCUSSION?

One of our responsibilities as teachers is to give everyone the opportunity to participate (see D&C 88:122). We want to be careful not to allow a few class members to dominate the discussion. On the other hand, we want to ensure that those who desire to share have ample opportunity to do so. We might achieve this balance by allowing learners to share in small groups or by saying something such as, "We have had some wonderful comments but for these next few questions let's hear from someone who hasn't shared yet" or "What do the rest of you think?"

CREATING AN ENVIRONMENT THAT PROMOTES AN INSPIRED DISCUSSION

The environment we create can promote an inspired discussion. Elder Richard G. Scott explained, "Creating an atmosphere of participation enhances the probability that the Spirit will teach more important lessons than you can communicate."[4] The Savior chose the Sea of Galilee, the upper room, and the Mount of Transfiguration for a reason. Each setting contributed to the gospel message He wanted to teach. Something as simple as arranging a room a certain way can make a difference. For example, when possible, we do not want the aisle to be in the center of the room. That is the sweet spot—the most desirable spot to teach because it allows for the best eye-to-eye contact. To put the aisle in the middle may be like discarding the center of the cinnamon roll and being left with only the outer crust.

Pictures, objects, and music can all add to the warmth and spirit of the classroom. In addition, our warm greeting to each class member at the beginning of class and calling each by name can spark their willingness to participate. These first few moments are prime time when the teacher can reverently but warmly greet each class member and make them feel welcome. It can set the spiritual tone for what will follow.

WHAT IF THE CONTINUATION OF A DISCUSSION PREVENTS COVERING ALL THE LESSON MATERIAL?

The intent of the teacher should not be to cover all the lesson material but to cover that portion that will best meet the needs of the class members. Curriculum lessons are somewhat like a dinner buffet; we do not eat everything on the table but rather choose those items that will result in a healthy and delicious meal for those partaking. Accordingly, it is entirely appropriate, even imperative at times, that we continue a good gospel discussion to its natural end, even though this may prevent us from covering other material in the lesson.

Steven Linford called this principle of continuing the discussion to its natural end "riding the wave." In his own words, he explained it as follows:

> Oftentimes, we feel the weight of the unfulfilled teaching outline, and we move the class away from a spiritually nourishing experience that is fortifying faith, renewing hope, and having a profound effect on our students. When we feel those times when the Spirit is rich and deeply edifying, it is wise to continue the discussion, even if we do not get to the end of the outline. I have heard this referred to as "riding the wave." Once you are on a great wave, continue to ride it while it lasts. If it lasts too long, you will feel it and know it is time to move on, but many times we can abandon the wave too early. By riding the wave, we allow the Holy Ghost time to testify of pure truth that is impressed into the minds and hearts of the listeners.
>
> Recently, I watched a class ride a wonderful wave. The class was speaking about times when they had "wrestled" with God in "mighty prayer" (Enos 1:2, 4). As the students shared their experiences, the Spirit washed over the entire class. One young man told of an experience where he had recently learned the Lord wanted him to focus on preparing for his mission rather than on obtaining an athletic scholarship. He had prayed to the Lord for direction in his life, and he gradually received perspective and peace. This young man concluded his experience by simply sharing pure truth. He said, "We must keep the Lord as our most important priority in our life." The teacher paused and then asked him to state the truth again. It was one of those spiritual moments, where pure truth was spoken, and the entire class became still. . . . The class had ridden a wonderful wave that was exhilarating and stimulating for the entire class.[5]

The simple question "What has the Holy Ghost taught you this past week as you have read the scriptural assignment?" can often lead to a spiritual wave.

ENDING THE DISCUSSION ON A SPIRITUAL NOTE

At the end of a discussion, we may choose to briefly summarize what has been said so as to reinforce key principles. In addition, we might conclude with a brief testimony, which will be most powerful if we attest to the truthfulness of the doctrine that has been taught.[6]

HOW CAN WE KNOW IF A DISCUSSION IS SUCCESSFUL?

As previously mentioned, the Lord gave this command to teachers: "Teach one another the doctrine of the kingdom" (D&C 88:77). Occasionally, there are discussions that are open and lively but have little, if any, doctrinal focus or emphasis. Perhaps some conversations were therapeutic and some experiences were shared, but they were minimally connected to doctrine. It is unlikely that a teacher would do this intentionally, but sometimes we may lose focus and think a vigorous discussion, independent of doctrine, equals a successful class. But it does not. Discussion is a means, not an end.

A discussion is not successful merely because it is robust or because many participated. Many robust discussions occur in business and secular settings and have nothing to do with building faith. *A gospel discussion is successful if it increases faith, leads to a greater understanding of the doctrine being taught, and inspires the participants to live more Christlike lives.*

The ideal teacher is constantly striving to connect class comments to doctrine. If a participant gets off topic, a teacher might say, "The experience you shared reminds me of a scripture" or "What gospel truths do we learn from the comments we have heard?" or

"Would someone like to bear their testimony of the power of that truth we have been discussing?" The teacher should always bring the discussion back to doctrine. Then discussion fulfills its rightful purpose.

CONCLUSION

Inspired discussions are often at the heart of an inspired lesson. The principles to effectively lead such discussions are common to both home and church settings. We can come to know these principles by learning from our leaders, by observing others, and by practicing them. Our ability to lead an inspiring discussion can then open the door to sharing spiritual experiences, bearing testimonies, and receiving divine impressions and insights.

CHAPTER 20

Extending Inspired Invitations

THE SAVIOR'S EXAMPLE

The Savior understood the significance of extending invitations. He invited people to "come, unto me" (Matt. 11:28), "do as I have done" (John 13:15), and "learn of me" (D&C 19:23). Likewise, the Savior spoke of the need for learners to make commitments to act: "bind yourselves to act in all holiness before me" (D&C 43:9).

Elder David A. Bednar emphasized the need for teachers to extend invitations: "As teachers, one of our most important responsibilities is to invite learners to act—to exercise their moral agency in accordance with the teachings of the Savior."[1] Invitations carry with them a sacred responsibility. A good invitation will inspire us to *do* something, but a great invitation will inspire us to *become* something. Such an invitation was extended by the Savior: "What manner of men ought ye to be? Verily I say unto you, even as I am" (3 Ne. 27:27).

When prompted by the Spirit, we may make invitations and

Extending Inspired Invitations

promises with the assurance of which Nephi spoke: "The Holy Ghost giveth authority that I should speak these things" (1 Ne. 10:22). We can always feel comfortable extending a promise that accompanies an invitation when the promise has the endorsement of the scriptures. For example, we can confidently promise people who read and pray about the Book of Mormon with "a sincere heart, with real intent, having faith in Christ" that God will "manifest the truth of it unto [them], by the power of the Holy Ghost" (Moro. 10:4).

Our lives usually change as we build good habits. Some habits may take months to develop. Accordingly, we may have a single invitation that extends over many months. For example, we might invite class members to consider one Christlike attribute or habit they would like to individually develop. Perhaps it is the habit of meaningful morning prayer or striving to be more humble or patient. Each week or so, those who feel inclined might share their progress or the challenges they are facing.[2] In addition, we might regularly follow up on invitations that Church leaders extend during general conference.

Our invitations need to be much more than perfunctory—more than numbers oriented. We are not just trying to get people to pray but to pray with sincere hearts and real intent—not just trying to get people to turn pages of the scriptures but to assimilate and live what they read. An uninspired invitation may be an irritant—even counterproductive. Hopefully we would never extend an invitation just to extend an invitation. On the other hand, inspired invitations can lift people to new spiritual heights.

On occasion we may feel inspired to extend an invitation that is directive, such as "Today we talked about speaking kindly to our brothers and sisters. I invite you to look for the good in your siblings, compliment them sincerely when possible, and then share in our next class what you have experienced." On most occasions, however, we will want to appeal to the individual agency of our class members. For example: "Would you consider one way you could strengthen your relationship with your siblings?" or "Would you consider one way you might invite the Spirit into your home and then, if you feel comfortable, share it with us the next time we meet?" or "Would you reflect for a moment on the spiritual impressions and promptings you have received in class today and then resolve to act upon one or more of them?"

With some frequency we should invite class members to read the next week's scriptural assignment. This invitation, however, could be much more than just a reminder; it could also serve as a powerful incentive to read. The entertainment world often promotes future movies with a trailer that whets the interest of its intended audience. Likewise, we might present "spiritual trailers" that accomplish a similar purpose.

At one zone conference, we showed our missionaries a short trailer for an upcoming movie thriller. All present sat in rapt attention. When the trailer was over, we asked how many would like to see the full-length movie. With great excitement they all raised their hands. We then replied, "Wonderful—when you get released from your mission, you can go see it." A brief discussion then followed. We asked them why they wanted to see this movie after seeing only a short preview. The answers were similar: "It was exciting; it got us involved; it was a cliff-hanger, and we wanted to see how it ended."

We then discussed the teaching principle we had just witnessed and how we often fail to use it when inviting those we teach to read the Book of Mormon. Instead, the invitation often goes "Here is a copy of the Book of Mormon. We placed a bookmark at 3 Nephi 11 and invite you to read that chapter, which tells about the visit

Extending Inspired Invitations

of Christ to the Americas." Instead of using that approach, we practiced various "trailers" we might use to introduce the Book of Mormon in a way that would make it seem exciting and capture the interest of those we were teaching.

Following that zone conference we helped teach a first lesson with a missionary who had caught the spirit of extending an invitation that was both spiritual and tantalizing. He invited the young man he was teaching to read 3 Nephi 11, but instead of just handing him the book with a bookmark, his invitation went something like the following: "Leading up to chapter 11 there was a colossal earthquake—major cities sank into the depths of the sea or were buried in the depths of the earth. Others were destroyed by fire. Thunder was so powerful that it shook the entire land. Many lost their lives, and there was a thick darkness, an all-consuming darkness that covered the land for three days, so much so that no light could be seen. Finally the righteous survivors, devasted by the destruction, heard a faint voice from heaven that pierced their souls. They looked up and saw a man descending from heaven." This missionary then asked the young man, who was now on the edge of his seat, "Do you know who that was and what He said to the people?"

"No," the man replied.

"Well, that is what you are going to read about in 3 Nephi 11."

The young man replied, "Wow, that's the best introduction I've ever heard."

Can you imagine what other spiritual trailers could entice young people to read the Book of Mormon? Cliff-hangers could be created around the story of Ammon protecting the king's sheep; or the intrepid Teancum creeping over the enemy wall to find the tent of the enemy king; or the two thousand teenage boys in the heat of battle, none of whom suffered death; or Samuel preaching on the city wall as arrows encircled him but miraculously were unable to hit him; or Korihor's confrontation with Alma. And the list goes on and on. The Book of Mormon is a treasure trove, not only of pure doctrine but of action-packed and real-life stories that teach the doctrine in unforgettable ways to which all ages can relate. We can make the scriptures sound exciting to read because, in fact, they are.

FOLLOW UP

If we extend invitations but do not follow up, they will quickly lose their power. Often teachers find that effective follow-up provides an additional incentive for class members to accomplish the invitation. This follow-up may come by way of text, email, or reporting in class.

CONCLUSION

Invitations can be powerful tools for good, but they should be used wisely. If given too frequently they can prove burdensome or discouraging or seem routine. On the other hand, when spiritually prompted, they can cause meaningful reflection and inspire Christlike action.

LOVE THOSE YOU TEACH

CHAPTER 21

Loving Those You Teach

WHY LOVE IS ESSENTIAL TO TEACHING

The Lord counseled us, "Love one another; as I have loved you" (John 13:34). Later He asked Peter, "Lovest thou me?" When Peter answered affirmatively, the Lord said, "Feed [i.e., teach and minister to] my sheep" (John 21:16). In this dispensation the Lord counseled, "No one can assist in this work except he shall be humble and full of love" (D&C 12:8). President Thomas S. Monson gave the underlying reasons for why love is so essential to teaching: "Love is the catalyst that causes change, love is the balm that brings healing to the soul. . . . Where love is, there God will be also."[1]

LOVE INSPIRES CHANGE

A friend of ours served as a mission president. On one occasion he asked President Spencer W. Kimball, "What can I do to motivate my missionaries?" President Kimball replied, "Lavish them with honest praise." Giving genuine compliments is a form of expressing love. Mark Twain once said, "I can live on a good compliment for two weeks with nothing else to eat."[2]

On one occasion President Kimball embraced Tad's father and said, "Reed, I love you." When sharing that experience, he said, "Tad, I would do anything for that man." Love is a powerful, motivating force for good.

We can express our love in both word and deed. It may be in the form of a sincere compliment or a short note expressing appreciation for someone's participation, respect, or kindness shown to others in class. We may show love by attending someone's ball game or recital. Love can be an antidote for disruptive behavior. *Teaching, No Greater Call* shares this experience:

> A new teacher was having problems with some misbehaving class members. She sought advice from a member of the Sunday School presidency, and he suggested that she conduct an experiment. She was to select a disruptive class member and then show that person in five different ways that she cared about him or her. A few weeks later, the leader asked the teacher how she was doing. She reported that the person she had selected had stopped misbehaving, so she was in the process of selecting another class member. After two more weeks the leader inquired again. The teacher said that she was having difficulty finding someone to work with. When he asked her a third time, she told him that she had selected three different class members, one after another, and that when she started to show that she cared about them they had ceased being disruptive. In each case, love had softened a heart.[3]

When reason falls short, it is love—unconditional and unwavering—that can be the last bright hope to soften hearts and change lives. One man spoke of his father (a former president of the United States) in this admiring way: "No matter how badly we misbehaved, he always loved us. . . . There was no point in competing with our father—no point in rebelling against him—because he would love us no matter what. I took that lesson to heart when I became a parent."[4] And we can take that lesson to heart as teachers.

Nephi observed that the Savior "layeth down his own life that he may *draw* all men unto him" (2 Ne. 26:24; emphasis added). In that act of supreme love there was no need to push or pull or prod; the Savior knew that love itself was a catalyst to draw us unto Him and His ways.

On one occasion, two full-time missionaries told us they were teaching a man named Bob Garcin. We were totally surprised. We knew the man as a tough, high-profile attorney in our city who had served as our mayor and city-council member for many years. The missionaries told us they had given him four lessons but that, in attorney-like fashion, he had scrutinized most every verse and questioned most every principle. It was at this point that the missionaries invited Tad to attend the next lesson with them, hoping that his legal background might be helpful in relating to Mr. Garcin.

When Tad and the elders arrived at Bob's home, he greeted them with a warm smile. They briefly talked about some mundane matters, and then Bob said, "Well, let's begin. We have more important things to talk about." He then took them into his den. Tad could see the Book of Mormon next to where Bob sat. It looked like he was about fifty pages into it. That, Tad thought, was a good sign. Then Bob said, "Would you mind if I gave the opening prayer tonight?" He then offered one of the sweetest, most humble prayers Tad had ever heard. Bob thanked the Lord for the gospel that had been brought to his home. He gave thanks for the missionaries, and then he said that he had come to know this Church was true and had decided to be baptized. The prayer ended, and everyone was stunned—totally stunned. Bob then made this observation: "There is much I do not know, but the Spirit has confirmed to me that this message is true."

Tad felt prompted to ask him what had changed from the time of his earlier meetings with the missionaries, when he seemed to scrutinize every verse with his legal analysis. His response was ever so enlightening: "As you know I have been in politics most of my life. Someone has always wanted something from me. Never outside of my own family have I met someone who I felt had no ulterior motive, who wanted something just for me, until I met these two young men. I know they came into my home for one purpose only—to do what was best for me. I do not understand everything they have taught me, but I believe them."

Shortly thereafter he was baptized. He and his wife were later sealed in the temple. As compelling as the doctrine is, it took the pure love of Christ, manifested by two humble missionaries, to touch Bob's heart in such a way that he became receptive to the truth.

At one teacher council meeting, the leader asked this question: "Who was your most influential teacher, and why?" Every response had the same common denominator—a teacher who cared about him or her and took a personal interest in their lives. One man told of not wanting to attend early-morning seminary as a youth but finally deciding to go anyway. After each class the teacher would casually ask him questions about his interests and how he was doing. Pretty soon he grew to like the teacher, and when that happened, he wanted to learn from him.

LOVE IS A HEALING BALM

Ann Madsen had been teaching the seventeen-year-olds' Sunday School class for about five years. During a sacrament meeting her train of thinking was interrupted and she received a prompting: "Tell each one of them you love them." She thought to herself, "I tell them all the time as a class that I love them." Then the prompting came again: "No, tell *each* one of them that you love them."

When next week's class came, she thought, "How can I implement what I heard in my heart and my mind?" When the closing prayer was offered, she stationed herself at the door, shook hands with each one, looked them in the eye, and said, "I love you." She noted that a few girls hugged her, while most of the boys looked at different corners of the room and avoided any eye contact.

Sister Madsen determined that she would repeat this after every class. She later commented on the remarkable change that eventually took place in her class. It was not long before all the girls were hugging her and saying in return, "I love you too, Sister Madsen." Miraculously, even some of the boys looked her in the eyes and said, "I love you too."

Some years later she talked with one of those boys. She asked him if he had been in the class when she had started saying "I love you" to each one of them. He said that he had and then expressed how much that moment had meant to him. In his own words he then noted: "I wasn't sure anybody *liked* me, let alone *loved* me, and when you said that to me week after week, I [looked] forward to coming to class because it was so predictable. It didn't matter if anybody else in the world liked me that week, but I knew that you loved me because you looked me in the face and told me." Sister Madsen then added, "That was one of the sweetest experiences of my life."[5]

Love not only comforts and gives solace to those in need but it can also open the hearts of those we teach. It is a powerful teaching tool.

LOVE IS AN EVIDENCE OF THE SPIRIT

Paul taught that one "fruit of the Spirit" is love (Gal. 5:22). In other words, if we have the Spirit, it will be manifested in our love toward God and others. Likewise, if we demonstrate love, we will invite the Spirit into our lives and classrooms. John taught this principle: "God is love; and he that dwelleth in love dwelleth in God, and God in him" (1 John 4:16). Not everyone is lovable at first sight, but John taught that we have the responsibility to reach out first: "We loved him, because *he first loved us*" (1 John 4:19; emphasis added). As we express and demonstrate true love for those in our class, even the seemingly "unlovable," hearts will soften and become more receptive to the message we have to share. As some have noted: "Where love is, there God is also."[6]

HOW TO ACQUIRE THE PURE LOVE OF CHRIST

President Dallin H. Oaks taught: "When we are called to teach, we should accept our calling and teach because of our love for God the Eternal Father and His Son, Jesus Christ. In addition, a gospel teacher should always teach with love for the students. . . . Love of God and love of His children is the highest reason for service. Those who teach out of love will be magnified as instruments in the hands of Him whom they serve."[7] So one might ask, "How can I increase my love?"

The gifts of the Spirit are, in truth, attributes and qualities of godliness. Accordingly, love, which is an attribute of God, is a gift of the Spirit. The Lord has told us repeatedly to acquire these gifts: "Covet earnestly the best gifts" (1 Cor. 12:31); "lay hold upon every good gift" (Moro. 10:30); and "seek ye earnestly the best gifts" (D&C 46:8). We can acquire greater love, but there must be a burning desire in our hearts for it. Mormon addressed this level of earnestness: "Charity is the pure love of Christ. . . . Wherefore, my beloved brethren, pray unto the Father *with all the energy of heart,* that ye may be filled with this love" (Moro. 7:47–48; emphasis added).

Love also increases as we give it away. It is one of those ironies of life—the more we give, the more we receive. Oscar Hammerstein put it this way:

> *A bell is no bell till you ring it,*
> *A song is no song till you sing it, . . .*
> *Love isn't love*
> *Till you give it away.*[8]

How simple it is for a teacher to give away love by simple acts of kindness—to warmly greet each class member by name and with a smile, to express love when appropriate, to write simple emails or notes of encouragement. As Alma taught, "By small and simple things are great things brought to pass" (Alma 37:6). To love is to do, however simple the act may be.

Our capacity to love is also increased by our knowledge of the talents, interests, weaknesses, and strengths of each student in our class. There is so much good in everyone if we will but take the time to discover it. This adage is laden with truth: "To know him is to love him." The Savior exemplified this truth: "I am the good shepherd, and *know* my sheep, and am known of mine" (John 10:14; emphasis added).

If we will take the time to get to know our class members, our love for them will almost always increase. And there are so many ways to do this. If we teach children or youth, there may be no better way than to talk to their parents to determine how we can support their goals for their children. Getting to know those we teach may be as simple as asking questions about their backgrounds, some of which may be asked in class or at more informal times. We can get to know them by observing them during church and other activities. We can also pray for understanding to know their hearts. If we care, there are many avenues to pursue that will help us get to know them. As that knowledge increases, our capacity to love them increases. On the other hand, it is hard for us to fully love someone whom we do not know.

FOCUS ON PEOPLE NOT LESSONS

Oftentimes our focus may be on the lesson: "What doctrine do I want to teach? What good stories can I use?" And so on. Hopefully we can shift the focus to people, to the one. We might ask ourselves: "How can I encourage them to change their lives? How can I build their faith? How can I inspire them to live more like Christ?" Then we might ask: "What doctrine, what questions, what stories will help accomplish this goal? How can I involve the class members individually and collectively to build faith?" Then the lesson becomes the means, not the end.

President David O. McKay taught: "The successful teacher is one who, with a spirit of discernment, can detect to a degree at least, the mentality and capability of the members of his class. He should be able to read the facial expressions and be responsive to the mental and spiritual attitudes of those whom he is teaching. . . . Too few teachers have this gift, even to a necessary degree."[9] Fortunately, we can acquire this gift through diligent prayer, by careful observation, and by learning more about each class member. As we develop this gift, it will help us focus on people, not lessons.

CONCLUSION

Fortunately, in many cases, love does soften hearts. When our class members know we love and care about them, they come to learn with more receptive hearts and minds. While serving in a certain priesthood leadership position in the Church, Tad had the good fortune of being assigned on repeated occasions to meet with one particular member of the Quorum of the Twelve. It seemed like he made a special effort to teach and befriend Tad. When he spoke at general conference, Tad's ears would perk up and he would think, "I need to listen to him carefully—he truly loves me and cares about me. What he says can help me." Our students can have that same response to us. Our love can open their hearts. It can create a climate of welcomed participation without worry of reprisal. It can facilitate divine learning and living.

CHAPTER 22

Reaching Out to Those Who Do Not Attend

GO GET THEM

President David O. McKay once shared a story that appeared in a schoolbook. The author pictured some youth sailing down the river toward Niagara Falls. A man on the shore cried: "Young men, look out! The rapids are below you!" But they went on laughing and ignored him. He cried again, "Young men, look out! The rapids are below you!" Nonetheless, they did not heed the warning call until they suddenly realized that they were in the midst of the rapids. With all the power they could command, they failed to turn their boat upstream; so shrieking and yelling, over they went!

President McKay said that the story "left an indelible impression" on him, but somehow it seemed incomplete. "It is one thing," he said, "for a teacher to stand on the shore and cry, 'Young men, look out! The rapids are below you!' It is quite another to get into the boat, row out to them, and with all the kindly force and persuasion one can muster cause them to turn upstream."[1] One of our

Reaching Out to Those Who Do Not Attend

duties and privileges as teachers is to go get the lost and turn their boats upstream.

As teachers our responsibility is not only to teach those who attend class but also to reach out to those who do not attend. Some teachers may feel that the responsibility to reactivate lies solely with ministering brothers and sisters or with the quorum and organizational presidents—that somehow reactivation rests outside the domain of a teacher. Some may innocently but incorrectly believe that the teacher's duty is to teach only those who are present. Teachers, however, are not called and set apart to teach only the active members. Rather, they have a responsibility for everyone in their class, especially the less active. Of course, teachers should work in harmony with ward leaders and ministers in a cooperative effort, but hopefully reactivation efforts are a central part of each teacher's endeavors.

There is much the teacher can do to help reactivate a lost sheep that others cannot easily do, and there is much a teacher can do to support the efforts of others. For example, the teacher can invite less-active members to participate in part of the lesson—perhaps to role-play or to share thoughts about a specific gospel principle or to help with an object lesson. The inspired teacher can make phone calls, send emails and texts, use social media, and make home visits to those who do not attend to let them know they are loved and missed and needed. Teachers might invite a class member or parent to provide transportation if necessary. In addition, teachers can pray for the one. This responsibility is important enough that the scriptures record the Savior's prayer for the one: "I have prayed for thee [Peter], that thy faith fail not: and when thou art converted, strengthen thy brethren" (Luke 22:32).

A couple in our stake visited the homes of every family who had a child in their Primary class. They met with the parents and explained what they would be studying in the coming year and asked for the parents' input and support. One of the parents, thrilled with the visit, said, "Have you ever had a teacher of one of your children visit your home?" The truth was, we could not recall such a case. Suffice it to say, those parents were committed to having their child attend class every Sunday.

One Sunday School teacher, Mary Menlove, told of the spiritual impression she had to reach out to those in her class: "I was at stake conference and listened to a talk regarding a Primary teacher's influence on her class members. The Spirit testified to me that day that just as a Primary teacher needs to watch over their flock or individual class members, the gospel doctrine teacher needs to do so as well. I thought of several friends in the neighborhood who are nonmembers or less active. I've tried to invite them to the lessons that I teach, and remember that Heavenly Father has given me this sacred responsibility."[2]

What an army for good we could be if all teachers reached out in love to those who do not attend. Instead of standing on the shore, we could join with the host of other reactivation forces and help bring these wonderful Saints who have temporarily gone astray back home.

NEVER GIVE UP

The Savior taught two parables to emphasize the principle of never giving up in our reactivation efforts. The first speaks of the good shepherd who had a hundred sheep but lost one of them in the wilderness. The Savior asked the pointed question: "What man of you . . . doth not leave the ninety and nine and go into the wilderness after that which is lost *until* he find it?" (JST Luke 15:4; emphasis added). We have been intrigued by the phrase "until he find it." This search is not a casual scanning of the area, not a one-shot attempt that ends at nightfall or when the first cold comes; rather this is an intense, all-out rescue that continues despite the inclement weather and wild beasts *until* the sheep is found and brought safely home.

No doubt we will often face one or more obstacles in our reactivation efforts, but the Lord has given us our marching orders to keep trying, keep searching, keep rescuing until we bring the lost sheep back. The Lord gave such counsel to the people in Book of Mormon times: "Unto such shall ye *continue to minister*; for ye know not but what they will return and repent . . . and I shall heal them; and ye shall be the means of bringing salvation unto them" (3 Ne. 18:32; emphasis added).

Of course, some teachers, such as those who teach adult Sunday School, may have more lost sheep than is reasonably possible for one man or woman to rescue. In these circumstances, the Lord expects us to use good judgment and prioritize those who are lost and to use other class members to assist.

Teachers have a great responsibility and privilege to seek out the lost sheep who have been assigned to their fold. Edwin Markham spoke of a way to reach out:

> *He drew a circle that shut me out—*
> *Heretic, rebel, a thing to flout.*
> *But Love and I had the wit to win:*
> *We drew a circle that took him in!*[3]

One day, during lunchtime at a high school near our home, many students were on the front lawn eating and enjoying the beautiful sunny day. Some students, maybe twelve to fifteen, were in a circle, socializing and having a good time as they ate together. About fifteen feet away, a young lady was seated on the grass, eating all by herself. It was heartbreaking to see her sitting alone. The thought came, "Couldn't the group reach out to her and bring her within their circle? What joy they could bring to this solitary soul." What an impact for good both teachers and active class members can be in the lives of those who struggle for one reason or another. Unconditional love, the Spirit, and creativity can often bring them back.

The second parable told by the Savior is known as the "parable of the lost coin": "What woman having ten pieces of silver, if she lose one piece, doth not light a candle, and sweep the house, and *seek diligently till she find it*" (Luke 15:8; emphasis added). If a woman would seek diligently for a lost piece of silver until she found it, what efforts should we put forth—to what extremes should we go—to diligently seek and bring back a lost child of God?

Naaman, the great captain of the Syrian hosts, had contracted leprosy. Elisha, a prophet of God, told him to dip himself seven times in the river Jordan in order to be healed. Finally, after some persuasion from a servant, Naaman reluctantly obeyed. But what if he had dipped himself only six times and then stopped? You know the result. Even if he had done six-sevenths of the work, he would not be six-sevenths clean. Perhaps with some of our less-active members, we have dipped ourselves three or four or even six times, and then seeing no results, have abandoned the cause. If we have not yet prayed or fasted for the lost in our class, then perhaps there are more dippings; if we have not yet visited their homes, spoken with their parents, or invited them to participate in the lesson, then perhaps there is still another dipping left undone.

Elder Mervyn B. Arnold tells about Brother José de Souza Marques, who was a great example of this principle. He was a member of the branch presidency in Fortaleza, Brazil. Brother Marques, with certain other priesthood leaders, developed a plan to rescue some less-active members, one of whom was a young man named

Reaching Out to Those Who Do Not Attend

Fernando Araujo. Elder Arnold shared, in Fernando's own words, his unique experience:

> I became involved in surfing competitions on Sunday mornings and stopped going to my Church meetings. One Sunday morning Brother Marques knocked on my door and asked my nonmember mother if he could talk to me. When she told him I was sleeping, he asked permission to wake me. He said to me, "Fernando, you are late for church!" Not listening to my excuses, he took me to church.
>
> The next Sunday the same thing happened, so on the third Sunday I decided to leave early to avoid him. As I opened the gate I found him sitting on his car, reading the scriptures. When he saw me he said, "Good! You are up early. Today we will go and find another young man!" I appealed to my agency, but he said, "We can talk about that later."
>
> After eight Sundays I could not get rid of him, so I decided to sleep at a friend's house. I was at the beach the next morning when I saw a man dressed in a suit and tie walking toward me. When I saw that it was Brother Marques, I ran into the water. All of a sudden, I felt someone's hand on my shoulder. It was Brother Marques, in water up to his chest! He took me by the hand and said, "You are late! Let's go." When I argued that I didn't have any clothes to wear, he replied, "They are in the car."
>
> That day as we walked out of the ocean, I was touched by Brother Marques's sincere love and worry for me. He truly understood the Savior's words: "I will seek that which was lost, and bring again that which was driven away, and will bind up that which was broken, and will strengthen that which was sick" (Ezekiel 34:16). Brother Marques

didn't just give me a ride to church—the quorum made sure I remained active. They planned activities that made me feel needed and wanted, I received a calling, and the quorum members became my friends.[4]

Following his reactivation, Brother Araujo served a full-time mission and thereafter as a bishop, stake president, mission president, and regional representative. His widowed mother, three sisters, and several cousins also entered the waters of baptism—all because some priesthood leaders continued to minister to a teenage boy.

SEARCH FOR THE CAUSE

Often the challenge is not in finding the one who is lost but in determining the cause for his or her inactivity. For example, suppose after being invited to church, someone said, "I don't want to go." Rather than being content with that answer, the valiant teacher might "dig" to the next level. Was the desire not to attend due to an absence of friends, a feeling of unworthiness, inadequate clothes, not feeling the Spirit, or a previous bad experience? It is difficult, if not impossible, to discover the right solution if we do not know the root of the problem. Searching out the cause will open the doors to enhanced revelation about what we can do to help.

USING CLASS MEMBERS TO ASSIST IN THE RESCUE

Teachers have other resources to assist in the rescue process besides their own prayers and efforts. One such resource is the members of our classes. Thirteen-year-old Erika Swainston was the president of her Young Women class. Tad was a stake missionary teaching the Johnson family, who had a thirteen-year-old daughter named Cindy. One day the Johnsons heard a knock on their door—there was Erika and the other girls in her Young Women class. They had baked a cake to welcome Cindy to their class. Later that night Cindy's mother told Tad that Cindy came to her with tears in her eyes and said: "Mother, did anyone ever do anything like this for you when you were my age?" It probably would not surprise you to know that Cindy and her mother joined the Church shortly thereafter. Oh, the power of one youth to touch the heart of another youth.

WE NEED THEM, AND THEY NEED US

While Tad was serving as a bishop, our ward council resolved to prioritize the less-active members and to reach out to them one by one. The first sister we reached out to was a convert who had been active for three to four years and then for some reason just stopped attending. Tad called her on the phone and invited her to speak at sacrament meeting. She said, "Bishop, you know I have not been active—what would I speak on?"

He replied, "You pray, don't you?"

"Yes," she said. "I do."

"Then why don't you speak on prayer?"

She gave a wonderful talk. The members flooded around her after sacrament meeting and expressed their love to her—she felt the Spirit.

After sacrament meeting the bishopric invited her to meet with them. They knew she played the organ and told her they needed a Relief Society organist and were extending the call to her to play each Sunday.

Obviously moved, she replied, "But I would have to change my lifestyle."

With a smile, they replied, "That's the point." To her credit, she accepted and became active once again.

Other calls were extended, one to a less-active sister and her nonmember husband to be greeters each week—they accepted.

Another call was extended to a good man and his nonmember wife to teach their granddaughter in Primary—they accepted. Not everyone accepted, nor did everyone steadily perform their callings, but the majority did. It was a great boon to our ward, and a great lesson was learned: There is power in an assignment, power in a calling, that comes from the Lord. Teachers can use this same principle. They can invite class members in advance to participate in their lessons and help them once again feel the Spirit in their lives, and in the process, both the active and the less active will be blessed.

Not only do the less active need the gospel, but the active members need the less active to help strengthen their own testimonies. The Savior taught this principle in the following way: "The body [i.e., the Church] hath need of every member, that all may be edified together, that the system may be kept perfect" (D&C 84:110). Suffice it to say, every member can benefit from the experiences and testimony of every other member.

Moses learned that callings are a two-way street that bless both the called and the beneficiaries of the called. Moses was in the wilderness with the tribes of Israel. He asked a local Midianite, Hobab, to be their guide. Then he told Hobab how fortunate he would be if he accepted: "Come thou with us, and we will do thee good: for the Lord hath spoken good concerning Israel." In other words, "Hobab, this is your lucky day. We are the chosen of God, and if you come with us, you will enjoy His blessings."

No doubt, to Moses's surprise, Hobab declined: "I will not go; but I will depart to mine own land, and to my kindred."

Moses then changed tactics: "Leave us not, I pray thee . . . [that] thou mayest be to us instead of eyes" (Num. 10:29–31). In other words, Moses was now pleading with Hobab to be their needed guide. Moses realized they needed him as much as Hobab needed them. So it is with every less active we bring back to the fold—we are all "edified together" (D&C 84:110).

CONCLUSION

Bishop Vaughn J. Featherstone once said: "I believe that when you care, when you love, when you pray—yes, when you have a supreme interest in others—we don't need to teach you the mechanics of activation—they will come by the Spirit."[5] That is good counsel for all of us who are teachers. Let us leave the comfort of our "shores" and by the Spirit go get the lost *until* we bring them safely home. May reaching, as well as teaching, be a significant part of our call as teachers.

CHAPTER 23

Making Teaching with Technology More Personal

The events of recent days have forced many teachers to rely much more extensively on virtual technology. While both of us have used virtual technology for Sunday School lessons, missionary-training sessions, devotionals, and leadership and business meetings, we do not feel like we have an expertise in this area. We do, however, have a daughter, Angela Dalebout, who extensively uses such technology in both an ecclesiastical capacity (as a seminary teacher) and in a professional setting (teaching English to students in China). Accordingly, we asked for her advice in this area. Below are some of her suggestions, in her own voice, as to how we might use technology without losing our personal touch with students and family in the process.

"SEE" THE STUDENT, NOT THE SCREEN

Through virtual teaching, I have learned the importance of truly "seeing" the student behind the screen. When you "see" the student, you forget about what is actually on the screen—often just a name, a black box, or a ceiling. This allows you to connect with them, even over the internet. Here is how I try "seeing" the student:

- I ask questions about their lives and what they are doing. In seminary, we often start out by asking a "question of the day," which can be fun or serious. For example, "What is your favorite ice cream flavor?" Or "Where do you like to travel?" Because these questions are fun and simple, the students are usually willing and eager to participate, and we often learn more about one another.
- Most importantly, I pray for sight. I pray that I can hear their answers. I pray that I can know when to press them for more and when they need a break. I pray that I can ask the right questions to help them feel the Spirit. I pray that I will share scriptures and experiences that will answer questions they may have. *I pray that they can feel my love through the computer.*

Zachary is a five-year-old Chinese boy who is one of my English students. He is fairly fluent in English. A couple of days ago I asked him what he had done that day. He said he had gone to swimming lessons. When I asked if he had had fun, he said, "No." I subsequently learned that he was afraid to put his face in the water. The teacher had been trying to help him, but he was afraid and didn't want to go back for more lessons. For part of our class we referred to his swimming experience. When we learned the word *strong*, I had him say, "Zachary is strong because he can put his face in the water." I kept bringing the lesson back to how he is brave and strong and can do hard things. Yesterday, his mother posted this message on my teacher page: "Thank you so much! I told Zachary your encouragement. The next day, he overcame his fear and was able to bury his face in the water while swimming." She then told me she would send me a video of him swimming.

I believe that when I pray to "see" a student, I can learn how to encourage them to be better, even while teaching virtually.

PRACTICE, PRACTICE, PRACTICE

You have to *be prepared* and know how to use the software. Practice using and sharing slides, again and again. If you are too worried about the technicalities, you forget to "see" the student.

EXPECT TECHNICAL DIFFICULTIES

Technical difficulties happen constantly, no matter how hard you prepare. I have found that if I expect there to be a few technical difficulties, I can move on when they happen and they don't trip me up. I can continue to focus on teaching and keeping the Spirit. Most students don't mind when there are technical difficulties. If a teacher handles it calmly, the students just wait patiently rather than being focused on (and entertained by) the frazzled teacher.

One should have a backup plan for when technical difficulties do occur. I usually print off my slides. If needed, I just hold up the slides to the camera if screen sharing is not working properly.

GIVE A HEADS-UP

Because students are often less willing to participate in a virtual discussion, I usually give them a heads-up that they will be called upon to answer a question. For example, I may say, "Jack, after Amber reads Doctrine and Covenants 8:2–3, would you please answer the question 'How does the Lord say we can receive revelation in this particular scripture?'" I usually get much more thoughtful answers this way, and it doesn't put the student on the spot.

SCREEN SHARING

I usually share my screen to show slides of the scriptures because most students toggle between the classroom and the scriptures on their phones, which can be disruptive. It is more effective for them to see the scriptures on the screen share rather than fumble around on their phones.

OVERCOMING THE BLACK BOX

In addition to our daughter's ideas and suggested solutions, we have confronted the problem of the black box appearing on the screen rather than a personal face. When someone does not turn on his or her video feed, it makes it difficult, if not impossible, for the teacher to "read" the expressions and responses of the listener and for others in the class to effectively interact with that person. While we don't have the magic answer, we have found that the following courses of action can help reduce this problem: One, the teacher can ask the ward to send out a communication inviting all ward members to show their faces on the screen so as to more closely simulate an in-person classroom encounter. And two, the teacher can make a comment such as, "Bill, we would love to see your handsome face" or "Jane, we would love to see your beautiful countenance." We have found that when we do the latter, most of the youth we teach will start their video feed. Then we can have a teaching experience that is much more personal.

CONCLUSION

While it is more difficult to have a personal experience over the computer than in person, there are ways to preserve and enhance the student-teacher relationship. In addition, technology now allows us to have extended family gatherings and devotionals that were previously impossible or difficult. Technology is one more tool the Lord has given us to reach out and touch our family and class members.

PARENTS: THE PRIME GOSPEL TEACHERS

CHAPTER 24

Teaching Ideas for the Home

How then can we fulfill our responsibility to teach our children and grandchildren the truths of the gospel of Jesus Christ? The following are some ideas that helped our family.

DISCOVER THEIR INTERESTS

One of our teenage sons, Nathan, loved sports. It was all he could talk about. Kathy, on the other hand, did not grow up in a sports-minded family. As such, she found it extremely difficult to have a meaningful conversation with him. When asked how his day at school was, he would respond: "Fine." When asked how he did on a certain test, the answer was "Fine." When asked about how he enjoyed the school dance: "It was fine." Everything was fine. It had become the universal one-word answer to all inquiries. Finally, Kathy sought the Lord in prayer. She desperately wanted to be a good mother but did not know how to unlock her son's heart and mind. Then one day an answer came.

As Kathy walked through the house, she saw a sports magazine sitting on a table. The thought came, "Read it. Nathan loves sports, and you know nothing about sports." She did read it. When Nathan came home, Kathy discussed with him the articles she had read—he was interested, and a real conversation began. She read more and more in this weekly sports magazine. She read about key players and their lives, major trades, the top twenty-five picks, and so on. The conversations between mother and son continued and grew. Nathan then asked her to read a book that he was reading for a class at school so they could discuss it together. They became great friends.

As Kathy was having this marvelous experience with Nathan, Tad remembers one particular day taking him to football practice. Nathan had just had one of those sports conversations with his mother. He said: "Dad, Mom knows a lot about sports." And Tad thought to himself, "If only you knew." Kathy's willingness to find one common interest was the key to opening Nathan's heart.

TEACH THEM THE POWER OF PRAYER

One of the most meaningful things we can do as parents is teach our children the *power* of prayer, not just the *routine* of prayer. One of us, or both, knelt by the side of each child as he or she said nightly prayers until we were assured each had developed the habit. We remember one of our young sons saying, "I think I can do it on my own." Obviously, he had reached the point when we could "let go of his hand."

When Tad was about seventeen years old, he was kneeling by his bed, saying his evening prayers. Unknown to him, his mother was standing in the doorway. When he finished praying, his mother said, "Tad, are you asking the Lord to help you find a good wife?" Her question caught him totally off guard. That was the furthest thing from his mind. He was thinking about basketball and school.

Teaching Ideas for the Home

And so he replied, "No," to which his mother responded, "Well, you should son; it will be the most important decision you will ever make." Those words sunk deep into his heart, and so for the next six years, he prayed that God would help him find a good wife. And, oh, how grateful he is that God answered those prayers.

As parents, we can teach our children to kneel and to pray for things of eternal consequence—to pray for the strength to be morally clean in a very challenging world, to be obedient, to do well at school, to develop a testimony, to have the courage to stand for the right, and to find a good eternal mate.

No doubt many of our youth have their evening prayers, but perhaps many of them struggle with the habit of personal morning prayer. Parents, as their prime gospel teachers, can correct this. Which parents in Book of Mormon times would have let their sons march out to the battlefront without a breastplate and shield and sword to protect them against the potentially mortal blows of the enemy? But how many of us let our children march out the front door each morning to the most dangerous of all battlefields—to face Satan and his myriad of temptations, without their spiritual breastplates, shields, and swords that come from the protective power of prayer? The Lord said, "Pray always, . . . that you may conquer Satan" (D&C 10:5). As parents, we can help protect our children by instilling within them the habit and power of meaningful morning prayer.

Family prayers can also be a magnificent opportunity to get by with some "free preaching." As our children grew up, there were only so many times we could preach morality without the concern they might respond negatively. But family prayers became a free forum for doing so. In most of our family prayers, we prayed that our children would be morally clean. We prayed that they would find good spouses when the time came. We prayed that they would prepare for missions and the temple. There was never any backlash on what we prayed for. Family prayer is a time when we can "preach" without being charged for it.

READ THE SCRIPTURES WITH THEM

We can help our children develop the habit of daily scripture study. Some years ago we invited our twin sons, then about nine years old, to read the Book of Mormon. After a few nights, one of them came into our bedroom and said, "I want to read the Book of Mormon, but it's hard for me to understand." We asked him if he would like us to read the Book of Mormon with him. He replied that he would. Then followed some of the sweetest, most memorable teaching moments we have ever had. Night after night, we would have one of our twins on each side of us as we slowly but carefully read the Book of Mormon. We would try to explain it the best we could to nine-year-old boys, and they in return would ask questions they had. We did not read every night, but perhaps three or four nights a week. After about a year and a half, we read the last chapter in the Book of Mormon together. We asked them what they wanted to do next—they said, "Let's read it again." These are some of the choicest moments we recall as parents—tender moments with our children discussing the great truths of the Book of Mormon night after night.

TEACH THE DOCTRINE TO THEM

Our children should not have to be set-apart missionaries before they learn the doctrine and how to teach it. As parents, we should not abdicate this responsibility to Sunday School and seminary teachers. Our children should understand the doctrine of the Savior's Atonement from us as parents. They should know and love the plan of salvation because we have taught it to them. They should

Teaching Ideas for the Home

understand from our lips and hearts the true nature of God, His overwhelming love for us, the doctrine of Christ, and the historical truth of the Apostasy and the Restoration. These are key doctrines that make up the foundation of a solid testimony. Teaching these truths is part of bringing up our children "in the nurture and admonition of the Lord" (Eph. 6:4). Consider for a moment the following chart. Your children could answer the questions on the left, and then you as a parent could make plans to follow up on the right:

What do my children know about the following doctrine?	What additional truths and feelings would I like to share with my children on this doctrinal subject?
The Savior's Atonement • What is the Atonement? How would they explain it to a friend of another faith? (See Bible Dictionary, "Atonement"; 2 Ne. 2:21–26; Hel. 14:15–18.) • Why was the Atonement necessary? (See Mosiah 4:8; Alma 34:9; 42:12.) • What price did the Savior have to pay to make the Atonement possible? (See Mosiah 3:7; Alma 7:11–12; D&C 19:16–19.) • What does it mean to be resurrected? (See Bible Dictionary, "Resurrection"; 1 Cor. 15:42–58; Alma 40:23–24.)	

What do my children know about the following doctrine?	What additional truths and feelings would I like to share with my children on this doctrinal subject?
• Why is repentance a positive concept, and how does it relate to the Atonement? (See Bible Dictionary, "Repentance"; 2 Ne. 10:23–25; 3 Ne. 9:13–14.) • Can the Atonement totally cleanse us of our sins? (See Isa. 1:18; D&C 1:31–32.) • Can the Atonement also remove our guilt, or will we be troubled by the pains of our sins even though we are forgiven? (See Enos 1:5–8; Alma 24:9–12; 36:17–21.) • How can the Atonement help me overcome my weaknesses and even perfect me? (See Ether 12:26–27; Moro. 10:32–34.) • How can I best express my love for the Savior? (See John 14:15.)	

You can also do this exercise with other key doctrinal principles of the gospel, such as the plan of salvation, the Apostasy and Restoration, and the doctrine of Christ.

As a parent you might ask, "Where and when can I teach these truths?" The opportunities are many—home evening, family scripture study and prayer, dinner conversations, informal discussions, virtual conferences, etc. One of our struggles during family scriptural discussions was capturing the interest of our younger children without losing the interest of the older ones. The difference in maturity and intellect was significant. On some occasions we found it helpful to divide the children into two or more age groups and then focus the gospel lesson to their level of maturity and receptivity. This was particularly beneficial to one of our older children. In fact, over twenty years later he still mentions how helpful it was to him. We would meet with him one-on-one, usually Sunday afternoon, and teach him about the plan of salvation, the Savior's Atonement, the Godhead, and other related gospel topics. Our teaching was geared to his intellect and spiritual maturity. He was very receptive to this individualized teaching.

Teaching the doctrine to our children may come in the form of questions, explaining gospel truths, routine conversations, watching videos, reading the scriptures together, bearing testimony, and the like. If the desire to teach the doctrine to our children is one of our priorities, then opportunities will arise to do so.

President Spencer W. Kimball gave this counsel: "What we do know is that righteous parents who strive to develop wholesome influences for their children will be held blameless at the last day, and that they will succeed in saving most of their children, if not all."[1] What a hopeful promise.

HOLD REGULAR SCRIPTURE STUDY IN OUR HOMES

The promises to those who hold regular, quality scripture study in their homes are remarkable. In 1974 the First Presidency promised: "We assure you that you will always have our blessings and our prayers to the end that you may be rewarded by a fulfillment of the promise that if fathers and mothers will discharge this responsibility [i.e., home evening], *not one in a hundred of your family, as has been said by the leaders who have preceded us, would ever go astray.*"[2] What a promise! And how much more the spirit of this promise must apply to those who hold not only home evening but regular scripture study in their homes. What greater promise could parents hope for than to know that not one in a hundred of their children would go astray *if* they faithfully hold regular family scripture study.

Of course, parents who hold regular scripture study may have one or more children temporarily go astray. But when this occurs—when their child has his or her own wrestle before God, such child may also have a spiritual experience like that of Enos: "The words which I had often heard my father [and mother] speak concerning eternal life, and the joy of the saints, sunk deep into my heart" (Enos 1:3). The words and spirit of our gospel discussions can be recalled when our children are ready. But what a tragedy if in our child's hour of need, there is no spiritual reservoir, no memories of family scripture study to draw upon. What if the well is dry at the time of their spiritual thirst because we as parents never filled it?

For our family scripture study, Kathy often used a flannel board to teach gospel principles (today, parents might use more sophisticated mediums). One flannel-board story concerned "garbage can" words. On one side of the flannel board was a big garbage can with the lid off. On the other side were words that were trash can words, such as "shut up" or "stupid" or "ugly." One by one, each child would take one of those words, stick it in the garbage can and put the lid on it, signifying, of course, that they were not to be used by them. The years passed, and Tad was with our four-year-old granddaughter Hannah. For some reason he said, "I must have been a dummy to have done that." Hannah responded, "Grandpa, we don't say that word, and we don't say *stupid* or *ugly* either, but some adults do." How wonderful—the garbage-can lesson passed on from our daughter to another generation.

The outcome of another of our family discussions was totally unanticipated, but never to be forgotten: As a young married couple we learned that Bishop Vaughn J. Featherstone, then a member of the Presiding Bishopric, would be attending our upcoming stake conference. We thought our children might have a better appreciation for him if we could share a story about his family that would be appealing to them. So we read his book titled *A Generation of Excellence* and told the story of his twelve-year-old son Scott, who had been in an accident. He wanted to be in an upcoming stake track and sports meet, but with his injury he was unable to run in any of the sprints. Finally, he learned they had a sit-up contest and decided to enter it.

At one point during the track meet, Sister Featherstone came to her husband and said, "I want you to go over and stop the boy. He's done over five hundred sit-ups!"

In essence, Bishop Featherstone replied, "No, let the boy go."

Later his wife returned again. "He's now done seven hundred and fifty sit-ups," she said. "His back is bleeding. Please get him to stop."

Bishop Featherstone replied, "No, Merlene. . . . He'll know when to stop." A short while thereafter, Scott approached his parents with a big grin and a blue ribbon in his hand: 1,001 sit-ups![3]

As we told the story, the eyes of our nine-year-old son, Rick, were as big as silver dollars. He was entranced by every word. He had been training for the Cub Scout Olympics, and a sit-up competition was one of the events. As soon as we finished the story, he blurted out, "I want to beat that boy's record." We said that was a great goal and maybe he could work on it every night until he had accomplished it, but he replied, "No, I want to beat it tonight." And so, he began. After about 250 sit-ups we remarked that it was getting late and he needed to go to bed. He replied that he didn't want to quit. As he continued, we could see a blazing determination in his eyes—he was not about to stop. Recognizing this fact, we quickly got our camera and started filming. His brothers and sisters walked in and out of the room watching and witnessing this heroic feat, wondering, "Will he stop, or will he reach this seemingly unattainable goal?" When Rick reached various milestones, his brothers and sisters made charts designating how many he had done: 550 . . . 600 . . . 700 . . . 800 . . . 900 . . . and, finally 1,004 sit-ups. Our family could have heard one thousand sermons from the pulpit on determination, but they never would have had the effect of this single experience during this time of gospel discussion. Of course there were many such discussions that were not so perfect, but paydays like this one far overshadowed the more chaotic ones.

Consistent family scriptural discussions are the glue that can hold a family together. They are an ideal forum for teaching the gospel of Jesus Christ and strengthening family relationships. Their impact on our family for good has been overwhelming.

TEACH THE VALUE OF HARD WORK

We can teach our children both to work hard and to do so with excellence. We had a wheel on our refrigerator door that rotated weekly with our children's names and work assignments. Our children often called it the "wheel of misfortune." In retrospect we hope it is now referred to as the "wheel of good fortune."

BE CONSISTENT

Elder David A. Bednar tells of a beautiful painting depicting a wheat field that hangs in his office. He said:

> The painting is a vast collection of individual brushstrokes—none of which in isolation is very interesting or impressive. In fact, if you stand close to the canvas, all you can see is a mass of seemingly unrelated and unattractive streaks of yellow and gold and brown paint. However, as you gradually move away from the canvas, all of the

individual brushstrokes combine together and produce a magnificent landscape of a wheat field. . . .

Each family prayer, each episode of family scripture study, and each family home evening is a brushstroke on the canvas of our souls. No one event may appear to be very impressive or memorable. But just as the yellow and gold and brown strokes of paint complement each other and produce an impressive masterpiece, so our consistency in doing seemingly small things can lead to significant spiritual results.[4]

Alma confirmed this truth: "By small and simple things are great things brought to pass. . . . And by very small means the Lord doth confound the wise and bringeth about the salvation of many souls" (Alma 37:6–7).

SHARE WHAT WE HAVE LEARNED AT CHURCH AND HOME

Each week at church we have the opportunity to gain greater doctrinal insights, to feel the Spirit, and to strengthen our testimonies. While these insights and feelings are fresh in our minds and hearts, we have a golden opportunity to share them with our spouse, children, and friends. Alma condemned the Zoramites, who worshipped only one day a week, for failing to do this: "Now, after the people had all offered up thanks after this manner, they returned to their homes, *never speaking of their God again until they had assembled themselves together again*" (Alma 31:23; emphasis added). In essence, they went to church, worshipped, and then returned home, never to speak of God until the following week's church service. They were nothing more than "Sunday Christians."

Fortunately, there is now an emphasis on sharing at church what we have learned at home—to have gospel learning that is home centered and Church supported. Doing so reinforces the principles we learned at home and helps us crystalize and articulate the truths we have learned so as to further embed them in our minds and hearts.

TEACH THE WISE USE OF TIME

We can also teach our children to use their time wisely. On occasion, we will need to put our foot down, lovingly but firmly, to restrict our children's time with television and other electronic devices that in many cases are monopolizing their lives. Instead we may need to redirect their time into more productive efforts. There may be some initial resistance, some complaining, but we need to have the vision and the will to stick with it. One day our children will understand and appreciate what we have done.

DEDICATE OUR HOMES

Our homes do not need to be paid for to be dedicated. At the dedication of our home, our children gave talks on the type of language, music, art, and spirit we wanted to enjoy in our home, and then our home was dedicated to be a refuge and sanctuary from the ills and temptations of the world. It was a memorable occasion that reminded us of the sanctity of the home. It was an opportunity to bless our home to become a bit of heaven on earth.

NEVER GIVE UP ON TEACHING AND REACHING

We must never give up on teaching and reaching and praying for our children. It is a lifelong pursuit. What if God had given up on Saul of Tarsus? What if, from the heavens above, God had seen this anti-Christ persecuting the Saints, even consenting to the death of Stephen (see Acts 22:20), and lost patience with him? What if Alma had lost hope in his rebellious son and stopped praying for him one day before the angel came? What if the father of the prodigal son, saddened by his profligate life, had turned him away in his hour of need? President Boyd K. Packer passionately pleaded: "You who have heartache, you must never give up. No matter how dark it gets or no matter how far away or how far down your son or daughter has fallen, you must never give up. Never, never, never."5 That is what the Atonement of Jesus Christ is all about—it provides a way back home for even the most hardened of sinners, even the most wayward of our children.

AVOID BEING OVERWHELMED OR DISCOURAGED

Perhaps some feel guilty or overwhelmed or discouraged when thinking of these multiple ideas for parental improvement. We often felt like that after we attended mission presidents' seminars. There were so many good ideas presented that we felt overwhelmed—incapable of implementing them all. We knew that we could not physically, spiritually, or emotionally do everything everyone else was doing. Any attempt to do so would probably be foolhardy, as well as frustrating. We needed to exercise some common sense—select one or two of the ideas we felt would be most helpful to our mission and focus on them. Then the guilt would subside and renewed energy and hope would fill our souls.

The Lord wants to stretch us—to take us out of our comfort zones, but He does not want us to become discouraged in the process. King Benjamin gave us this wise counsel: "See that all these things are done in wisdom and order; *for it is not requisite that a man should run faster than he has strength.* And again, it is expedient that he should be diligent, that thereby he might win the prize; therefore, all things must be done in order" (Mosiah 4:27; emphasis added).

In other words, use good judgment, set realistic goals, and then proceed at a diligent but doable pace.

When we use common sense and prioritize, then our guilt and feelings of being overwhelmed can be replaced by constructive energy and enthusiasm that will help us complete the selected and realistic tasks at hand. Then we can proceed with the assurance that we are following the Lord's counsel to proceed in "wisdom and order" (Mosiah 4:27).

CONCLUSION

God has temporarily given us the custody of His spirit children—to train and nurture them in the way of the Lord. If we honor that parental responsibility, then these children that we love so much may become ours forever and ever.

CHAPTER 25

Informal Teaching Moments

The Savior gave this command: "Therefore, *strengthen your brethren in all your conversation*, in all your prayers, in all your exhortations, and *in all your doings*" (D&C 108:7; emphasis added). Such counsel reminds us that teaching moments are everywhere to be found. President Henry B. Eyring gave this sobering counsel:

> A wise parent would never miss a chance to gather children together to learn of the doctrine of Jesus Christ. Such moments are so rare in comparison with the efforts of the enemy. For every hour the power of the doctrine is introduced into a child's life, there may be hundreds of hours of messages and images denying or ignoring the saving truths.
>
> The question should not be whether we are too tired to prepare to teach doctrine or whether it wouldn't be better to draw a child closer by just having fun or whether the child isn't beginning to think that we preach too much. The question must be, "With so little time and so few opportunities,

what words of doctrine from me will fortify them against the attacks on their faith which are sure to come?" The words you speak today may be the ones they remember. And today will soon be gone.[1]

The Savior knew that not all teaching moments are found in formal or prearranged settings. On one occasion, He watched with His disciples as people cast money into the treasury. With His observant eye, He noticed that "many that were rich cast in much." He then noted that "there came a certain poor widow, and she threw in two mites, which make a farthing." The Savior knew this was a golden teaching moment, and He did not want the lesson to be lost on His disciples, so He called it to their attention. Perhaps prior to this point, His disciples thought that this day was more or less a routine one at the treasury or that the widow was penurious or that a simple fact of life is that the rich give more because they have more, and thus they may not have contemplated the underlying lesson to be discovered. But the Master Teacher seized upon the moment to teach a great truth: "Verily I say unto you, That this poor widow hath cast more in, than all they which have cast into the treasury: for all they did cast in of their abundance; but she of her want did cast in all that she had, even all her living" (Mark 12:41–44). A magnificent lesson had been taught: generosity is not measured by how much we give, but rather by what we have left after we give. This same principle might have been taught in the abstract, but how much more poignant when taught at the precise moment it was being demonstrated.

There are many teaching moments around us, often informal, if we but seek them. Our son Rick was about to ordain his twelve-year-old son a deacon. Before inviting others to join with him in the ordination, Rick sensed a teaching moment: "Do any of you have a spiritual experience about the priesthood you would like to share?"

Informal Teaching Moments

That simple invitation opened the door. Several moving experiences were shared, and the Spirit filled the room. He then proceeded with the ordination, but only after we were all reminded of the power and reality of the priesthood that was about to be bestowed.

While we were attending a stake conference in Toronto, Canada, the stake president spoke of a Saturday morning when two young boys were fighting over the first pancakes that would come off the griddle. The mother, seeing this as a teaching moment, said, "Boys, if Jesus were here, He would say: 'Here, you have the first pancake.'" The older boy turned to the younger one and said, "Kevin, you be Jesus today." Somehow that teaching moment did not turn out exactly as planned, but without some failures there will be few, if any, successes.

Tad can relate to the foregoing experience. Many years ago our family traveled to Argentina to pick up our son who was finishing his mission. Tad thought it might be useful to learn some Spanish and practice it while there. After several days of annoying and amusing people with his heavy accent, our kids (some of whom were studying Spanish in school) said, "Dad, please stop. It's embarrassing. You are butchering the language."

Finally, after their repeated petitions to quit, Tad said to them, "I want to teach you a lesson. It has been said that if you want to learn a language you must be willing to go out there and make ten thousand mistakes." One of our sons responded, "Yes, Dad, but not all in the same day." Another quipped, "You are already over the limit." So much for that informal teaching moment.

Perhaps the lesson to be learned is that even Babe Ruth, perhaps the greatest baseball hitter of all time, did not get a hit every time he came to bat. Sometimes he struck out, but it never diminished his enthusiasm for stepping up to the plate and swinging away once again, knowing that, in due course, many hits would come, even some home runs.

On one occasion we were part of a group touring the Payson Utah Temple before its dedication. As we neared the end of the tour, Kathy overheard a mother of two young girls turn to them and say, "What do you think the Holy Ghost was trying to teach us today?" After a short pause one of the girls responded, "That temples are very sacred buildings and are very important to us." That wise and sensitive mother understood the value of that informal teaching moment and readily seized upon it. Sometimes there is a certain spirit in the moment that cannot be captured or duplicated at a later time.

Informal teaching moments will come if we are striving to be observant of what is around us and actively thinking how we might transform such moments into valuable teaching lessons. Perhaps asking our children questions, such as those below, will help create such teaching moments:

- What do you think the Lord wanted you to learn from your lesson at church today?
- What did you feel as Sister Jones bore her testimony?
- What has the Holy Ghost taught you during our scripture study?

Some of the best informal teaching moments may be our quiet, anonymous examples—the unplanned moments when our children see us praying or reading the scriptures or rendering some act of kindness, not as part of a formal teaching moment, but because it is who we really are and what we really do. Sister Neill F. Marriott, of the Young Women General Presidency and a mother of eleven, was asked to give some thoughts on how she helped her children keep the Sabbath day holy. She invited her children, now grown, to share their memories in this regard. With her permission, we share one of her children's responses that evidence the power of a quiet example:

Informal Teaching Moments

Her son Daniel, age thirty-eight, wrote:

> You always closed your eyes and bowed your head during the passing of the sacrament. We seven sons did a lot of misbehaving during the meeting and we knew we could get away with plenty of things while your eyes were closed, but for some reason, we just didn't want to try. I can't really explain it, but I felt like you trusted us, and you had sincere reverence for the sacrament, so I just sat still. I remember, as a young teenager, doing something goofy during the sacrament. Then I looked at you and you had your head bowed and your eyes closed. I lost my appetite for goofing off in those moments because I could see how much you cared about this part of the meeting.[2]

Sister Marriott was teaching at her best when she may not have even known she was teaching. Her silent example thundered with positive repercussions.

A MOTHER'S HAT AS A TEACHER

In a conversation with our daughter Rebecca (the mother of six children), she commented on Sister Joy Jones's observation that "women wear many hats."[3] Rebecca then indicated that one of those hats is that of a teacher. Her spontaneous comments on the subject were so insightful and eloquent that we invited her to share them with us to include in this book:

> As a mother, I can recognize those small teaching moments that are woven into the fabric of our daily lives. While I am wearing my taxi driver's hat, my children and I can discuss the architecture of the beautiful buildings we are passing or ways we can help those in need as we drive past a homeless person. While I am wearing my chef's hat,

we can discuss mathematics as we carefully measure out the ingredients, the science of how the baking soda will affect the cookies we are baking or who we can deliver these cookies to when they are done. While I am wearing my nurse's hat, we can discuss why the body feels pain or how amazing our God-given bodies are and what a divine gift they are to us. Teaching moments surround us as we live our daily lives. It is up to us as parents, grandparents, aunts, and uncles to recognize and seize these teaching opportunities.

How grateful we can be for mothers, and others, who never cease teaching the gospel of Jesus Christ and other important truths to their children.

CONCLUSION

We should be constantly teaching our children and grandchildren the gospel of Jesus Christ, which includes everything that is "virtuous, lovely, or of good report or praiseworthy" (A of F 13). We should be eager to impart to our children every gospel truth and insight that has blessed our lives and strengthened our testimonies.

If we read a scripture that touches us or a good book that inspires us or witness a painting that stirs our finest emotions or listen to some uplifting music or see an act of kindness—then we have a wonderful opportunity to share these experiences with our children, whether in the car, at the dinner table, or at any other informal moment, and thus fulfill our role as the prime gospel teachers of our children.

CHAPTER 26

Teaching Our Children to Recognize the Spirit

WHY IS IT SO IMPORTANT TO RECOGNIZE THE PROMPTINGS OF THE SPIRIT?

One critical skill we can teach our children is how to recognize the promptings of the Spirit. In fact, so critical is this need that President Russell M. Nelson observed: "In coming days, it will not be possible to survive spiritually without the guiding, directing, comforting, and constant influence of the Holy Ghost."[1]

Sometimes these promptings of the Spirit may be the light of Christ, which is given to all men and women; other times they may be the Holy Ghost. The important point is that we want our children to be able to recognize these divine promptings and then follow them. If we can assist in this endeavor, then they will have a constant, reinforcing witness of the reality and divinity of God the Father, His Son Jesus Christ, and the Restoration. Then our children will know for themselves, in spite of any secular or theological arguments to the contrary, that the gospel of Jesus Christ is as true as true can be. Then their testimonies will be founded on the personal light of divine revelation, not the borrowed light of another. And then they will have the witness of the Spirit, which trumps and transcends every conceivable counterargument of man. When all is said and done, the Spirit is the ultimate witness, the consummate test of truth.

President Boyd K. Packer tells of an experience that the naturalist John Burroughs had:

> One summer evening [he] was walking through a crowded park. Above the sounds of city life he heard the song of a bird. He stopped and listened! Those with him had not heard it. He looked around. No one else had noticed it. It bothered him that everyone should miss something so beautiful. He took a coin from his pocket and flipped it into the air. It struck the pavement with a ring, no louder than the sound of a bird. Everyone turned; they could hear that! It is difficult to separate from all the sounds of city traffic the song of a bird. But you can hear it. You can hear it plainly if you train yourself to listen for it.[2]

In a similar manner, the whisperings and impressions of the Spirit are all around us, but they will be drowned out and smothered by the noise of the secular world if we do not train our ears to hear them and our hearts to feel them. This training is part of the spiritual education parents can give to their children.

A friend of ours became one of the premier radiologists in Hawaii. Other radiologists would send him their X-rays when they had difficulty interpreting them. Somehow, through his experience and schooling he had acquired an expertise that eluded many others. In each case he saw the same film as his colleagues, but the difference was his ability to recognize and read what was seemingly indiscernible to them. Perhaps a similar experience happens with the Spirit. No doubt the Spirit sends many messages, but they are discernable only to those whose spiritual education and experience have trained them to recognize and comprehend them.

Missionaries teach the truths of the gospel, often with great power and authority. The people they teach may feel good when they hear these truths, but if they are unable to recognize the accompanying impressions as promptings of the Spirit, they may dismiss them as mere psychological feelings. That is why it is so important for missionaries to not only teach the doctrine by the Spirit but also educate those they teach to recognize the Spirit when it comes—to connect the dots, so to speak—the impression on one hand and the cause on the other.

HELPING OUR CHILDREN RECOGNIZE THE PROMPTINGS OF THE SPIRIT

How then can we as parents help our children recognize the Spirit when it comes? We need to teach them that the voice of God is vastly different from the voice of the world. We live in a world of high drama and action thrillers, fast-paced entertainment, and loud music. As a result, many people expect spiritual impressions in a dramatic way—an audible voice or a vision or some thunderous witness from the heavens. But the Lord usually works in much more subtle and serene ways. The newly born Savior was laid in a manger. His Atonement commenced in a quiet garden. The Restoration of His Church began in a secluded grove. And His truths are often revealed in the intimacy of a searching heart. There is something sacred and divine in the quiet and seemingly anonymous works of God. The Lord taught this lesson to Elijah: "And he said, Go forth, and stand upon the mount before the Lord. And, behold, the Lord passed by, and a great and strong wind rent the mountains, and brake in pieces the rocks before the Lord; but the Lord was not in the wind: and after the wind an earthquake; but the Lord was not in the earthquake: And after the earthquake a fire; but the Lord was not in the fire: *and after the fire a still small voice*" (1 Kings 19:11–12; emphasis added).

The Savior's appearance to the Nephites is another case in point. The Father's voice, which introduced His Beloved Son, was described as follows: "It was not a harsh voice, neither was it a loud voice; nevertheless, and notwithstanding it being a small voice it did pierce them that did hear to the center" (3 Ne. 11:3).

One way to help our children recognize the Spirit is to ask a simple question at those times when we are feeling the Spirit and then bear a confirming testimony of its presence. For example, suppose you are having a family discussion and you feel a particular influx of the Spirit. You might pause and ask one or more of your children, "What are you feeling right now?"

They might respond, "A peace or warmth or desire to be better." If they struggle to define their feelings, then you might help with some suggestions.

After they have expressed themselves, you might bear your testimony: "I had the same feelings you did and that is a witness of the Spirit. God, in His merciful way, sent us that feeling and impression as a witness that the doctrine we are discussing is true. No matter what anyone else may tell you, you just had a personal witness from God of its truthfulness." Moments like this are opportunities for parents to help their children connect the divine dots—to understand that certain feelings and impressions are promptings of the Spirit.

A similar experience might occur when discussing sacrament meeting around the dinner table. The question might be asked, "How did you feel or what did you learn when Sister Barnes spoke and bore her testimony of the Atonement of Jesus Christ?" That simple question might unleash a powerful teaching moment on how to recognize the Spirit.

As parents we have all had experiences when we felt the Spirit. Some of these may have occurred when we were the ages of our children. As we appropriately share these experiences with our children, they may in some way feel the spirit of that moment and then recognize the promptings of the Spirit for themselves.

The question is often asked, "How can I distinguish between my own psychological feelings and the still, small voice of the Spirit?" For us, this has been an educational process that requires pondering, studying the scriptures, exercising spiritual integrity, and testing the promptings that come against the promises of the Lord. Fortunately, there are certain feelings of the heart and impressions of the mind that come only from heaven. These feelings and impressions are divinely directed. Even Satan, the great counterfeiter, cannot duplicate them. A few such feelings and impressions are as follows.

A Feeling of Peace

The Savior said, "My peace I give unto you: not as the world giveth, give I unto you" (John 14:27). Oliver Cowdery, an early leader in the Church, had been in the home of Joseph Smith's father and prayed to know the truth of the Book of Mormon. While there, he received a convincing witness of its truthfulness, which came in the form of an undeniable peace. Time passed and human nature took its toll. Perhaps Oliver wondered if that experience had really been an impression from heaven or just some psychological feeling or passing moment of self-delusion. To resolve his anxiety, he went to Joseph Smith and asked him to request a revelation from God that would be a witness to him of the truthfulness of the Book of Mormon. Joseph Smith sought such a revelation. It came as follows: "Verily, verily, I say unto you [Oliver], if you desire a further witness, cast your mind upon the night that you cried unto me in your heart, that you might know concerning the truth of these things. *Did I not speak peace to your mind concerning the matter? What greater witness can you have than from God?*" (D&C 6:22–23; emphasis added).

Oliver had received peace. The Lord reaffirmed his prior experience and confirmed that peace comes only from Him. Joseph Smith had no knowledge of these circumstances; in fact, he only learned of Oliver's earlier experience through this revelation. Oliver now knew with certainty that peace is a divine witness from God. Oliver connected the dots—peace and the prompting of the Spirit. Alma also recognized this truth when he exclaimed: "Behold, I did cry unto him [God] and I did find peace to my soul" (Alma 38:8).

An Intent to Do Good

If you have a desire to be a better person after reading the scriptures, hearing a talk, following a class discussion, or at any other time, then that is a divine witness of the presence of the Spirit. The prophet Mormon taught: "Every thing which inviteth and enticeth to do good, and to love God, and to serve him, is inspired of God" (Moro. 7:13). The Lord spoke further on this subject: "*Put your trust in that Spirit which leadeth to do good*—yea, to do justly, to walk humbly, to judge righteously; and this is my Spirit" (D&C 11:12; emphasis added). If you feel an impression to be a better person, that is the Spirit working upon you.

An Enlightened Understanding

Another divine witness comes in the form of increased enlightenment and understanding. The Lord said, "I will impart unto you of my Spirit, which shall enlighten your mind" (D&C 11:13; see also D&C 6:15).[3] This enlightenment literally causes our minds to transform. It elevates us to a loftier plane and gives us a higher intellectual and spiritual IQ, so to speak—perhaps a more infinite-like capacity to think and reason like God. Paul observed, "Be ye transformed by the renewing [or enlightening] of your mind" (Rom. 12:2). Joseph Smith added: "A person may profit by noticing the first intimation of the spirit of revelation; for instance, when you feel pure intelligence flowing into you, it may give you sudden strokes of ideas."[4] I think we have all felt such promptings when we have diligently sought God's help in solving a problem or received ideas for a talk or teaching a class or giving counsel to someone in need.

This enlightenment will help us understand, perhaps for the first time in our lives, that we are the literal spirit children of God and what our divine destiny can be. It will unfold to us the truths of where we came from, why we are here, and where we are going. It will fill the doctrinal blind spots in our minds with heavenly light. These truths and insights will quicken our minds and give us newfound reservoirs of direction and hope. The scriptures will take on a new vibrancy—they will be more readable and desirable and understandable than ever before. This enlightenment is a form of mental expansion and divine confirmation.

An Increased Love

The word of God and the Spirit have the capacity to "enlarge" our souls (see Alma 32:28), meaning, among other things, to give us a greater capacity to love. Scrooge, much like the Grinch, had a heart "two sizes too small." Then, through a series of visions—past, present, and future—his heart "enlarged," and he was filled with compassion and love.[5] When that happens—when we are forgiving and concerned about others—it is a witness that the Spirit is working upon us.

Other Divine Witnesses

Sometimes the divine witness comes as a burning in the bosom. The two disciples who walked with the Savior on the road to Emmaus acknowledged, "Did not our heart burn within us, while he talked with us by the way?" (Luke 24:32; see also D&C 8:2–3; 9:7–9). On other occasions, the doctrine we hear or the impressions we receive are "delicious" to us—they taste good spiritually (Alma 32:28). In other words, we do not need external evidence to verify these truths or logic to prove them—we just know. Our hearts have tasted of their goodness, and that is sufficient.

Paul tells us that other fruits of the Spirit are "joy, peace, long-suffering, gentleness, goodness, faith" (Gal. 5:22–23).[6] When any of these virtues or impressions envelop our hearts or minds, it is a witness from God that what we are listening to, what we are feeling, is from Him. Thereafter, God holds us accountable for these divine witnesses and our subsequent conduct.

CONCLUSION

If we have felt peace or an intent to be a better person or any of the other witnesses described above, that is God's quiet but certain witness to us that what we are hearing or feeling is the truth, that we are on the right course—God is speaking to us. As we teach these truths and bear our testimony of them, then we as parents can fulfill the Lord's command: "All thy children shall be taught of the Lord." And then our children can be recipients of the accompanying promise: "and great shall be the peace of thy children" (Isa. 54:13).[7]

CHAPTER 27

Teaching Our Children Morality

WHY IS IT SO IMPORTANT TO TEACH MORALITY TO OUR CHILDREN?

In Psalms we find this sobering truth: "Who shall ascend into the hill of the Lord? or who shall stand in his holy place? He that hath clean hands, and a pure heart" (Ps. 24:3–4). Lest there be any question about this truth, Nephi taught that "no unclean thing can dwell with God" (1 Ne. 10:21). Purity of mind and heart is a fundamental element of godhood. It is a gauge of our receptivity to the Spirit, our self-mastery, and our integrity.

Immorality may be Satan's deadliest arrow in his quiver of evil. Certainly it is among the most flagrant and frequent temptations he directs at our youth today. If we teach God's laws of morality with love and testimony, we will provide our children with a shield of faith that can thwart Satan's every blow and a sword of truth that can counter his every specious argument. This is all-out war, and parents are the spiritual generals who are divinely commissioned to prepare and train their children for the inevitable battles they will face.

TEACH CORRECT DOCTRINAL PRINICPLES

How can we as parents teach our children God's moral law without being overbearing but with such clarity, dignity, and power that it infuses within their souls a burning desire and discipline to be clean? We do not claim to know the best way for parents to teach their children God's moral laws and how to counter a society that opposes many of them. We do believe, however, that the best way must be done in a loving, sensitive environment that includes a teaching of correct doctrinal principles, an explanation of the blessings of living or consequences of failing to live God's laws, and our own personal testimony that living God's laws brings happiness, while violation of them brings misery.

Following are some of the key doctrinal principles that constitute the foundation for God's moral laws. It is critical for our children to understand these doctrinal principles because they are the key to understanding God's moral laws. Hopefully this understanding will help bless our children with the resolve and discipline to be morally clean.

Our Divine Identity

We are the spirit offspring of God (see Acts 17:28)[1] and thus have inherited spiritual traits that give us the divine potential to become like Him. The family proclamation reads: "Each [of us] is a beloved spirit son or daughter of heavenly parents, and, as such, each has a divine nature and destiny."[2] And that destiny is to become like God our Father (see Matt. 5:48).[3]

If we do not correctly understand our divine identity as sons and daughters of God, then we will never fully comprehend our divine destiny—to become like Him. These truths are inseparable partners.

But why is it so important for us to understand that we can become like God? Because He has what we all desire—a fullness of joy. He is the happiest person in the universe, and He wants us to have that same happiness, which is only possible if we become like Him, and we can become like Him only if we keep His moral laws.

Accordingly, every law God gives us has one underlying objective—to help us become as He is. This condition is known as exaltation. Exaltation is not so much a place as a state of being. God gives us moral laws because they are a reflection of who He is and serve as the basis for who we may become.

Our Bodies Are Holy Temples

Our bodies are not just temporal objects designed to seek physical pleasure. King Benjamin described this mindset as "the natural man [who] is an enemy to God" (Mosiah 3:19). To the contrary, God has decreed that our bodies are holy temples. Paul confirmed this truth: "Know ye not that your body is the temple of the Holy Ghost, which is in you, which ye have of God, and ye are not your own? For ye are bought with a price: therefore glorify God in your body, and in your spirit, which are God's" (1 Cor. 6:19–20). This makes perfect sense. Among His many titles, God is known as "Man of Holiness" (Moses 7:35). Since we are created in "the image of his own body" (Moses 6:9), it stands to reason that we too can become holy as He is holy. For this reason, God has given us moral laws, which if obeyed, will help us become holy—the ultimate pursuit of our mortal lives.

God Gave to Us the Sacred Power of Procreation

Because we are created in God's holy image and because He loves us immensely, He has shared with us that power which is most prized and sacred to Him—the power of procreation. God's moral laws are designed to help us use those creative powers in such a way that will (1) best fulfill God's purposes on earth by having children in the marriage relationship, (2) facilitate our ability to become holy like He is holy by learning and exercising self-control over these powers, and (3) maximize our joy in the use of such powers.

God's moral laws are not arbitrary or unnecessarily restrictive. Suppose parents were to give a car to their teenage son and say: "You don't need to obey the speed limit, you don't need to stop at red lights, and you don't need to signal when turning. Just go out there, do what you want, and have a good time." What would you think of those parents? Instead, as a parent, you would explain to your son that a car is a powerful instrument—if used wrongly it could maim, even destroy lives; if used correctly, it is a means to accomplishing much good. We know from years of experience that the rules of the road are a formulation of what society deems best—what will best protect the driver and innocent bystanders.

So it is with our God-given procreative powers. Like cars they can be a powerful force for good or evil. The restrictions imposed on the use of our creative powers are given to protect both the ones using such powers and potentially innocent victims. The powers of procreation should not be used unchecked—without rules, without restraint, without regard to God's will. Fortunately, God's moral laws have been defined by His prophets. The First Presidency and Quorum of the Twelve Apostles have declared, "God commanded that the sacred powers of procreation are to be employed only between man and woman, lawfully wedded as husband and wife."[4] These are God's "rules of the road" for the use of this prized power.[5]

Will and Ariel Durant, the world-renowned historians, wrote of society's need for moral standards:

> No man [or woman], however brilliant or well informed, can come in one lifetime to such fullness of

understanding as to safely judge and dismiss the customs or institutions of his society, for these are the wisdom of generations after centuries of experiment in the laboratory of history. *A youth boiling with hormones will wonder why he should not give full freedom to his sexual desires; and if he is unchecked by custom, morals, or laws, he may ruin his life [or hers] before he matures sufficiently to understand that sex is a river of fire that must be banked and cooled by a hundred restraints if it is not to consume in chaos both the individual and the group.*[6]

Marriage and Families Are Meant to Be Eternal

One purpose of the creative powers is to bind husbands and wives more fully in the marriage covenant. Another purpose is to "multiply, and replenish the earth" (Gen. 1:28). The original Hebrew word for replenish means "fill."[7] As a consequence, God wanted men and women in the marriage relationship to fill the earth with His spirit children (see 1 Ne. 17:36) so that all spirits in the premortal existence who chose God's plan of salvation would have the opportunity to come to earth in fulfillment of that plan, preferably in a family setting.

God's prophets have spoken of the divine and eternal nature of the family: "The family is ordained of God. Marriage between man and woman is essential to His eternal plan. Children are entitled to birth within the bonds of matrimony, and to be reared by a father and mother."[8] That is the ideal. Of course, many children are raised by wonderful single parents who live exemplary lives and are to be commended for what they do, often in the most difficult of circumstances. Kathy's mother was one of these.

Our experience in mortality was not designed as some random probationary test that, if passed, would then qualify us for some completely unrelated blissful life in the hereafter. Rather, mortality has a much deeper purpose; it is intended to be a prototype and preparation for a similar yet more exalted state of life, for which marriage and families continue to be the foundation. In other words, this life is a pattern for the next. The Savior so spoke: "I will give unto you a pattern in all things" (D&C 52:14). That is why marriage between a man and woman is so critical: because it mirrors marriage in heaven, where husbands and wives are "*heirs together* of the grace of life" (1 Pet. 3:7; emphasis added).[9] Likewise, it mirrors the ability of eternal spouses to have children, referred to in the scriptures as "a continuation of the seeds forever and ever" (D&C 132:19). Under these latter conditions the scriptures confirm that these eternal spouses "shall . . . be gods" (D&C 132:20). Why? Because they have the power to do what Gods do—have eternal offspring and thus have worlds without number. This is the crowning blessing God can bestow upon men and women, but it is available *only* if a man and woman keep God's moral laws and thus are eligible to be sealed together for eternity.

The Lord is clear on this point: "In the celestial glory there are three heavens or degrees; and in order to obtain the highest, a man *must* enter into this order of the priesthood [meaning the new and everlasting covenant of marriage]; and if he does not, he cannot obtain it. He may enter into the other, but that is the end of his kingdom; he cannot have an increase" (D&C 131:1–4; emphasis added).[10] That is why it is so critical to follow God's decreed path of marriage between a man and a woman and to reserve the creative powers for that relationship, so as to prepare us and help us be worthy for those similar but even greater responsibilities and blessings in the life to come.

GOD'S MORAL LAWS AND THE BLESSINGS OF KEEPING THEM

The doctrinal principles discussed above serve as the foundation for God's moral laws, some of which are discussed below.

Fornication and Adultery

Because our bodies are holy temples and the Lord has commanded us to reserve the powers of procreation for a lawful marriage, fornication and adultery are prohibited. No wonder Paul taught, "Know ye not that the unrighteous shall not inherit the kingdom of God? Be not deceived: neither fornicators, nor idolaters, nor adulterers" (1 Cor. 6:9).[11] Lest there be any question about God's position on premarital relations, Paul wrote, "For this is the will of God, . . . that ye should abstain from fornication" (1 Thes. 4:3).

Sometimes people do not realize the seriousness of these transgressions, or, in some cases, they rationalize them away. Corianton, son of the prophet Alma, did not seem to realize the gravity of what he had done when he sinned with Isabel. Some of our youth may have that same misconception unless we help correct it. Alma candidly taught his son Corianton the truth: "Know ye not, my son, that these things are an abomination in the sight of the Lord?" (Alma 39:5). Joseph also spoke of this great evil. When he was tempted by Potiphar's wife—who said, "Lie with me"—he replied: "How . . . can I do this great wickedness, and sin against God?" (Gen. 39:7, 9).

God has given us additional guidelines regarding the use of these sacred creative powers. The inappropriate touching of someone else, or of one's self, is the smaller sibling of fornication and adultery. The First Presidency has spoken directly to this point: "Before marriage, do not . . . touch the private, sacred parts of another person's body, with or without clothing. . . . Do not arouse those [sexual] emotions in your own body."[12] Any conscious thoughts or voluntary actions that stimulate or result in the expression of the creative powers outside the marriage relationship are disapproved of by the Lord and will ultimately bring guilt and remorse. And why did God give us this restriction? Because ironically, this moral law is a restriction that, in truth, liberates us. If some yield to the creative urge at every whim, especially when restricted by God, they will soon find that this urge controls them, not the reverse—they have become the slave, and the urge has become the master. Control and discipline are essential elements of freedom and godhood.

Despite God's clear condemnation of the use of the creative powers outside the marriage relationship, some might say, "But these acts are between consenting parties; they bring immediate pleasure and allow individual choice; therefore they are to be condoned, not condemned." But in truth, these acts violate God's moral laws and thus are an obstacle to our spiritual growth. The consequences of using the creative powers outside the marriage relationship can include broken homes, children born out of wedlock, denigration of the marriage covenant, and abortions, and they will always result in guilt, lack of self-esteem, and the loss of the Spirit. Simply said, these actions hinder our pursuit of becoming like God. Every decision we make to become more like God increases our capacity for freedom; every decision to the contrary decreases that capacity.

Immodesty

True to the Faith defines modesty as "an attitude of humility and decency in dress, grooming, language, and behavior. If you are modest, you do not draw undue attention to yourself. Instead, you seek to 'glorify God in your body and in your spirit' (1 Cor. 6:20; see also verse 19)."[13]

We should all have a great respect for our bodies, which are temples of God (see 1 Cor. 3:16–17). Part of our respect is shown by the way we dress. Does our clothing dignify our body? Does it say, "This body is sacred and holy"? *For the Strength of Youth* teaches: "Your dress and grooming influence the way you and others act."[14] We can dress fashionably but also modestly. As we act and dress modestly, we invite the Spirit, we treat our bodies with the respect they deserve, and we engender the respect of others as disciples of Jesus Christ.

Pornography

God is desirous that none of His children view or listen to anything that is pornographic. It is *repulsive* to the Spirit of the Lord. It is inconsistent with our bodies being sacred and holy temples of God. Pornography undermines marriages, demeans women and men, and fosters deceit (see D&C 38:13, 28). Pornography has no redeeming moral value whatsoever. It is a moral evil. Fortunately, it can be overcome with discipline, the Lord's Atonement, prayer, fasting, and, when appropriate, proper counseling.

The story is told of a lone man who ascended a high mountain. The weather was bitter cold at the summit. He looked around and saw a rattlesnake. He withdrew a safe distance. The rattlesnake then spoke to him in pleading tones: "Please take me to the valley below where the weather is warmer and I can survive; otherwise I will die."

The man replied, "But you will bite me."

"No," came the reply from the snake, "you are different. You are special. I promise I will not bite you if you carry me to safety below."

The believing man picked up the snake, held it next to the warmth of his body, and carried it to the valley below. Just as he released it, the snake struck and bit him. The man cried out, "But you promised!" to which the snake replied, "You knew what I was when you picked me up."[15]

No one can claim to be fooled regarding the effects of pornography when one "picks it up." It is a poisonous, venomous, unforgiving snake that will strike the moment a person takes a first look and continue to strike with a full portion of venom at each look thereafter.

No doubt you can recall your visits to the dentist's office and the shots of anesthetic you received to deaden the nerves and senses. The affected area had no feeling; in fact, the numbness may have lasted even after you left the office. Pornography is Satan's "shot of anesthetic"—it dulls our spiritual senses until we become like Laman and Lemuel, to whom Nephi said, "He [God] hath spoken unto you in a still small voice, *but ye were past feeling, that ye could not feel his words*" (1 Ne. 17:45; emphasis added). Pornography has the power to spiritually numb us, making us "past feeling" to the impressions of God.

If we or our children ever encounter pornography, whether it be in a movie or on the internet or otherwise, we should do as Joseph of the Bible did when he was tempted: he "fled, and got him out" (Gen. 39:12). As parents we can be proactive in inoculating our children against this pernicious evil. We can warn them of its highly destructive effects in one's life, we can place filters on computers, establish "safe areas," and counsel them what to do if they involuntarily encounter it, and we can teach and testify of the beauty and blessings of a clean mind and a pure heart.

Nonetheless, however hard we try, we cannot protect our children against pornography that may be displayed outside the home, such as at school, at work, on the internet, on billboards, or the like. Somehow we must so instill in their hearts and minds the evils of pornography and the beauties of chastity that they will have the self-discipline to reject it, wherever and however it may be thrust upon them. And there is no better way to do this than to help them develop the habits of daily prayer and scripture study, to teach them correct moral principles, to provide a receptive environment to hear their concerns and challenges, and to live an exemplary life consistent with such principles.

Unclean Thoughts

King Benjamin taught, "If ye do not watch yourselves, *and your thoughts*, and your words, and your deeds, and observe the commandments of God, . . . ye must perish" (Mosiah 4:30; emphasis added). We cannot avoid seeing every improper thing that may spark an unclean thought, but we can drive out improper thoughts if they arise. The sin is not in accidentally seeing something improper; the sin is in voluntarily seeking out evil or nurturing an improper thought once it comes. The scriptures tell us, "For as he thinketh in his heart, so is he" (Prov. 23:7). Our thoughts are the seeds of our words and actions.

Good and evil cannot simultaneously exist in our minds any more than light and darkness can exist at the same time and in the same place. At some point we must decide which will be our master—unclean thoughts or pure thoughts. One choice will free us; the other will enslave us. If we so desire, we can drive out every evil thought and immediately replace it with an uplifting song, poem, scripture, or prayer. Just as darkness flees at the presence of light, so evil flees at the presence of good.

Because the Lord has commanded us to have clean thoughts, He has given a magnificent promise to those who do so: "Let virtue garnish thy thoughts unceasingly; *then shall thy confidence wax strong in the presence of God*" (D&C 121:45; emphasis added).[16] In other words, if our thoughts are pure, we can have a clear conscience and approach God with confidence that He will answer the righteous desires of our hearts. If we conscientiously strive and seek God's help, we can control our thoughts. We can teach this truth to our children with the power of our speech and the force of our example.

THE GREAT LIE

Unfortunately, there are many who fail to understand God's moral laws or, worse, elevate their own wisdom and ideology above His, or perhaps they have fallen prey to the social pressures of the day. Whatever the reason may be, no reason is good enough to endorse violating God's moral laws. We must clearly and powerfully teach God's doctrinal principles that underlie His moral standards.

God has taught the nature of true compassion and love. For example, we can abhor the act of fornication or adultery but still love the individual who committed it. Certainly we can love our children even though we may disagree with some of the choices they make. The world would have us believe otherwise—if you disagree with the act, you must despise the person—that is a great lie perpetuated by the evil one and unfortunately fostered by much of society.

True love is to kindly and patiently encourage those we have stewardship over to turn from their immoral conduct and help them get back on the road that leads to exaltation. Who is more loving—the parent who never disciplines his or her child or the parent who kindly and patiently, but honestly, points out what the child is doing wrong and helps him or her get back on the right road? It is a misguided compassion, a misguided love—even counterproductive—to encourage someone in actions that lead him or her away from becoming like God. Parents who truly love their children will never endorse immoral actions. Instead, with true love and patience, they will use their example and kindly influence to reverse the destructive course and bring them back to God.

It can be difficult as a parent when a child chooses to not live God moral's laws. To such parents, the Church has counseled, "Be sure to charge your spiritual battery by spending quality time in sacred places. . . . As you seek the companionship of the Spirit, you will draw near to God, your child, and, if applicable, your spouse.

Teaching Our Children Morality

Remember to honor agency. If your spouse disagrees with how you want to handle things, work it out respectfully. If your child makes choices you disagree with, kindly let them know how you feel. Never try to control or manipulate them. Give them your time and assure them of your love."[17]

Similarly, President Dallin H. Oaks has given us this guidance for how we can balance teaching the law with showing our love:

> As Latter-day Saints, many of us, not all of us, but many of us are inclined to insist on the law and do so in an unloving way. . . . We have to have in mind the commandments of the Lord, which I'll refer to as the law, and also the great commandment to love one another. . . . When we obey those commandments, we are obedient. The consequence of being obedient to commandments is to put ourselves in harmony with the eternal law that permits us to grow and progress toward eternal life. The Savior commanded His followers to "love one another, as I have loved you." So we look at how He loved us. He sacrificed Himself for us. He was concerned always with the individual. He had a wonderful outreach for people. I think those are all indicators of how we can love one another like He loved us. If we make Him our role model, we should always be trying to reach out to include everyone.[18]

IDEAS FOR PARENTS

Though parents can teach their children the correct doctrinal principles underlying God's moral laws, what happens when one of our children says, "I want to be morally clean but have difficulty resisting the temptations that confront me"? While serving as a Church leader, Tad had a young man come to him who had difficulty keeping his thoughts clean. He said that improper thoughts would often pop into his mind and then he would strive to drive them out. Tad asked him if he had a song he would sing or a scripture he would recall that would help him. He said he did and it helped, but some thoughts still lingered or returned.

Further inquiry was then made: "Do you pray daily?"

"Not always" was the response.

Tad asked about his daily scripture reading; it was sporadic. Did he attend all his Church meetings regularly?

"Not always," came the answer.

Tad pondered for a moment, and then an impression came: "You like to play basketball, don't you?"

"Oh, yes!" came the reply. "I love basketball."

"Well, suppose for a moment that at your next game the coach called all the players together just before the tip-off and said: 'Tonight, players, we are going to try a new strategy—no one is to take a shot. We are going to save all our energy and play the best defensive game anyone has ever played.' What is the best your team could hope to do?"

He looked somewhat puzzled and replied, "Break even, a zero-to-zero tie."

"That's right," Tad replied, "and that's exactly what you are doing. You have been playing defense. When some evil thought crosses your mind, you try to drive it out. That is good, but it is the lesser part of what you ought to be doing. You need to take the offense. For, in truth, the best defense is a good offense. When you have the ball, the other team *cannot* score."

This young man's spiritual offense was sporadic at best. One cannot play defense alone and expect to beat Satan. That was the counsel of Paul: "Be not overcome of evil, but overcome evil with good" (Rom. 12:21). Fortunately, this young man was receptive to this counsel and made an effort to be more proactive in his spiritual growth.

Parents can help their children learn to take the spiritual offense. They can ensure they are having morning as well as evening prayers. They can encourage them to pray for moral strength and discipline and to study the scriptures daily. Where possible they can encourage them to attend the temple to perform proxy work for the dead. They can inspire them to do family history research and indexing. They can help them get patriarchal blessings as soon as they are spiritually mature, knowing that these blessings will reinforce their child's divine identity and destiny. They can hold family scripture discussions regularly and bear witness of these moral principles. They can have family prayer and pray that their children will be morally clean. They can give priesthood blessings that will strengthen resolves and extol the virtues of a clean life. They can have candid but sensitive talks with each child. They can keep computers in visible sight and refrain from giving out cell phones to children with internet access until they are mature enough to handle them. They can make sure their children have uplifting pictures in their room, such as pictures of the Savior and temple, and that they are listening to uplifting music. If parents seek the Spirit, guidance will come that will help them know how to get their children on spiritual offense and thus best be protected from the evils of the world. In fact, when our children take such offense, Satan is relegated to defense.

WHEN SHOULD WE TEACH THESE MORAL LAWS?

The timing as to when we should teach God's moral laws is governed in large part by the age and maturity of our children. This can often differ from child to child and culture to culture. Perhaps a guideline could be as follows: our children should learn about morality from parents before the world (i.e., peers, teachers, television, or the like) teaches them false doctrines, but not before they are physically, emotionally, and spiritually mature enough to understand and receive these moral laws. This can be a delicate balance, and thus we as parents need spiritual guidance to determine when and how to teach such sacred concepts.

Rosemary M. Wixom, former Primary General President, offered this helpful counsel: "The world will teach our children if we do not, and children are capable of learning all the world will teach them at a very young age. What we want them to know five years from now needs to be part of our conversation with them today. Teach them in every circumstance; let every dilemma, every consequence, every trial that they may face provide an opportunity to teach them how to hold on to gospel truths."[19]

CONCLUSION

God's moral standards are positive and uplifting and liberating. They build relationships of trust, they enhance self-esteem, they foster a clear conscience, they invite the Spirit of the Lord into our individual and married lives, and they maximize our happiness. Regardless of all the rationalization to the contrary, there is no lasting joy in immorality. The prophet Samuel spoke directly to that point: "Ye have sought all the days of your lives for that which ye could not obtain; and ye have sought for happiness in doing iniquity, which thing is contrary to the nature of that righteousness which is in our great and Eternal Head" (Hel. 13:38).[20]

If we teach God's moral laws with clarity and conviction, as taught in the scriptures and by the living prophets and with our own personal testimony, our children will recognize these moral laws as a true source of happiness and will have an enhanced desire and discipline to live them.

CHAPTER 28

The Refining Influence of Culture in Our Homes and Classes

CULTURE REFINEMENT IS A RELIGIOUS PURSUIT

Elder Douglas L. Callister made this important connection between culture and spirituality: "The nearer we get to God, the more easily our spirits are touched by refined and beautiful things. . . . Refinement is a companion to developed spirituality. Refinement and spirituality are two strings drawn by the same bow."[1] With each degree of refinement, we become more like Him who is the most refined of all beings. And as we become more like Him, we inevitably become more in tune with His Spirit. Thus, cultural refinement is not just an academic endeavor—it is also a religious pursuit. The thirteenth article of faith reads in part, "If there is anything virtuous, lovely, or of good report or praiseworthy, we seek after these things." What an ennobling and uplifting thought.

The account is told of a young boy who visited the Grand Canyon for the first time and looked over the canyon rim at the breathtaking view below. He then wrote home to tell his mother of the experience. "Today," he said, "I spit two miles." Tragically, he had missed it all—the grandeur, the splendor, the compelling witness of God's creative powers.[2]

Karl G. Maeser, a highly refined German convert and former president of Brigham Young Academy, once had a wealthy, well-educated friend who invited Brother Maeser and some missionaries to have dinner with him at a hotel. The table manners of the missionaries were so distressing that upon reflection Brother Maeser later said, "I will go through poverty, I will suffer persecution, I will go to hell with the elders, but I will not go to dinner with them again."[3] It was a sad commentary on their cultural refinement.

As Charles Darwin focused solely on his scientific discoveries, he lamented his loss of appreciation for the cultural arts. He wrote: "The loss of these tastes is a loss of happiness, and may possibly be injurious to the intellect, and more probably to the moral character, by enfeebling the emotional part of our nature."[4] It was a startling admission of the role culture can play in our intellectual and moral development.

Fortunately, we can all learn to refine our lives. In this regard Bertrand Russell, the British philosopher, made this observation about our need to expand our circle of interests: "There is no abstract and impersonal proof either that strawberries are good or that they are not good. To the man who likes them they are good, to the man who dislikes them they are not. But the man who likes them has a pleasure which the other does not have; to that extent his life is more enjoyable and he is better adapted to the world in which both must live. . . . The more things a man is interested in, the more opportunities of happiness he has."[5]

In other words, it is neither moral nor immoral to like or dislike strawberries. But if you develop a liking for them, you have one more enjoyment in life than the man or woman who does not. And

The Refining Influence of Culture in Our Homes and Classes

so it is as we develop our cultural sensitivities. In addition, as we do so, we enhance our spiritual sensitivity.

DEVELOPING OUR CULTURAL SENSITIVITIES

Those who expand their interests and gain an appreciation for the cultural arts will find a subtle refining of their souls. It may not be dramatic, but it will be steady and sure. President J. Reuben Clark Jr. expressed his feelings about the role of culture on our spirituality:

> Music, art, literature, and the drama, looked at from the point of view of the Church, are priceless to us because of the ennobling effect they have upon the spirit of man. . . . They are the things which administer to our intelligence; they are the things which cultivate and make us grow spiritually, and even though they may not, in the narrow sense, be from the point of view of the Church an end in themselves, they are such an adjunct, such a cultural aid to the spiritual aim of the Church, that they may not be overlooked, forgotten, or neglected.[6]

President Brigham Young echoed this same sentiment: "Every accomplishment, every polished grace, every useful attainment in mathematics, music, and in all science and art belong to the Saints."[7] Robert K. Thomas, a respected author and former professor of English at Brigham Young University, added this insight: "The whole life is the happy, significant life. How embarrassing it is to hear someone say that he is not interested in music, art, drama, or literature. It is not a question of substituting these for something else. These are never adequate substitutes, but they are necessary supplements if we are not to be victims of cultural poverty."[8] This thought reminds us of Truman Madsen's observation, quoting

William James, that someone "may define a Bach quartet as 'the moving of horsehair over catgut,' or he may be transformed by the music."[9] How tragic if it is the former.

It is not always easy to stretch ourselves outside our cultural comfort zones, but it is possible. Elder Quentin L. Cook loved sports. He said that early in marriage his wife was concerned he "might overemphasize sporting events, so she negotiated that . . . there would be two musicals, operas, or cultural activities for each paid ball game [they attended]." He then added this significant statement: "Initially I was resistant to the opera component, but over time I changed my view. I particularly came to enjoy the operas by Giuseppi Verdi."[10] Likewise, we can all develop a taste for cultural arts if we give them an honest chance. They can become appealing and enriching to our soul; they are a necessary adjunct to and integral component of our spirituality.

In addition to enhancing our own spirituality, President Spencer W. Kimball had a far-reaching vision of what the cultural arts could do for the Church:

> We are proud of the artistic heritage that the Church has brought to us from its earliest beginnings, but the full story of Mormonism has never yet been written nor painted nor sculpted nor spoken. It remains for inspired hearts and talented fingers *yet* to reveal themselves. They must be faithful, inspired, active Church members to give life and feeling and true perspective to a subject so worthy.
>
> Take a Nicodemus and put Joseph Smith's spirit in him, and what do you have? Take a da Vinci, Michelangelo, or Shakespeare and cleanse him and give him a total knowledge of the plan of salvation of God and personal revelation, and then take a look at the statues he will carve and the murals he will paint and the masterpieces he will produce.

Take a Handel—with his purposeful effort, his superb talent, his earnest desire to properly depict the story—and give him inward vision of the whole true story and revelation, and what a master you have![11]

Orson F. Whitney shared a similar vision. He wrote: "We shall yet have Miltons and Shakespeares of our own. God's ammunition is not exhausted. His highest spirits are held in reserve for the latter times."[12]

MAKING OUR HOMES A BIT OF HEAVEN ON EARTH

The home and the classroom are ideal forums where we can not only breed individual cultural appreciation but inspire budding artists, musicians, sculptors, and writers who can support the gospel message with their unique talents. As parents and teachers we can help whet and develop the cultural appetites of those we teach and inspire them to embrace President Kimball's vision.

On repeated occasions we have been invited to make our homes a bit of heaven on earth. Can we imagine a heaven without music to stir our souls—without the "Hallelujah Chorus" to transport our thoughts and feelings to celestial realms. Can we imagine a heaven without art to kindle our passions—with no Sistine-like chapels or statues of David to tap the boundaries of our creativity. Or a heaven without literature—without Shakespearian plays and insights, without Miltonian poetry that lifts our thinking to the highest and noblest within us. Our homes and classrooms should be a bit of heaven on earth; they should be both a prototype and preparation for that which is to come.

In that spirit we can fill our homes with inspiring music; we can adorn our walls with uplifting and beautiful art; we can fill the air with kind and stimulating conversation; we can teach the heartfelt and mind-expanding truths of the gospel. Amid all the mortal failings we possess, we can strive little by little to make our homes a bit of heaven on earth. The Lord gave this wise counsel: "Continue in patience until ye are perfected" (D&C 67:13). In other words, don't give up. Don't get discouraged; the Lord does not expect instant perfection but rather honest, regular efforts to refine and sanctify our homes little by little.

As parents and teachers, we can include culture in our teaching diet. It is an integral part of the spiritual feast we can serve to our children and students.

HOW CAN WE BRING CULTURE INTO OUR HOMES AND CLASSES?

This is easier said than done. On one occasion we wanted our children to see a movie on TV that we thought they would enjoy and hoped would be good for them. After about fifteen minutes of an admittedly slow start, one of our teenage boys blurted out: "There better be a CIA agent jumping through a window any moment now, or I'm out of here." In spite of such moments, we did our best to forge ahead with some cultural training.

As part of General Authority and leadership training at general conference, President Russell M. Nelson delivered a masterful message on the Savior's Atonement. But what added to the stirring nature of his talk was the use of art and music. He showed a portion of a video that had been produced by Brigham Young University on the life of George Frideric Handel and focused on his writing of *The Messiah*. The premiere performance had been played in Dublin, Ireland. Handel and the performers, in an act of extraordinary compassion and generosity, used the proceeds of the concert to pay off the obligations of some of those in debtors' prison. This video portrays the release of these prisoners. One sees the downtrodden and unfortunate who are imprisoned for no other reason than an inability to pay their debts. The prison gate is then opened, and one by one these poor victims are liberated. As they line up before the court clerk, each name is read, and the number of guineas he or she owes is confirmed by the debtor and creditor. In a touching scene, the clerk then takes the necessary coins available from the proceeds of the premiere and pays off the creditor. There is inexpressible joy and gratitude on the faces of those who previously had little to no hope of being rescued.

Wives, husbands, and children burst into tears of ecstasy as they throw their arms around their loved ones in blessed reunions. Meanwhile, the inspired music of Handel plays: "Lift up your heads . . . ; the King of Glory shall come. Who is the King of Glory? The Lord of Hosts, He is the King of Glory." The symbolism of the Savior's redemption was inescapable.[13]

Amid many tears, those present at the meeting realized even more keenly, even more deeply, the love and sacrifice of the Savior, who freed us from the debt of sin. Words alone could not have evoked such tender feelings, but when combined with the moving depiction of debtors being liberated and music that was divine, the moment became an unforgettable spiritual feast.

President Nelson is an exemplary teacher. He demonstrated how we can use art and music to support the doctrine we are teaching. Following are some other ideas as to how we might incorporate culture into our teaching.

Art

The Savior used visuals, such as His reference to the lilies of the field or the barren fig tree.[14] While some teachers may seldom use visuals, others use art in ways that stir our compassion, quicken our minds, and provide insights into the doctrine being taught. Much of the art we have available today is literally breathtaking, both visually and mentally. It can be one of a teacher's best friends.

Kathy uses a painting to effectively demonstrate the importance of the family. It was painted by Angelica Kauffmann and is entitled *Cornelia, Mother of the Gracchi*. Two women are featured. One is Cornelia, a Roman widow, with three of her children. The other is a visitor who has come to Cornelia's home to show off her costly jewels. When the visitor asks Cornelia to show her jewels, Cornelia points to her children as if to say, "These are my jewels—these are my treasures." The visitor, with surprised expression, seems caught off guard by this simple but poignant answer. Kathy then asks questions such as: "What is the difference between these two treasures? What rewards does each treasure offer? What responsibilities? Which treasures are the prime focus of our lives?" There is something about visualizing this scene versus just hearing the narrative that adds another dimension to our learning.

We have two different pictures in our home of the Savior in the Garden of Gethsemane, accompanied by an angel. In one picture, the angel has his hands over the Savior's head as though he is about to bless Him. In the other, the angel has one hand tenderly placed on the Savior's head, the other wrapped around His shoulder. Both of these pictures could lead to an inspired discussion: Who might this angel have been? Why did he come? What could he do to comfort and strengthen the Savior? What couldn't he do that the Savior had to do on His own? How does the Savior's experience in the garden affect our love for Him? Some artists are so gifted that they recreate not only the facts but also the passion of the moment and thus add to the depth of insights we might gain and the gratitude we might feel.

We attended President Boyd K. Packer's funeral, where President M. Russell Ballard spoke. He said that President Packer had a copy of the statue *Winged Victory* on his desk. The original statue, which now sits in the Louvre Museum, is missing its head and arms. Elder Ballard then explained that President Packer loved this statue because it was not perfect, but it was still a masterpiece. As my wife related this story to our eleven-year-old granddaughter Naomi, she replied: "Grandma, we aren't perfect either, but we are masterpieces because we are God's children." Art had been used to teach a central gospel truth in a very powerful way.

President Thomas S. Monson, a master speaker and teacher, used art to teach the importance of rescuing the one. Following is one such example:

> I made [a visit] to one of the great art galleries of the world—the famed Victoria and Albert Museum in London, England. There, exquisitely framed, is a masterpiece painted in 1831 by Joseph Mallord William Turner. The painting features heavy-laden black clouds and the fury of a turbulent sea portending danger and death. A light from a stranded vessel gleams far off. In the foreground, tossed high by incoming waves of foaming water, is a large lifeboat. The men pull mightily on the oars as the lifeboat plunges into the tempest. On the shore stand a wife and two children, wet with rain and whipped by wind. They gaze anxiously seaward. In my mind I abbreviated the name of the painting. To me it became *To the Rescue*.
>
> Amid the storms of life, danger lurks. Men and women, boys and girls find themselves stranded and facing destruction. Who will guide the lifeboats, leaving behind the comforts of home and family, and go to the rescue? . . .
>
> Ours is the duty to reach out to rescue those who have left the safety of activity, that such might be brought to the table of the Lord to feast on His word, to enjoy the

companionship of His Spirit, and to be "no more strangers and foreigners, but fellowcitizens with the saints, and of the household of God" [Eph. 2:19].[15]

President Monson shared his moving insights about this rescue at a priesthood leadership meeting while all present viewed Turner's painting on a large screen. His message was masterful and moving, but the painting added to the drama and intimacy of the moment that otherwise would have been lost. There are many such paintings, drenched in doctrine, just waiting for the observant teacher to disclose and unleash their gospel truths.

To a large extent, we become like the things we habitually love and admire. If we love and admire and study the life of the Savior, it is likely we are becoming more like Him. Likewise, if we love and revere the temple, it is likely we will strive to live a life of purity that will allow us to enter its holy rooms and partake of its holy ordinances and spirit. No doubt, that is why President Spencer W. Kimball (and later President Thomas S. Monson) counseled about the importance of young children having a picture of the temple in their bedroom: "It would be a fine thing if every set of parents would have in every bedroom in their house a picture of the temple so the [child] from the time he is an infant could look at the picture every day and it becomes a part of his life. When he reaches the age that he needs to make this very important decision, it will already have been made."[16]

Art can be uplifting and inspiring and heart rending. It is a reservoir from which we should frequently draw.

Music

Music is another medium through which the Spirit operates. The scriptures record that the "morning stars sang together, and all the sons of God shouted for joy" (Job 38:7) when they learned of

The Refining Influence of Culture in Our Homes and Classes

their earthly advent. It was music that soothed and "refreshed" the soul of King Saul (1 Sam. 16:23). When the Lord directed Emma Smith to compile a selection of hymns, He said, "My soul delighteth in the song of the heart" (D&C 25:12). Years later, the Saints were instructed to "praise the Lord with singing [and] with music" (D&C 136:28). And the First Presidency noted: "Some of the greatest sermons are preached by the singing of hymns. Hymns move us to repentance and good works, build testimony and faith, comfort the weary, console the mourning, and inspire us to endure to the end."[17]

President George Albert Smith told of the power of music that overcame an armed mob about to harm two missionaries. After these humble missionaries had walked some distance, they came to a small house in the late afternoon. Some kindly people there invited them to partake of some simple refreshments. Outside in the cool of the afternoon shade, they began to sing some hymns. Unbeknownst to them, a lookout sent word to his fellow mobsters that the missionaries had been sighted. President Smith described what happened next:

> [The mobsters] saddled their horses and took their guns, and rode to the top of the hill overlooking the little house. The missionaries knew nothing about it; they did not know that right over their heads, not very far away, were a considerable number of armed horsemen. But they had the spirit of the Lord, and as they sat there in the cool of the afternoon and sang hymns, the one hymn that seemed to have been prepared for the occasion was, "Do What Is Right." They happened to be good singers, and their voices went out into the quiet air. They had only sung one verse when the leader of the mob took off his hat. They sang another verse, and he got off his horse, and the others got off their horses, and by the time the last verse had been sung, those men

were repentant. Upon the advice of their leader, they rode away without making their presence known. The leader was so impressed with what he heard the missionaries sing that he said to his associates: "We made a mistake. These are not the kind of men we thought they were. Wicked men can't sing like angels, and these men sing like angels. They must be servants of the Lord."

The result was that this man became converted to the Church and later was baptized. And I never hear that hymn sung but I think of that very unusual experience when two missionaries, under the influence of the spirit of God, turned the arms of the adversary away from them and brought repentance into the minds of those who had come to destroy them.[18]

Music has a way of softening the heart and reaching a spiritual depth that words alone cannot always do. On one occasion, we attended a Sunday School class in which the teacher focused on John 15. In doing so, she highlighted the scripture "This is my commandment, that ye love one another, as I have loved you" (John 15:12). Before commencing her lesson, however, she invited a young girl to come forward and play on the piano "Love One Another." That music invited the Spirit into the room in an even greater proportion than otherwise would have been present.

Music is a heaven-sent tool that can help us invite the Spirit into our classrooms and homes and set the tone for the doctrine to be taught. Music can be used in many ways—the class might sing a hymn together and discuss the words; an individual might be invited to sing or play a solo; a family might be asked to sing a hymn, such as "Families Are Forever," or a Primary child might be invited to sing a song, such as "I Am a Child of God." A teacher might play a portion of some inspired music, such as the *Messiah*, and ask questions like "What titles were given to the Savior?" Class members might respond with, "Wonderful, Counselor, the Mighty God, the Everlasting Father, the Prince of Peace." The teacher may then ask, "What do those titles mean?" and "What other titles have been given to the Savior in the scriptures, and what do they teach us about His attributes and mission?"

Music can both invite the Spirit and be a trigger for a meaningful gospel discussion. President Dallin H. Oaks spoke of the refining influence of music: "I wonder if we are making enough use of this heaven-sent resource [music] in our meetings, in our classes, and in our homes. . . . Our sacred music is a powerful preparation for prayer and gospel teaching."[19]

Literature

The Lord has commanded us to "seek . . . out of the best books words of wisdom" (D&C 88:118) and on another occasion to "study and learn, and become acquainted with all good books" (D&C 90:15). President Russell M. Nelson echoed this sentiment: "Expose yourselves broadly to the great literature of other eras and of other disciplines. In them you will find teachings of invaluable worth."[20]

Certainly poetry is included in the spirit of these injunctions. Elder George F. Richards said: "I believe there is much inspiration from the Lord outside the Church of Jesus Christ of Latter-day Saints, in various ways, not the [least] of which is found among the poets."[21] Paul cited the Greek poets in order to prove his case that we are literally the offspring of God (see Acts 17:28–29). The Church has produced some magnificent poets in Orson F. Whitney, Eliza R. Snow, and others.

The writings of inspired poets are deserving of our attention. Inspired poets who were not Latter-day Saints have testified of the premortal existence,[22] the Resurrection,[23] the cleansing power of

Christ's Atonement,[24] the eternal nature of spouses and family,[25] and many other gospel truths.

The world of literature is filled with divine insights and majestic language that is spiritually akin to and supportive of the doctrine we teach. Elder Bruce R. McConkie, one of the greatest scriptural scholars of this dispensation, who was not predisposed to surrendering his words for another's, quoted extensively from Frederic W. Farrar of the Church of England. In fact, he so admired Farrar's writings that he quoted him extensively in his Messiah series. He even prayed that Farrar would receive the gospel in the spirit world. Of Farrar, he paid this tribute: "No man of whom I know has written so consistently and so well—in such shining English prose—about the dramatic and miraculous happenings in the life of our Lord as has Canon Farrar, whose words I have freely quoted from time to time in this work."[26] When we ourselves read Farrar's *Life of Christ,* we were so taken by the book, the penetrating insights, the majesty and eloquence of the language, and the spirituality that oozed from every page, that we felt we were on a spiritual high.

There is so much literature that is uplifting and appropriate to share in family and church settings. When speaking of integrity, one might refer to the book *To Kill a Mockingbird,* in which Atticus Finch, a lawyer, is assigned to defend a Black man who was falsely charged with committing a crime. Many people in the town are racially prejudiced and harass Atticus and his two children because of Atticus's defense. At one point Atticus says to his children: "They're [the townspeople] certainly entitled to think that, and they're entitled to full respect for their opinions, *but before I can live with other folks I've got to live with myself. The one thing that doesn't abide by majority rule is a person's conscience.*"[27] The lesson taught is powerful.

In *Les Misérables,* Javert says to Jean Valjean, "A man like you can never change,"[28] and then Jean Valjean spends a lifetime proving him wrong—demonstrating that we can all become new creatures in Christ (see 2 Cor. 5:17) regardless of our past.

In *The Adventures of Huckleberry Finn*, we hear Huck introspectively admitting, "You can't pray a lie—I found that out."[29] Contemplation of such a statement and what it means can cause a healthy evaluation of our own prayers.

In setting forth the foregoing there is a caution: art, music, and literature can be wholesome and inspiring adjuncts to the lesson, but if they become the main course, if they replace the focus on the scriptures and words of the prophets, if they transform a doctrinal lesson into a sociology class or book club or feel-good presentation, then we have missed the mark.

CONCLUSION

We happen to love mashed potatoes with gravy, but not for breakfast, lunch, and dinner every day. We all recognize the need for a varied diet, to get all the nutrients our bodies need. Likewise, various teaching resources can supply our spirits with the multiple spiritual nutrients they need. Some of the people we teach respond to certain types of teaching resources better than others. For example, some are more visual learners or are touched by music or understand a principle best when reinforced by a literary story.

The resources in the world of art, music, and literature are almost limitless in their ability to support and enhance the doctrine of the kingdom. They provide one more dimension to know and feel the truth. As parents and teachers we should drink from these wells often.

LEARNING

CHAPTER 29

The World Is Our Classroom

Ideal teachers are always preparing future lessons. The world is their classroom, and they are the students. Like the young boy Mormon, they are "quick to observe" (Morm. 1:2). They are observant of nature, science, sports, and culture—always seeking to discover a new analogy, a new story, a new insight. In truth, ideal teachers are ideal learners. There are no time parameters or classroom boundaries to their learning experience—they are learners day and night, in and out of class. They save articles, copy stories, and record thoughtful quotes and insights. They have a reservoir of ideas, not only for next week's lesson, but for future lessons, home evenings, and family scripture discussions—some of which may be years down the road. In essence they are intellectual and spiritual sponges, from which the Holy Ghost may draw a treasure trove of truth.

As Shakespeare noted, there are "tongues in trees, books in the running brooks, sermons in stones and good in everything."[1] For

Shakespeare, the world was his classroom. Robert G. Ingersoll explained this principle as follows:

> Some have insisted that Shakespeare must have been a physician, for the reason that he shows such knowledge of Medicine—of the symptoms of disease and death—was so familiar with the brain, and with insanity in all its forms. . . . Others maintain that he was a lawyer, perfectly acquainted with the forms, with the expressions familiar to that profession. . . . Some think that he was a botanist, because he named nearly all known plants. Others, that he was an astronomer, a naturalist, because he gave hints and suggestions of nearly all discoveries. Some have thought that he must have been a sailor, for the reason that the orders given in the opening of "The Tempest" were the best that could, under the circumstances, have been given to save the ship. For my part, I think there is nothing in the plays to show that he was a lawyer, doctor, botanist, or scientist. He had the observant eyes that really see, the ears that really hear, the brain that retains all pictures, all thoughts, logic as unerring as light, the imagination that supplies defects and builds the perfect from a fragment. . . . He lived the life of all.[2]

In order to be a great teacher, we need to be looking for the good and uplifting in everything. Then the world becomes our teacher and we become its student.

Brigham Young also knew that the world was our classroom and thus enjoined the Saints to learn both secular and spiritual truths. He said: "Educate your children in all the knowledge the world can give them. . . . Every true principle, every true science, every art and all the knowledge that men possess, or that they ever did or ever will possess, is from God."[3] Brigham Young was echoing the words of the Lord that we should learn "of things both in heaven and in the earth, and under the earth; things which have been, things which are, things which must shortly come to pass; things which are at home, things which are abroad; the wars and the perplexities of the nations, and the judgments which are on the land; and a knowledge also of countries and of kingdoms." And then the Lord added: "that ye may be prepared in all things" (D&C 88:79–80).

Without minimizing our need to learn secular truths, President Henry B. Eyring put our learning in perspective: "It is clear that our first priority should go to spiritual learning. For us, reading the scriptures would come before reading history books. Prayer would come before memorizing those Spanish verbs. A temple recommend would be worth more to us than standing first in our graduating class. But it is also clear that spiritual learning would not replace our drive for secular learning. . . . On the contrary, it gives our secular learning purpose and motivates us to work harder at it."[4] And what is that purpose? It is to become more like God in our character and in our intellect.

No wonder the scriptures teach us "Whatever principle of intelligence we attain unto in this life, it will rise with us in the resurrection. And if a person gains more knowledge and intelligence in this life through his diligence and obedience than another, he will have so much the advantage in the world to come" (D&C 130:18–19).

CONCLUSION

In order to become more like God we need to understand the world He has created and its underlying operative principles. As we make the world our class of study, we increase our knowledge and thus the potential for receiving greater power from the Spirit. And in the process of becoming a master learner, we lay the foundation for becoming a master teacher.

CHAPTER 30

What Responsibilities Do I Have as a Learner?

TEACHERS AND LEARNERS HAVE EQUAL RESPONSIBILITIES

The story is told of a man who became known as the town idler. He was unwilling to work, unwilling to seek employment; he simply lived off the efforts of others. Finally, the townspeople had had enough. They decided to banish him. One of the townspeople escorted him in a wagon to the edge of town. The driver felt a wave of compassion sweep over him. Perhaps, he thought, the derelict should be given one more chance. Accordingly, he asked, "Would you like a bushel of corn to get a new start?" The derelict replied, "Is it husked?"[1]

Sometimes we find people on the scriptural dole—they want the scriptures husked before they partake. They want the gospel in a series of entertaining sound bites or video clips. They want their Sunday School teacher or parent to prepare and spoon-feed them the doctrine with little preparation or participation on their part. In

What Responsibilities Do I Have as a Learner?

contrast to this, the Savior commanded the Nephites to pray, ponder, and "prepare [their] minds" to hear His word (3 Ne. 17: 3). The lesson was this: just as the teacher has the responsibility to teach by the Spirit, the learner has the responsibility to learn by the Spirit (see D&C 50:13–21). In the book of Alma we read: "The preacher was no better than the hearer, *neither was the teacher any better than the learner; and thus they were all equal*" (Alma 1:26; emphasis added).

Elder Bruce R. McConkie taught of the need for speakers [and teachers] and learners to be equal:

> Sometimes a speaker brings a jug of living water that has in it many gallons. And when he pours it out on the congregation, all the members have brought is a single cup and so that's all they take away. Or maybe they have their hands over the cups, and they don't get anything to speak of.
>
> On other occasions we have meetings where the speaker comes and all he brings is a little cup of eternal truth, and the members of the congregation come with a large jug, and all they get in their jugs is the little dribble that came from a man who should have known better and should have prepared himself and talked from the revelations and spoken by the power of the Holy Spirit.[2]

If teachers and learners are equally yoked, then the Lord promises that they shall be "edified and rejoice together" (D&C 50:22). Unfortunately, some teachers pull the bulk of the lesson load alone, while the learners passively sit by, hoping to benefit from the pull. The classroom experience was meant to be a team effort. Imagine if the orchestra conductor raised the baton to begin the concert and no one played, or the quarterback took the snap and no one blocked, or the teacher asked questions and no one participated. In order to avoid these latter conditions, we might appropriately ask, "What can we do as learners to be better team players, to pull our equal share of the load and thus contribute to more inspired lessons?" Following are some suggestions:

BE AN ACTIVE LEARNER

There is no short supply of scriptures setting forth our responsibility to be *active learners*. In Proverbs, we read, "A wise man will hear, and will increase learning" (Prov. 1:5). In the New Testament, the Savior commanded "learn of me" (Matt. 11:29). And Paul counseled, "Study to shew thyself approved unto God" (2 Tim. 2:15). In our dispensation, we have been instructed to "seek learning, even by study and also by faith" (D&C 88:118).[3] In addition, we have been commanded: "Organize yourselves; prepare every needful thing; and establish a house, even . . . *a house of learning*" (D&C 88:119; emphasis added). No doubt this reference to a house of learning applies to both our personal houses and our houses of worship. They are both to be centers of learning.

The Lord spoke candidly, perhaps even harshly, to those who failed to learn from His teaching: "Perceive ye not yet, neither understand? have ye your heart yet hardened? Having eyes, see ye not? and having ears, hear ye not? and do ye not remember?" (Mark 8:17–18). There is no place for complacency in God's kingdom—either in the home or classroom. He desires us to be active, alert, avid learners of His gospel.

J. B. Priestly, the English novelist, was once asked how he became such a famous writer since some of his gifted peers, as youth, had not so excelled. He responded: "The difference between us was not in ability, but in the fact that while they . . . merely toyed with the fascinating idea of [writing], *I cared like blazes!*"[4] Somewhere, sometime, we must care like blazes if we really want to learn. In

What Responsibilities Do I Have as a Learner?

essence, we must come to our meetings and our classes with our minds in gear, not in neutral. When all is said and done, each of us is responsible for our own rate and depth of learning. As President Russell M. Nelson said: "We are each responsible for our individual spiritual growth."[5]

Socrates understood this principle. The account is told of a young man who came to Socrates and requested that he teach him all he knew. Without responding, Socrates took him to a pool of water, walked out a few feet, and then held the young man under water until he almost lapsed into unconsciousness. The young man was irate: "Why did you do that?" Socrates allegedly replied, "When you want to learn from me as much as you wanted air, come see me."

The Lord gives liberally to all who want to learn from Him, but there is a price tag. We must "care like blazes" about learning. The Lord made this wonderful promise to the active learner: "Unto you that hear shall more be given" (Mark 4:24). If at home and church we have a burning desire to learn, not just endure, it will happen.

President Boyd K. Packer became a rapid learner simply because he wanted to learn. He noted: "Elder Harold B. Lee and Elder Marion G. Romney were always teaching, and they would, in a sense, go out of their way to tell me something or teach me something. I think the reason they did it—I'm not sure they ever saw me in this position or calling—is *that I had one virtue: I wanted to learn, and I didn't resent it. And if you don't resent it, and if you want to learn, the Lord will keep teaching you, sometimes things you really didn't think you wanted to know.*"[6]

It is said that you can lead a horse to water, but you cannot make it drink. While individuals must develop their own thirst for learning, sometimes great teachers can whet that appetite. Below are some further thoughts about how learners and, in some cases, teachers can help elevate the role of the learner.

PRAY FOR THE LEARNERS AS WELL AS THE TEACHERS

We often hear prayers on behalf of the teacher, and rightfully so, but that is only half the equation. How wonderful it would be if our prayers also petitioned for the learners to be spiritually attentive and participatory. We can pray that the Lord will "pour out his Spirit" upon all class members "to prepare their hearts to receive the word" (Alma 16:16).

BE HUMBLE

If we are not humble, not teachable, then the greatest teacher in the world can do nothing for us. It would be like hammering on cold steel. Alma rejoiced in the Saints who were in exceeding poverty—not because they were poor but because their poverty had so humbled them "that they were in a preparation to hear the word" (Alma 32:6). Now he knew he could teach them the pure truths of the gospel and they would be receptive.

PREPARE IN ADVANCE

We can carry our share of the learning load by coming to class better prepared, having read the assigned materials, and being ready to share insights. Our preparation can be a spiritual gift we share with all class members. Fortunately, we have many teachers who assist learners in this regard by sending emails and texts in advance of class. These electronic communications may remind the learners of the upcoming lesson to be studied or pose a question that captures their interest.

What Responsibilities Do I Have as a Learner?

PARTICIPATE IN CLASS

The Lord has taught the doctrinal principle underlying the need for individual participation: "Appoint among yourselves a teacher, and let not all be spokesmen at once; but let one speak at a time and let all listen unto his sayings, that when all have spoken *that all may be edified of all,* and that every man may have an equal privilege" (D&C 88:122; emphasis added). This same principle was taught by King Mosiah when he explained the responsibility each person bears to maintain a righteous government: "And he told them that these things ought not to be, but that *the burden should come upon all the people, that every man might bear his part"* (Mosiah 29:34; emphasis added).

The command to open our mouths (see D&C 60:2–3) may apply not only to a missionary setting but also to a classroom setting. When we participate, we invite the Spirit, who can then bear witness of the truth of our comments and enlighten our minds with further insights. In addition, our participation may inspire the thoughts of others and thus encourage additional input. Sometimes we need to step outside our comfort zone and participate even when it is not easy, realizing that with increased exercise of our agency can come increased growth for all.

Certainly the learner should contribute in an effort to edify others with his or her insights, but there is another reason it is important to contribute. The scriptures declare the divine principle that "in the mouth of two or three witnesses shall every word be established" (2 Cor. 13:1). As we contribute in class, we provide multiple witnesses to the doctrine being taught.

President Boyd K. Packer spoke of the value of participation by sharing a related principle in the life of Belle Spafford. He said that shortly after Sister Spafford had been called as Relief Society General President, she met with President George Albert Smith. In the course of this meeting, she recommended the Church drop its membership in one national and one international women's organization. The prophet inquired, "Had they not held membership for well over a half century in these organizations?"

Sister Spafford acknowledged that was true but then explained how costly it was to travel to these board meetings and that occasionally they even became the subject of humiliation. Then she added: "We don't get a thing from these councils."

The wise prophet responded, "You want to withdraw because you don't get anything out of it?"

"That is our feeling," she replied.

He then responded: "Tell me, what is it that you are putting into it?" He then extended his hand and with considerable firmness said: "You continue your membership in these councils and make your influence felt."

She followed the prophet's counsel. Later she shared how she had become the president of one of these organizations.[7]

The lesson taught was critical. If we do not put anything into our Church classes or family discussions, we are unlikely to get much out of them. Suffice it to say, the learner has an equal responsibility to that of the teacher to contribute to the well-being of Church and family discussions.

ASK QUESTIONS

Questions are often the precursor to knowledge and revelation. Indeed, one of the quickest ways to learn is to ask questions—in essence to demonstrate a spiritual curiosity. Moses had that curiosity. He said: "I will not cease to call upon God, I have other things to inquire of him" (Moses 1:18). Joseph Smith was a kindred spirit. He was a master learner because first and foremost he was a master asker. He asked the question that triggered the First Vision, the

What Responsibilities Do I Have as a Learner?

question that triggered the Word of Wisdom, and the question that triggered the glorious revelation on the three kingdoms of glory. He was living proof of the scripture "Ask, and ye shall receive" (3 Ne. 27:29).

On one occasion we spoke with Sister Sheri Dew, who wrote the biography of President Gordon B. Hinckley. She mentioned that he was a voracious reader of newspapers, the Harvard Classics, and anything that was good and ennobling. He could converse with the chairman of the Federal Reserve at one moment and the man installing your plumbing the next. Whether at dinner or elsewhere, he had a string of unending questions. After doing this for many years, he was conversant on most any topic. No wonder Sister Dew observed: "Asking questions leads to knowledge. It leads to revelation. It leads to greater faith. And it leads to peace."[8]

President Russell M. Nelson noted this same talent after observing President Hinckley at a regional conference: "One of the security officers assigned to us worked for the local police department. We had time between sessions, and President Hinckley grilled that officer for an hour about their procedures, techniques, and even the equipment they used. I marveled that he knew which questions to ask, each of which was law-enforcement specific." Elder Robert D. Hales added: "I have never met an individual who can become so well informed through reading and through contact with people. When he spends an evening at dinner with someone, he leaves knowing something about that individual's expertise."[9]

RECORD INSPIRED THOUGHTS AND IMPRESSIONS

It is important not only for the teacher and parent to record inspired thoughts but also for the learner. Once we began carrying note cards or notepads to church, seeking for doctrinal insights and impressions, we can honestly say that we were richly rewarded. This approach has changed our perspective; it has focused our attention, accelerated our learning, and increased our anticipation for church.

Our experience reminds us of the quote attributed to Mark Twain: "When I was a boy of fourteen, my father was so ignorant I could hardly stand to have the old man around. But when I got to be twenty-one, I was astonished at how much he had learned in seven years."[10] In some ways that experience applies to us. When we started recording impressions in church, we were pleasantly surprised at how much better the speakers and teachers had become in such a short period of time.

Joseph Smith spoke of the importance of recording inspired insights and impressions: "Here is another important item. If you . . . proceed to discuss important questions . . . and fail to note them down, . . . perhaps, for neglecting to write those things, when God revealed them, not esteeming them of sufficient worth, the spirit may withdraw and God may be angry; *and here is or was a vast knowledge of infinite importance, which is now lost.*"[11]

In essence, every time we record a spiritual impression, we demonstrate to the Lord that we appreciate His guidance and want more. When recorded, these truths can be repeatedly savored as well as shared more easily with friends and family. One ward mission leader noted that when new converts were about to be baptized, he would invite them to record the spiritual impressions they felt on that occasion. Then, if at a later date they ever struggled with their testimony, they could read and relive the spiritual experience of that day. Recording these experiences allows us to preserve the spiritual impressions of past moments and thus keep our testimonies strong (see Mosiah 1:4). In addition, it is a reminder that not all spiritual truths are conveyed in cerebral communications, but that many come as impressions to the heart.

What Responsibilities Do I Have as a Learner?

OUR RESPONSIBILITY FOR INDIVIDUAL STUDY

In addition to learning in class, we all have the responsibility to regularly study the scriptures on our own. Elder Bruce R. McConkie repeatedly taught the principle: *"Each person must learn the doctrines of the gospel for himself.* No one else can do it for him. Each person stands alone where gospel scholarship is concerned; each has access to the same scriptures and is entitled to the guidance of the same Holy Ghost; each must pay the price set by a divine Providence if he is to gain the pearl of great price."[12] Learning was never intended to be a "one-shot" experience on Sunday, any more than eating was intended to be a once-a-week event. Both body and spirit need daily nourishment.

President Harold B. Lee observed: "If we're not reading the scriptures daily, our testimonies are growing thinner."[13] Paul noted that the Saints in Berea "were more noble than those in Thessalonica, in that they received the word with all readiness of mind," and then he shared the reason for such receptivity: "they ... *searched the scriptures daily"* (Acts 17:11; emphasis added). In other words, daily scripture study is an essential ingredient to our spirituality. It should be one of our non-negotiables in life. Nothing else can fully compensate for its absence in our daily routine. For this reason, scripture study should be set-aside time, not leftover time.

On occasion some may say, "But I don't have time for daily scripture study amid all my other duties in life." This is somewhat reminiscent of the two axmen who held a contest to determine who could cut down more trees in a day. At sunrise, the contest commenced. Every hour the smaller man was seen wandering off into the forest for ten minutes or so. Each time he did so, his opponent smiled and nodded, assured he was forging ahead. The larger man never left his post, never stopped cutting, never took a break. When the day ended, the larger man was shocked to learn that his opponent, who had seemingly wasted so much time, had cut many more trees than he. "How did you do it when you took so many breaks?" he asked. The winner replied, "Oh, I was sharpening my ax."

Every time we study the scriptures, we are sharpening our spiritual ax. And the miraculous part is that when we do so, we are able to use the remainder of our time more wisely and productively than if we had not done so.

The question is frequently asked, "What is the best way to study the scriptures?" Joseph Fielding McConkie said he was confident that if his father, Elder Bruce R. McConkie, or his grandfather, President Joseph Fielding Smith—both of whom were magnificent scholars of the scriptures—were asked the best method of scripture study, they would respond that what mattered was not so much the method but that "the great and grand key was the frequency, intensity, and consistency with which they studied."[14] In other words, effective scripture study is not a matter of turning pages or seeing how many times one can read a book of scripture, but rather one of intensely absorbing the word of God. This seems consistent with the fact that the Lord uses such words and phrases as *feast upon, treasure up, ponder, meditate*, and *search* when referring to our scripture study. We cannot merely tiptoe through the scriptures and enjoy them or be edified by them. We must immerse ourselves in them. They demand our highest attention, our most concentrated effort, to yield their precious fruit.

THE POWER OF OBSERVATION

When Mormon was only ten years of age, Ammaron informed him that he would one day be entrusted with the records of the Nephites. Then he gave one of the reasons for his selection: "I perceive that thou . . . art quick to observe" (Morm. 1:2). We too can be nonstop students—quick to observe—listening and learning not just in class, but at all times.

Louis Pasteur said that "in the field of observation, chance favors only those minds that are prepared."[15] Alexander Fleming was such an example. On September 28, 1928, Fleming noticed a petri dish containing staphylococcus bacteria that had been accidentally left open. It had been contaminated with some mold, but he noticed that the bacterial growth had been restrained by the mold. He then discovered it emitted an antibiotic, later developed into the wonder drug known as penicillin. His powers of observation, coupled with preparation and reflection, turned this seemingly insignificant event into a profound learning experience that no doubt has blessed millions of lives. Being observant is a habit we can develop—it is keeping our cerebral, hearing, and seeing capabilities on alert when others may have tuned out. It is doing what the angel constantly reminded Nephi to do—namely, to "look" (1 Ne. 11:8, 12, 19, 24, 26, 30–32), meaning to be aware and observant.

If in the field of secular study, chance favors the prepared mind, then perhaps in the field of spiritual truth, revelation favors the observing, pondering mind.

LIFELONG LEARNING

Learning is an ongoing endeavor. It is not relegated to our school years or preretirement life but is a lifelong pursuit, even extending beyond the grave. Joseph Smith declared, "It will be a great work to learn our salvation and exaltation even beyond the grave."[16] The Lord spoke of the great advantage we will have in the life to come if we use our time wisely in this life to learn: "Whatever principle of intelligence we attain unto in this life, it will rise with us in the resurrection. And if a person gains more knowledge and intelligence in this life through his diligence and obedience than another, he will have so much the advantage in the world to come" (D&C 130:18–19).

George W. Bush told of his hunger for learning even after his tenure as president of the United States. In those postpresidency years he developed a passion for painting. He took lessons and worked every day on improving. He painted birds, cats, dogs, world leaders, and so on. He observed: "You know what the interesting lesson is though, *that you can keep learning in life*. I mean, some guy one time said to me, 'Man, you deserve to rest.' I replied, 'I don't wanna rest . . . I wanna follow the example of President 41 [his father, George H. W. Bush], you know, sprint into the grave.'"[17] Don't you love that phrase, "sprint into the grave"?

We can put our learning in "sprint mode" all the days of our lives. Grandma Moses commenced painting in earnest at age seventy-eight. Initially her paintings sold for three to five dollars; years later one of her paintings sold for $1.2 million. Tad's father took up organ lessons in later life, and his mother was attending gospel study classes in her nineties. Lifelong learning is invigorating; it accelerates our pursuit of godhood, especially as we learn the doctrine of the kingdom.

ACT ON THE DOCTRINE

Learners have the responsibility to not only learn the doctrine but to act on it. President Joseph F. Smith taught: "I cannot save you; you cannot save me; we cannot save each other, only so far as we can persuade each other to receive the truth. . . . [A man] will not be saved merely because someone taught it to him, but because he received and acted upon it."[18] Once we have learned the doctrine, our agency "kicks in" and we are accountable from that point forward to live it.

What Responsibilities Do I Have as a Learner?

THE JOY OF LEARNING

Learning, however, is meant to be much more than a divine duty. It is also meant to be an exquisite joy. On one occasion, an ancient mathematician named Archimedes was asked by his king to determine if the king's new crown was solid gold or if the goldsmith had dishonestly substituted some silver for gold. Archimedes pondered the solution, and finally an answer came. So overjoyed was he by this discovery that legend has it he ran about the city crying, "Eureka, Eureka!" meaning "I have found it! I have found it!"

As great as was his joy, there is a far greater joy in discovering truths about the gospel of Jesus Christ—those truths that not only inform us but also save us (see 2 Ne. 4:5). For this reason, the Savior said, "These things I have spoken unto you, . . . that your joy might be full" (John 15:11). For this reason, Alma, reflecting upon the truths his father had taught about the Savior's Atonement, exclaimed, "There can be nothing so exquisite and sweet as was my joy" (Alma 36:21). And for this reason, "the sons of God shouted for joy" when they learned the plan of salvation in the premortal life (Job 38:7). Just as seeds have the inherent power to grow, so gospel truths have the inherent power to bring joy.

CONCLUSION

It was the Passover immediately preceding the Crucifixion. The Savior "sat down with the twelve." He then made the startling announcement that one of them would betray Him. The scriptures record that "they were exceedingly sorrowful." Human nature might have driven them to accuse someone else, to point their fingers and say, "Is he the one?" but instead the integrity of their character was revealed as they inquired, "Is it I?" (Matt. 26:20–22). In other words, "Am I the one at fault?"

Before concluding that a teacher is boring or uninformed or not up to our expectations, perhaps we could adopt the "Is it I?" principle. For example, we might ask ourselves: "Did I read the lesson material in advance? Did I pray for the teacher and for the Spirit to be present in our classroom? Did I contribute by participating in class or coming with an intense desire to learn? Did I seek divine impressions and record them? Did I share what I learned with others?" If we have somehow fallen short in these endeavors, then we might further ask: "Am I partially to blame for the class not being all I hoped it would be, and if so, how can I improve? How can I be a better class member? If the teacher were our own son or daughter, what would I do differently as a class member—to what extremes would I go—to help him or her have the most successful class possible?"

No doubt you recall the famous words of President John F. Kennedy: "Ask not what your country can do for you—ask what you can do for your country."[19] Perhaps in the classroom setting this statement might be revised to read, "Ask not what the teacher and class can do for you—ask what you can do for the class." In one of those ironies of life, if we do the latter, somehow the former will also be achieved.

Every time we come to class a little better prepared or participate or ask questions or record sacred impressions or ponder the scriptures more meaningfully, we are hastening our godlike pursuit (see D&C 130:18–19) and thus increasing our capacity to experience His quality of joy. As we strive to become more committed learners, more divine learners—in class, at home, and elsewhere—we will experience the supernal joy that comes from learning and living the gospel of Jesus Christ.

CONCLUSION

How Can I Honor My Calling as a Teacher and Parent?

The need for inspired teachers will always be in great demand. Philip saw "an eunuch of great authority" sitting in his chariot and reading. The Spirit directed Philip to approach the chariot, and as he did so, he heard the eunuch reading aloud from the book of Isaiah. He then asked the eunuch if he understood what he was reading. The eunuch replied, "How can I, except some man should guide me?" (Acts 8:26–31). In other words, "I need a teacher." The eunuch then asked Philip to sit with him, implying that he wanted him to instruct him.

In a similar manner Paul spoke to the Romans of the need to call upon the Lord to be saved and then inquired of them: "How shall they believe in him of whom they have not heard? and how shall they hear without a preacher? [i.e., a teacher]" (Rom. 10:13–14). Teachers always have been and always will be crucial to furthering the gospel of Jesus Christ.

Paul, speaking of the organization of the Church, emphasized the importance of teachers: "And God hath set some in the church, first apostles, secondarily prophets, thirdly teachers" (1 Cor. 12:28). In many respects our buildings and organizational structure are but resources to facilitate teaching and the performance of ordinances.

The Church is such a vast organization that sometimes we may think our contribution is of little significance, perhaps even meaningless. But parents and set-apart teachers are engaged in the same work and mission as Jesus Christ—to teach His gospel to others, one by one. With all the power the Savior possessed, He continually focused on the one. He invited the Book of Mormon Saints to come forth, "one by one," to feel the prints of the nails in His hands and feet (3 Ne. 11:15); the people who believed in Jesus were baptized one by one; He healed their sick one by one (see 3 Ne. 17:9); He blessed their little children one by one (see 3 Ne. 17:21); and He touched with His hand the disciples whom He had chosen one by one (see 3 Ne. 18:36).

Ordinances are performed one by one, both for the living and the dead. This gospel is the gospel of the one. In that spirit, we focus on the one, striving to assess the needs of each child, youth, and adult and then filling his or her well with the living water of God's word.

We are the designated instruments in the hands of God to teach His flock, whether it be one child or a hundred mature Saints. And fortunately, we are never alone in this endeavor, for the Savior has promised, "I am with you alway, even unto the end of the world" (Matt. 28:20).

President Boyd K. Packer taught: "I believe that to the degree you perform according to this challenge and charge which you have [as teachers], the image of Christ does become engraved upon your countenances. And for all practical purposes, in that classroom at that time and in that expression and with that inspiration, *you are*

How Can I Honor My Calling as a Teacher and Parent?

He and He is you."[1] What a sobering, majestic thought—when you teach with inspiration, "you are He and He is you."

The Savior underscored the importance of teaching: "Whosoever shall do and teach them [the commandments], *the same shall be called great in the kingdom of heaven*" (Matt. 5:19; emphasis added). President David O. McKay taught the same: "No greater responsibility can rest upon any man [or woman], than to be a teacher of God's children."[2] We can magnify that responsibility with the divine assurance that God will be with us in this endeavor, for He has promised, "I will never leave thee, nor forsake thee" (Heb. 13:5). With that promise, we can all become "a teacher come from God" (John 3:2) at home and church. We can all "teach one another the doctrine of the kingdom" (D&C 88:77). And like the sons of Mosiah, we can all teach "with power and authority of God" (Alma 17:3).

NOTES

CHAPTER 1

1. In "President David O. McKay," 980.
2. In Kimball, "Education for Eternity," educationforeternity.byu.edu.
3. Nelson, "Salvation and Exaltation," 9.
4. Lee, "Stand Ye in Holy Places," 123.
5. Oaks, "The Challenge to Become," 32; emphasis in original.
6. Oaks, "Gospel Teaching," 80.

CHAPTER 2

1. In *Teaching, No Greater Call*, 151; emphasis in original.
2. *Teachings of Presidents of the Church: Gordon B. Hinckley,* 30; emphasis added.
3. This includes the references in the chapter headings of the Latter-day Saint edition of the King James Version.
4. See also D&C 43:8–10, 15–16; D&C 88:77.
5. See also Mosiah 29:14.
6. Packer, *Teach Ye Diligently*, 3–4; emphasis added.
7. Packer and Perry, "Principles of Teaching and Learning," 82.
8. Monson, "The Priesthood—a Sacred Gift," 89.

NOTES

CHAPTER 3

1. See also Moses 6:57–59; Prov. 22:6.
2. On yet another occasion, Nephi spoke of parents' duty in the home: "We talk of Christ, we rejoice in Christ, we preach of Christ, we prophesy of Christ, and we write according to our prophecies, that our children may know to what source they may look for a remission of their sins" (2 Ne. 25:26; see also 2 Ne. 2:30; 3 Ne. 22:13).
3. "Letter from the First Presidency," Feb. 11, 1999.
4. See Carson and Murphey, *Gifted Hands*, 26–28.
5. See Carson and Murphey, *Gifted Hands*, 16–17, 32–33, 38, 69, 97, 108.
6. "The Family: A Proclamation to the World," ChurchofJesusChrist.org.
7. Nelson, *From Heart to Heart*, 155.
8. In Bush, *41: A Portrait of My Father*, 258.

CHAPTER 4

1. Paul said he had been given "a thorn in the flesh" (2 Cor. 12:7). Three times he approached the Lord and asked that it be removed, but instead the Lord responded: "My grace is sufficient for thee: for my strength is made perfect in weakness." Paul, understanding the Lord's response, then shared a new insight regarding his infirmity: "For when I am weak, then am I strong" (2 Cor. 12:8–10).
2. Faust, "Acting for Ourselves and Not Being Acted Upon," 47.
3. Packer and Perry, "Principles of Teaching and Learning," 85.
4. Maxwell, "It's Service, Not Status, That Counts," 7.
5. Young, *Discourses of Brigham Young*, 32; emphasis added.
6. See also D&C 42:61.
7. Nelson, "Revelation for the Church, Revelation for Our Lives," 96.
8. Nibley, *Approaching Zion*, 5.

CHAPTER 5

1. The Savior reprimanded the lawyers because they took "away the key of knowledge" (Luke 11:52). In other words, they traded the spirit for the letter of the law and, in the process, lost the key that unlocks the treasury of heavenly truths.
2. In Butterworth, "Eight Presidents: A Century at BYU," 23.
3. See also D&C 50:1.
4. Smith, *Doctrines of Salvation*, 1:47–48.
5. Hinckley, "Five Million Members—A Milestone and Not a Summit," 45.
6. Paraphrased from Cervantes, *Don Quixote de la Mancha*, 319. The actual statement reads, "'A good liver is the best preacher,' replied Sancho, 'and that is all the divinity I know.'"
7. Guiterman, "Education," 185.
8. Maxwell, "But a Few Days," 2.

NOTES

9. Hinckley, in Conference Report, Oct. 1965, 52.
10. See also Mark 6:46.
11. Matthew says He "fell on his face" (Matt. 26:39).
12. See also D&C 42:14.
13. In Clarke, "My Soul Delighteth in the Scriptures," 15.
14. Bednar, "The Spirit of Revelation," 87.
15. Scott, "Acquiring Spiritual Knowledge," 88.
16. President Russell M. Nelson told of the following experience: "Years ago, while immersed in the task of preparing a talk for general conference, I was aroused from a sound sleep with an idea impressed strongly upon my mind. Immediately I reached for pencil and paper near my bed and wrote as rapidly as I could. I went back to sleep, knowing I had captured that great impression. The next morning I looked at that piece of paper and found, much to my dismay, that my writing was totally illegible! I still keep pencil and paper at my bedside, but I write more carefully now" (Nelson, "Ask, Seek, Knock," 81).
17. See also Jarom 1:4.
18. Nelson, "Revelation for the Church, Revelation for Our Lives," 94.
19. Eyring, *Waiting upon the Lord*, 3.
20. See also D&C 100:5–8.
21. Holland, *Broken Things to Mend*, 61.

CHAPTER 6

1. Milton, *Paradise Lost*, book 12, lines 646–49.
2. *Hymns*, nos. 49, 136.

CHAPTER 7

1. See also D&C 18:5.
2. See Alma 16:21.
3. Eyring, CES Satellite Training Broadcast, Aug. 10, 2003.
4. See Alma 5:46; Moro. 10:5; Heb. 10:15.
5. See Heb. 4:12.
6. See Ps. 91:4.
7. See Alma 16:21.
8. Holland, "A Teacher Come from God," 26–27.
9. Packer, "The Mediator," 56.

CHAPTER 8

1. Even angels quote scripture, as evidenced by Moroni's repeated visits to Joseph Smith.
2. Benson, "The Gospel Teacher and His Message," 3.
3. See also Joseph Smith Translation, John 1:18 (in John 1:18, footnote *c*).

NOTES

4. Bednar, "A Reservoir of Living Water," 3; emphasis in original.
5. See Ether 2:16–3:6; see also Acts 12:6–11.
6. Clark, "The Charted Course of the Church in Education," 3, 9.
7. Taylor, "Discourse," 238.
8. While reason does not, in and of itself, bring about conversion, it does create a climate in which doctrine and testimony can flourish. No doubt, that is why the Lord said: "Come now, and let us reason together" (Isa. 1:18). And on another occasion He said, "I will reason as with men in days of old, and I will show unto you my strong reasoning" (D&C 45:10; see also 1 Sam. 12:7). For further information on developing a lesson plan, see chapter 6.
9. Roberts, *New Witness for God*, 2:vii.
10. Scott, "The Power of Scripture," 6.
11. Scott, "He Lives," 88.
12. Shakespeare, *The Merchant of Venice*, act 4, scene 1, line 173.
13. Pearce, "The Ordinary Classroom—a Powerful Place for Steady and Continued Growth," 12. Sister Cowley's name was Virginia H. Pearce at the time this address was given.

CHAPTER 9

1. *Teachings of Presidents of the Church: Joseph Smith*, 284.
2. See also D&C 97:14.
3. Scott, "Acquiring Spiritual Knowledge," 86.
4. See also Mark 2:27.
5. Confirmed in an email from President Russell M. Nelson to Tad R. Callister dated January 7, 2016.
6. Nelson, "Missionary Fireside Satellite Program," Apr. 24, 1994.
7. A similar situation occurred in Acts 16. The Church leaders had just decided that circumcision was not necessary among the Gentile converts (see Acts 15). Nonetheless, Paul had Timotheus (whose father was a Greek Gentile) circumcised "because of the Jews which were in those quarters" (see Acts 16:1–3) where they would be preaching the gospel. In other words, Paul knew that Timotheus did not need to be circumcised to meet the law of the gospel, but Paul also knew that circumcision would make it much easier to teach the gospel to the Jews. Like the meat of idols, or earrings, it was not a moral issue, but rather a practical stepping-stone to becoming a more effective minister of Christ.

CHAPTER 10

1. See also D&C 88:6.
2. Mark Pace made this statement when he reviewed this book as a courtesy to the authors.

NOTES

CHAPTER 11

1. In Smith, *The Life and Letters of Martin Luther*, 269.
2. Lewis, *Letters of C. S. Lewis*, 432.
3. For other scriptures used to support this position, see Isa. 64:6; Rom. 3:20, 27–28; 10:9–13; Gal. 2:16; Titus 3:5.
4. See also John 8:17.
5. See Foschini, "Those Who Are Baptized for the Dead," 98.
6. Dane, "A Survey and Analysis of the Interpretations of 1 Corinthians 15:29," 75.
7. Maxwell, *A More Excellent Way*, 66.
8. Milton, *Paradise Lost*, book 6, line 148.
9. See Luke 24:36–43; Rom. 6:9–10; Philip. 3:21; Heb. 1:3.
10. See also D&C 45:10; 71:8.
11. See also D&C 68:1.
12. See 1 Pet. 3:18–19; 4:6.
13. Lewis, *Letters of C. S. Lewis*, 432.
14. See also 1 Cor. 2:12–16.

CHAPTER 12

1. For other examples of divine repetition, see Ps. 102:1–2; 3 Ne. 11:3–5, 32–39.
2. Grant, in Conference Report, Oct. 1935, 7.
3. See, for example, the repetition in D&C 58:52; 61:22, 35; 80:3.
4. One of the authors heard President Oaks give this message in training to a stake presidency. The language as set forth is contained in a memo from President Oaks to the author dated January 13, 2016.
5. This story was told by Max Molgard, who personally heard it told by Elder L. Aldin Porter at a General Authority training meeting on October 3, 2000. On September 16, 2014, Max Molgard sent an email to one of the authors and others setting forth the story as it is presented in this book.
6. The same principle of repetition applied to the law of sacrifice. In the epistle to the Hebrews we read, "In those sacrifices there is a remembrance again made of sins every year" (Heb. 10:3).

CHAPTER 13

1. "Frequently Asked Questions: October 6, 2018," ChurchofJesusChrist.org.
2. McConkie, "The How and Why of Faith-Promoting Stories," 4–5.
3. Packer, "Where Much Is Given, Much Is Required," 89–90.
4. See Zobell, ed., *The Parables of James E. Talmage*.
5. Packer, "The Cloven Tongues of Fire," 7.
6. *Teachings of Presidents of the Church: Joseph Smith*, 132.

NOTES

CHAPTER 14

1. Uchtdorf, "A Matter of a Few Degrees," 58–59; emphasis added.
2. Packer, *Teach Ye Diligently*, 270–71.
3. Packer, *Teach Ye Diligently*, 37.

CHAPTER 15

1. In Prescott, "An Evening with Elder Ballard," 5, 11.
2. See also Mosiah 4:9; D&C 58:3.
3. See also D&C 78:17–19; 50:40; 1 Cor. 3:2.
4. See also 1 Ne. 13:21–22; Alma 37:1–11; 40:16–23.
5. De Tocqueville, *Democracy in America*, 1:11; emphasis added.
6. See also 1 Cor. 2.
7. Holland, "Lord, I Believe," 93–94.
8. See "Gospel Topics Essays," ChurchofJesusChrist.org.
9. Packer, "The Great Plan of Happiness," 1.

CHAPTER 16

1. Clark, "The Charted Course of the Church in Education," 6–7.
2. Smith, *Gospel Doctrine*, 206.
3. McConkie, "The Teacher's Divine Commission," 24.
4. Others have used similar phrases, but we do not know whom to credit for the initial thought.
5. In Weaver, "The Lord Sustains, Supports His Children in Missionary Service," 7.
6. Ballard, "Pure Testimony," 40.
7. Roberts, *The Life of John Taylor*, 40. Fortunately Parley P. Pratt's testimony returned, and he became a mighty preacher of righteousness.
8. Packer, "The Candle of the Lord," 54–55; emphasis in original.
9. Bednar, *Act in Doctrine*, 83.

CHAPTER 17

1. The story of the rich young ruler further emphasizes this expectation. He asked the Savior what he had to do to inherit eternal life. The Savior listed some commandments, and the young man responded that he had kept these commandments from his youth. Then he asked: "What lack I yet?" Jesus responded, "If thou wilt be perfect, go and sell that thou hast, and give to the poor" (Matt. 19:16–23). The Savior never lowered His standard—it was and always will be perfection.
2. See Menéndez and Musca, *Stand and Deliver*.

NOTES

CHAPTER 18

1. Eyring, "The Lord Will Multiply the Harvest," 6.
2. *Gospel Teaching and Learning*, 62; emphasis in original.
3. Eyring, "The Lord Will Multiply the Harvest," 6.
4. Confirmed in an email from President M. Russell Ballard to Tad R. Callister dated January 6, 2016.
5. Linford, "Icebergs, Point Guards, Waves, and Softballs," 131.
6. See also Mark 10:2–3.
7. See Mosiah 3:13; Alma 39, chapter heading.

CHAPTER 19

1. Monson, "Examples of Great Teachers," 106.
2. Holland, "Witnesses unto Me," 15.
3. Some people do not feel comfortable in smaller groups. Accordingly, each teacher needs to be sensitive to these feelings so that no class member feels pressure to participate.
4. Scott, "To Learn and to Teach More Effectively," 6.
5. Linford, "Icebergs, Point Guards, Waves, and Softballs," 138–39.
6. For more information, see chapter 16.

CHAPTER 20

1. Bednar, *Power to Become*, 162.
2. Those invitations that are subject to class discussion, however, should not involve worthiness issues. These matters should remain private—to be discussed with parents or bishops as needed.

CHAPTER 21

1. Monson, "A Doorway Called Love," 66–67.
2. Twain, *Mark Twain's Aquarium*, 16.
3. *Teaching, No Greater Call*, 31.
4. Bush, *41: A Portrait of My Father*, 82.
5. "Love Those You Teach" (video), ChurchofJesusChrist.org.
6. "Where Love Is," *Children's Songbook*, 138.
7. Oaks, "Gospel Teaching," 79.
8. Hammerstein, "Sixteen Going on Seventeen (Reprise)," *The Sound of Music*.
9. McKay, "The Opportunities of the Class Teacher," 722.

CHAPTER 22

1. See McKay, in Conference Report, Oct. 1920, 41–42.
2. Email received by one of the authors on June 5, 2014.

NOTES

3. Markham, "Outwitted," in *The Shoes of Happiness and Other Poems*, 2.
4. Arnold, "Strengthen Thy Brethren," 46–47.
5. Confirmed by phone call with Vaughn J. Featherstone on January 12, 2016.

CHAPTER 24

1. Kimball, "Ocean Currents and Family Influences," 111–12.
2. *Family Home Evening Manual*, 2; emphasis added.
3. Featherstone, *A Generation of Excellence*, 49.
4. Bednar, "More Diligent and Concerned at Home," 20.
5. Packer, "Families and Fences," 109.

CHAPTER 25

1. Eyring, "Teaching True Doctrine," 6–7.
2. Email received from Neill F. Marriott on May 5, 2015.
3. Jones, "An Especially Noble Calling," 17.

CHAPTER 26

1. Nelson, "Revelation for the Church, Revelation for Our Lives," 96.
2. Packer, "Prayers and Answers," 19.
3. See also Alma 32:28, 34; D&C 8:2–3.
4. *Teachings of Presidents of the Church: Joseph Smith*, 132.
5. Dr. Seuss, *How the Grinch Stole Christmas*; Dickens, *A Christmas Carol*.
6. See also D&C 11:13.
7. See also 3 Ne. 22:13.

CHAPTER 27

1. See also Gen. 1:27; Rom. 8:16–17; Heb. 12:9.
2. "The Family: A Proclamation to the World," ChurchofJesusChrist.org.
3. See also 3 Ne. 27:27.
4. "The Family: A Proclamation to the World," ChurchofJesusChrist.org; emphasis added.
5. Edmund Burke, a brilliant philosopher and statesman, addressed this same issue: "Men are qualified for civil liberty in exact proportion to their disposition to put moral chains upon their own appetites. . . . Society cannot exist, unless a controlling power upon will and appetite be placed somewhere; and the less of it there is within, the more there must be without. It is ordained in the eternal constitution of things, that men of intemperate minds cannot be free. Their passions forge their fetters" (*The Works of the Right Honorable Edmund Burke*, 4:51–52).
6. Durant and Durant, *The Lessons of History*, 35–36; emphasis added.
7. See Gen. 1:22, 28 footnote *c*; Ps. 127:3, 5.

8. "The Family: A Proclamation to the World," ChurchofJesusChrist.org.
9. See also 1 Cor. 11:11; D&C 131:1–3; 132:15–24.
10. See also D&C 132:22, 24.
11. See also 1 Cor. 10:8; D&C 42:24.
12. *For the Strength of Youth*, 36.
13. *True to the Faith*, 106.
14. *For the Strength of Youth*, 6.
15. See Harbertson, "Restoration of the Aaronic Priesthood," 77.
16. See also 1 John 2:28.
17. "Same-Sex Attraction: Family and Friends," ChurchofJesusChrist.org.
18. "Same-Sex Attraction: Family and Friends," ChurchofJesusChrist.org.
19. Wixom, "Stay on the Path," 9.
20. See also Job 20:4–5; 3 Ne. 27:11.

CHAPTER 28

1. Callister, "Your Refined Heavenly Home," speeches.byu.edu.
2. God's creations are not just functional but also aesthetical. The Lord declared: "All things which come of the earth, in the season thereof, are made for the benefit and the use of man, *both to please the eye and to gladden the heart*" (D&C 59:18; emphasis added). In the Sermon on the Mount the Lord referred to one of His glorious creations when He said: "Consider the lilies of the field" (Matt. 6:28).
3. Packer, "Follow the Brethren," speeches.byu.edu.
4. Darwin, *The Autobiography of Charles Darwin*, 51.
5. Russell, *The Conquest of Happiness*, 111–12.
6. Clark, *Selected Papers*, 155.
7. *Teachings of Presidents of the Church: Brigham Young*, 196.
8. Thomas, "Cultural Clues to the Abundant Life," 60.
9. In Nibley, *Nibley on the Timely and the Timeless*, xxvi–xxviii.
10. Cook, "Lamentations of Jeremiah: Beware of Bondage," 88.
11. Kimball, "The Gospel Vision of the Arts," 5; emphasis added.
12. In Packer, "The Arts and the Spirit of the Lord," 61.
13. See the video *Handel's Messiah: Debtor's Prison*, ChurchofJesusChrist.org.
14. See Matt. 6:28; Luke 13:6–9.
15. Monson, "Our Responsibility to Rescue," 4–5.
16. Kimball, *The Teachings of Spencer W. Kimball*, 301. In 1978 Diane Hallstrom attended the rededication of the Laie Hawaii Temple and some of the accompanying events. While there, she heard President Spencer W. Kimball counsel them "to have a picture of the temple in our children's bedrooms. He said that would be a visual reminder of the covenants they would one day make there. He also suggested we regularly ask our children why there was a picture of the temple in their room. He said it would lead to meaningful gospel discussions." Sister Hallstrom said that declaration was good enough for her. "Within a matter of days," she said, "we had large temple pictures hanging in each of our children's bedrooms. . . . At night when our children

would kneel down to say their prayers, I would ask them questions about the temple, [pointing] to the pictures in their rooms. . . . Following the counsel of a prophet has greatly blessed our lives."

17. In *Hymns*, ix.
18. Smith, in Conference Report, Oct. 1945, 116.
19. Oaks, "Worship through Music," 10–12.
20. Nelson, "Reach, Teach, and Serve," May 21, 1944.
21. Richards, in Conference Report, Oct. 1920, 40.
22. See Wordsworth, "Ode: Intimations of Immortality from Recollections of Early Childhood," 461–66.
23. See Donne, "Holy Sonnets," nos. VII, X, 250–51.
24. See Donne, "Holy Sonnets," no. V, 249.
25. See Browning, "Sonnets from the Portuguese," 2:285–307.
26. McConkie, *The Mortal Messiah*, vol. 4, 180–81, note 1.
27. Lee, *To Kill a Mocking Bird*, 105; emphasis added.
28. Boublil, *Les Misérables*.
29. Twain, *The Adventures of Huckleberry Finn*, 295.

CHAPTER 29

1. Shakespeare, *As You Like It*, act 2, scene 1, lines 16–17.
2. Ingersoll, *Shakespeare*, 68–70.
3. Young, *Discourses of Brigham Young*, 230.
4. Eyring, "Education for Real Life," 17–18.

CHAPTER 30

1. See Christofferson, "Free Forever, to Act for Themselves," 19.
2. McConkie, "The Seven Deadly Heresies," speeches.byu.edu.
3. See also D&C 130:18–19.
4. Priestly, *Rain upon Godshill*, 176; emphasis added.
5. Nelson, "Opening Remarks," 8.
6. Packer and Perry, "Principles of Teaching and Learning," 84; emphasis added.
7. See Spafford, *A Woman's Reach*, 96–97.
8. Dew, *Worth the Wrestle*, 12.
9. Dew, *Go Forward with Faith*, 449–50.
10. This sentiment is often attributed to Mark Twain, but that attribution is questionable, since Twain's father died when he was eleven. Nonetheless, many can relate to the underlying principle taught.
11. Smith, "Discourse," 87, josephsmithpapers.org; emphasis added.
12. McConkie, *Doctrines of the Restoration*, 234.
13. *Teachings of Presidents of the Church: Harold B. Lee*, 66.
14. Joseph Fielding McConkie, *The Bruce R. McConkie Story*, 274.
15. In *Respectfully Quoted*, 38.
16. *Teachings of Presidents of the Church: Joseph Smith*, 268.

NOTES

17. In Rubin, "George Bush: Renaissance Man," washingtonpost.com; emphasis added.
18. Joseph F. Smith, in Conference Report, Apr. 1902, 86.
19. Kennedy, "Inaugural Address," Jan. 20, 1961, presidency.ucsb.edu.

CONCLUSION

1. Packer, "The Ideal Teacher," 5–6; emphasis added.
2. McKay, in Conference Report, Oct. 1916, 57.

WORKS CITED

Arnold, Mervyn B. "Strengthen Thy Brethren." *Ensign,* May 2004, 46–48.
Ballard, M. Russell. "Pure Testimony." *Ensign*, Nov. 2004, 40–43.
Bednar, David A. *Act in Doctrine.* Salt Lake City: Deseret Book, 2012.
_____. "More Diligent and Concerned at Home," *Ensign*, Nov. 2009, 20.
_____. *Power to Become: Spiritual Patterns for Pressing Forward with Steadfastness in Christ.* Salt Lake City: Deseret Book, 2014.
_____. "A Reservoir of Living Water." Brigham Young University fireside, Provo, UT, Feb. 4, 2007. speeches.byu.edu/wp-content/uploads/pdf/Bednar_David_2007_02.pdf.
_____. "The Spirit of Revelation." *Ensign*, May 2011, 87.
Benson, Ezra Taft. "The Gospel Teacher and His Message." Address to Church Educational System religious educators, Sept. 17, 1976.
Boublil, Alain. *Les Misérables* (musical). 1980.
Browning, Elizabeth Barrett. "Sonnets from the Portuguese." In *Poems*. Vol. 2. New York: James Miller, 1862.
Burke, Edmund. *The Works of the Right Honorable Edmund Burke.* 5th edition. Vol. 4. Boston: Little, Brown, and Company, 1877.

WORKS CITED

Bush, George W. *41: A Portrait of My Father*. New York: Random House, 2014.

Butterworth, Edwin, Jr. "Eight Presidents: A Century at BYU." *Ensign*, Oct. 1975, 23–30.

Callister, Douglas L. "Your Refined Spiritual Home." Brigham Young University devotional, Provo, UT, Sept. 19, 2006. speeches.byu.edu/talks/douglas-l-callister/refined-heavenly-home.

Carson, Ben, and Cecil Murphey. *Gifted Hands: The Ben Carson Story*. Grand Rapids, MI: Zandervan, 1996.

De Cervantes Saavedra, Miguel. *Don Quixote de la Mancha*. Translated by Motteux, Jarvis, and Smollett. Revised edition. New York: D. Appleton and Company, 1863.

Children's Songbook of The Church of Jesus Christ of Latter-day Saints. Salt Lake City: The Church of Jesus Christ of Latter-day Saints, 1997.

Christofferson, D. Todd. "Free Forever, to Act for Themselves." *Ensign*, Nov. 2014, 16–19.

Clarke, J. Richard. "My Soul Delighteth in the Scriptures." *Ensign*, Nov. 1982, 13–15.

Clark, J. Reuben, Jr. "The Charted Course of the Church in Education." Address to seminary and institute of religion leaders, Aspen Grove, UT, Aug. 8, 1938. Revised edition. 1994.

———. *Selected Papers: On Religion, Education, and Youth*. Edited by David H. Yarn. Provo, UT: Brigham Young University, 1984.

Cook, Quentin L. "Lamentations of Jeremiah: Beware of Bondage." *Ensign*, Nov. 2013, 88–91.

Dane, Warren Talmage. "A Survey and Analysis of the Interpretations of 1 Corinthians 15:29." Thesis, Talbot Theological Seminary, June 1965.

Darwin, Charles. *The Autobiography of Charles Darwin*. Edited by Francis Darwin. London: J. Murray, 1908.

Dew, Sheri L. *Go Forward with Faith: The Biography of Gordon B. Hinckley*. Salt Lake City: Deseret Book, 1996.

———. *Worth the Wrestle*. Salt Lake City: Deseret Book, 2017.

Dickens, Charles. *A Christmas Carol*. London: Chapman & Hall, 1843.

Donne, John. "Holy Sonnets." In *Collected Poems of John Donne*. Edited by Roy Booth. Hertfordshire, England: Wordsworth Editions Limited, 1994. 247–55.

Durant, Will, and Ariel Durant. *The Lessons of History.* New York: Simon & Schuster, 1968.

Eyring, Henry B. CES Satellite Training Broadcast, Aug. 10, 2003.

———. "Education for Real Life." *Ensign,* Oct. 2002, 14–21.

———. "The Lord Will Multiply the Harvest." Address to Church Educational System religious educators, Feb. 6, 1998.

———. "Teaching True Doctrine." *Ensign,* Apr. 2009, 5–9.

———. "Waiting upon the Lord." Brigham Young University fireside, Sept. 30, 1990. speeches.byu.edu/talks/henry-b-eyring/waiting-upon-lord.

"The Family: A Proclamation to the World." ChurchofJesusChrist.org.

Family Home Evening Manual. Salt Lake City: The Church of Jesus Christ of Latter-day Saints, 1974.

Faust, James E. "Acting for Ourselves and Not Being Acted Upon." *Ensign,* Nov. 1995, 45–47.

Featherstone, Vaughn J. *A Generation of Excellence: A Guide for Parents and Youth Leaders.* Salt Lake City, Bookcraft: 1975.

For the Strength of Youth. Salt Lake City: The Church of Jesus Christ of Latter-day Saints, 2011.

Foschini, Bernard M. *"Those Who Are Baptized for the Dead," 1 Cor. 15:29: An Exegetical Historical Dissertation.* Worcester, MA: Heffernan Press, 1951.

"Frequently Asked Questions, October 6, 2018." The Church of Jesus Christ of Latter-day Saints. ChurchofJesusChrist.org/study/manual/frequently-asked-questions-october-6-2018/faq-october-6-2018.

Gospel Teaching and Learning: A Handbook for Teachers and Leaders in Seminaries and Institutes of Religion. Salt Lake City: The Church of Jesus Christ of Latter-day Saints, 2012.

"Gospel Topics Essays." The Church of Jesus Christ of Latter-day Saints. ChurchofJesusChrist.org/study/manual/gospel-topics-essays/essays.

WORKS CITED

Grant, Heber J. In Conference Report, Oct. 1935, 2–12.

Guiterman, Arthur. "Education." *School Life* 17, no. 10 (June 1932): 185.

Hammerstein, Oscar, II. *The Sound of Music* (musical). 1959.

Handel's Messiah: Debtor's Prison (video). 2017. ChurchofJesusChrist.org/media/video/2017-04-0001-handels-messiah-debtors-prison.

Harbertson, Robert B. "The Restoration of the Aaronic Priesthood." *Ensign*, July 1989, 76–77.

Hinckley, Gordon B. In Conference Report, Oct. 1965, 50–54.

_____. "Five Million Members—A Milestone and Not a Summit." *Ensign*, May 1982, 44–46.

_____. *Teachings of Presidents of the Church: Gordon B. Hinckley*. Salt Lake City: The Church of Jesus Christ of Latter-day Saints, 2016.

Holland, Jeffrey R. *Broken Things to Mend*. Salt Lake City: Deseret Book, 2008.

_____. "Lord, I Believe." *Ensign*, May 2013, 93–95.

_____. "A Teacher Come from God." *Ensign*, May 1998, 25–27.

_____. "Witnesses unto Me." *Ensign*, May 2001, 14–16.

Holzapfel, Richard N. *Every Stone a Sermon: The Magnificent Story of the Construction and Dedication of the Salt Lake Temple*. Salt Lake City: Deseret Book, 1992.

Hymns of The Church of Jesus Christ of Latter-day Saints. Salt Lake City: The Church of Jesus Christ of Latter-day Saints, 1985.

Ingersoll, Robert G. *Shakespeare: A Lecture*. New York: C. P. Farrell, 1895.

Jones, Joy D. "An Especially Noble Calling." *Ensign*, May 2020, 17.

Kennedy, John F. "Inaugural Address," Jan. 20, 1961. presidency.ucsb.edu/documents/inaugural-address-2.

Kimball, Spencer W. "Education for Eternity." Pre-school address to Brigham Young University faculty and staff, Sept. 12, 1967. educationforeternity.byu.edu/w_swk67.htm.

_____. "The Gospel Vision of the Arts." *Ensign*, July 1977, 2–5.

_____. "Ocean Currents and Family Influences." *Ensign*, Nov. 1974, 110–13.

_____. *The Teachings of Spencer W. Kimball*. Edited by Edward L. Kimball. Salt Lake City: Bookcraft, 1982.

WORKS CITED

Lee, Harold B. "Stand Ye in Holy Places." *Ensign*, July 1973, 121–24.

———. *Teachings of Presidents of the Church: Harold B. Lee.* Salt Lake City: The Church of Jesus Christ of Latter-day Saints, 2000.

Lee, Harper. *To Kill a Mockingbird.* Philadelphia: J. B. Lippincott, 1960.

"Letter from the First Presidency," Feb. 11, 1999. In *Liahona*, Dec. 1999.

Lewis, C. S. *Letters of C. S. Lewis.* Edited by W. H. Lewis. Revised and enlarged edition. San Diego: Harcourt Brace, 1993.

Linford, Steven T. "Icebergs, Point Guards, Waves, and Softballs: The Power of Good Questions and Discussions." *Religious Educator* 12, no. 1 (2011): 127–49.

"Love Those You Teach" (video). The Church of Jesus Christ of Latter-day Saints. ChurchofJesusChrist.org/media/video/2012-03-002-love-those-you-teach.

Markham, Edwin. *The Shoes of Happiness and Other Poems.* Garden City, NY: Doubleday, Page, & Co, 1922.

Maxwell, Neal A. "But a Few Days." Address to CES religious educators, Sept. 10, 1982.

———. "It's Service, Not Status, That Counts," *Ensign*, July 1975, 5–7.

———. *A More Excellent Way: Essays on Leadership for Latter-day Saints.* Salt Lake City: Deseret Book, 1967.

McConkie, Bruce R. *Doctrines of the Restoration: Sermons and Writings of Bruce R. McConkie.* Edited by Mark L. McConkie. Salt Lake City: Bookcraft, 1989.

———. "The How and Why of Faith-Promoting Stories." *New Era*, July 1978, 4–5.

———. *The Mortal Messiah: From Bethlehem to Calvary.* Vol. 4. Salt Lake City: Deseret Book, 1981.

———. "The Seven Deadly Heresies." Brigham Young University fireside, Provo, UT, June 1, 1980. speeches.byu.edu/talks/bruce-r-mcconkie/seven-deadly-heresies.

———. "The Teacher's Divine Commission." *Ensign*, Apr. 1979, 21–24.

McConkie, Joseph Fielding. *The Bruce R. McConkie Story: Reflections of a Son.* Salt Lake City: Deseret Book, 2003.

McKay, David O. In Conference Report, Oct. 1916, 57–61.

WORKS CITED

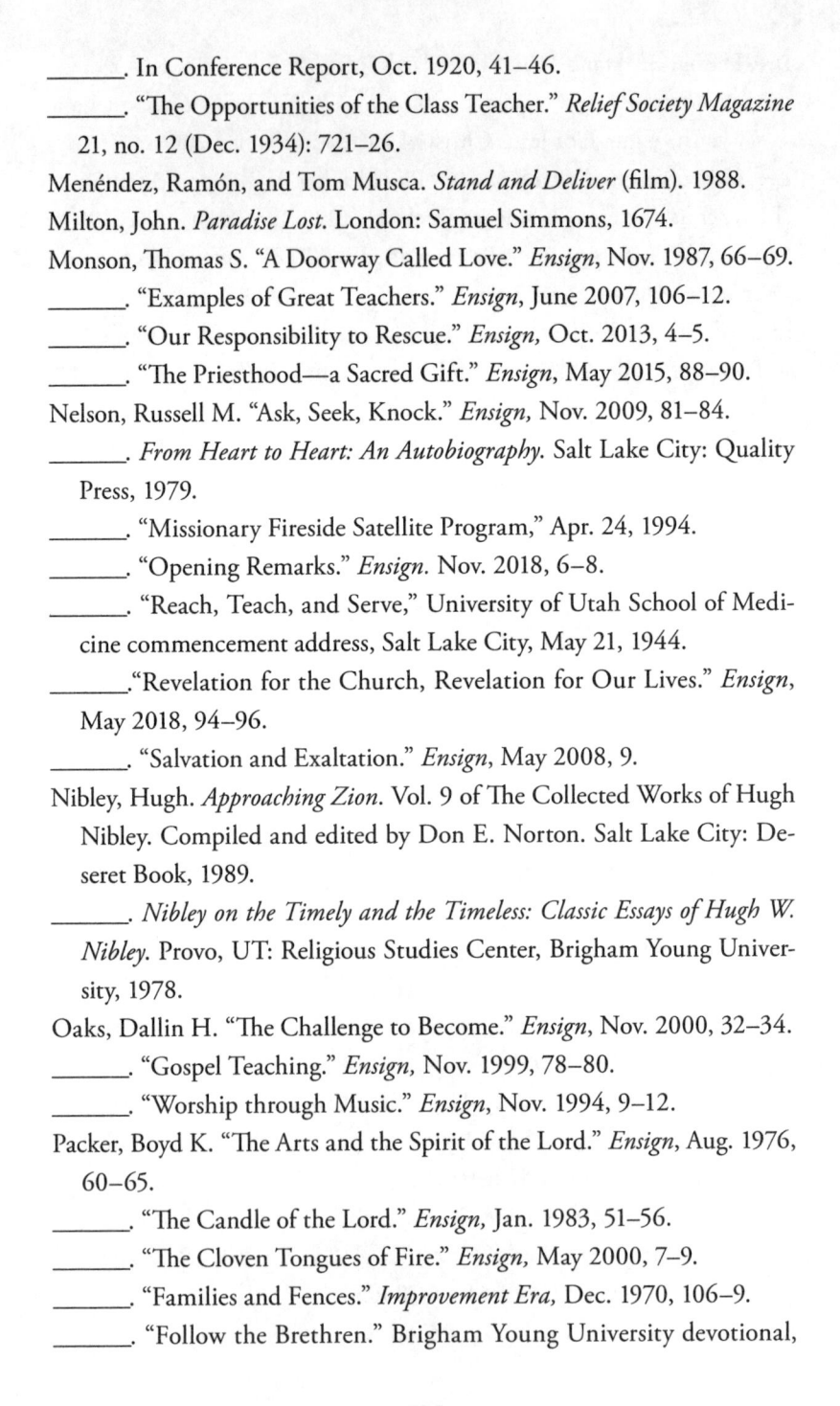

———. In Conference Report, Oct. 1920, 41–46.

———. "The Opportunities of the Class Teacher." *Relief Society Magazine* 21, no. 12 (Dec. 1934): 721–26.

Menéndez, Ramón, and Tom Musca. *Stand and Deliver* (film). 1988.

Milton, John. *Paradise Lost*. London: Samuel Simmons, 1674.

Monson, Thomas S. "A Doorway Called Love." *Ensign*, Nov. 1987, 66–69.

———. "Examples of Great Teachers." *Ensign*, June 2007, 106–12.

———. "Our Responsibility to Rescue." *Ensign*, Oct. 2013, 4–5.

———. "The Priesthood—a Sacred Gift." *Ensign*, May 2015, 88–90.

Nelson, Russell M. "Ask, Seek, Knock." *Ensign*, Nov. 2009, 81–84.

———. *From Heart to Heart: An Autobiography*. Salt Lake City: Quality Press, 1979.

———. "Missionary Fireside Satellite Program," Apr. 24, 1994.

———. "Opening Remarks." *Ensign*. Nov. 2018, 6–8.

———. "Reach, Teach, and Serve," University of Utah School of Medicine commencement address, Salt Lake City, May 21, 1944.

———. "Revelation for the Church, Revelation for Our Lives." *Ensign*, May 2018, 94–96.

———. "Salvation and Exaltation." *Ensign*, May 2008, 9.

Nibley, Hugh. *Approaching Zion*. Vol. 9 of The Collected Works of Hugh Nibley. Compiled and edited by Don E. Norton. Salt Lake City: Deseret Book, 1989.

———. *Nibley on the Timely and the Timeless: Classic Essays of Hugh W. Nibley*. Provo, UT: Religious Studies Center, Brigham Young University, 1978.

Oaks, Dallin H. "The Challenge to Become." *Ensign*, Nov. 2000, 32–34.

———. "Gospel Teaching." *Ensign*, Nov. 1999, 78–80.

———. "Worship through Music." *Ensign*, Nov. 1994, 9–12.

Packer, Boyd K. "The Arts and the Spirit of the Lord." *Ensign*, Aug. 1976, 60–65.

———. "The Candle of the Lord." *Ensign*, Jan. 1983, 51–56.

———. "The Cloven Tongues of Fire." *Ensign*, May 2000, 7–9.

———. "Families and Fences." *Improvement Era*, Dec. 1970, 106–9.

———. "Follow the Brethren." Brigham Young University devotional,

WORKS CITED

Provo, UT, Mar. 23, 1965. speeches.byu.edu/talks/boyd-k-packer/follow-brethren.

———. "The Great Plan of Happiness." Address given at the Church Educational System symposium, Aug. 10, 1993.

———. "The Ideal Teacher." Address to seminary and institute faculty, June 28, 1962.

———. "The Mediator." *Ensign*, May 1977, 54–56.

———. "Prayers and Answers." *Ensign*, Nov. 1979, 19–21.

———. *Teach Ye Diligently*. Revised edition. Salt Lake City: Deseret Book. 1991.

———. "Where Much Is Given, Much Is Required." *Ensign*, Nov. 1974, 87–90.

Packer, Boyd K., and L. Tom Perry. "Principles of Teaching and Learning." *Ensign*, June 2007, 82–87.

Pearce, Virginia H. "The Ordinary Classroom—a Powerful Place for Steady and Continued Growth." *Ensign*, Nov. 1996, 11–14.

Prescott, Marianne Holman. "An Evening with Elder Ballard." *Church News*, Mar. 6, 2016, 5, 11.

"President David O. McKay." *Improvement Era*, Nov. 1966, 980.

Priestly, John Boynton. *Rain upon Godshill*. New York & London: Harper & Brothers, 1939.

Respectfully Quoted: A Dictionary of Quotations. Compiled by the Library of Congress. Mineola, NY: Dover Publications, 2010.

Richards, George F. In Conference Report, Oct. 1920, 37–40.

Roberts, B. H. *The Life of John Taylor, Third President of The Church of Jesus Christ of Latter-day Saints*. Salt Lake City, 1892.

———. *New Witnesses for God*. Vol. 2, *The Book of Mormon*. Salt Lake City: Deseret News, 1920.

Rubin, Jennifer. "George Bush: Renaissance Man." *Washington Post*, Apr. 26, 2013. washingtonpost.com/blogs/right-turn/wp/2013/04/26/george-bush-renaissance-man.

Russell, Bertrand. *The Conquest of Happiness*. London and New York: Routledge Classics, 2006.

"Same-Sex Attraction: Family and Friends," The Church of Jesus Christ of Latter-day Saints. ChurchofJesusChrist.org/study/manual/same-sex-attraction-family-and-friends?lang=eng.

Scott, Richard G. "Acquiring Spiritual Knowledge." *Ensign*, Nov. 1993, 86–88.

———. "He Lives." *Ensign*, Nov. 1999.

———. "The Power of Scripture." *Ensign*, Nov. 2011, 6–8.

———. "To Learn and to Teach More Effectively." *The Religious Educator* 9, no. 1 (2008): 1–11.

Seuss, Dr. *How the Grinch Stole Christmas*. New York: Random House, 1958.

Shakespeare, William. *As You Like It*. 1599.

———. *The Merchant of Venice*. 1596–99.

Smith, George Albert. In Conference Report, Oct. 1945, 115–20.

Smith, Joseph. "Discourse, 27 February 1835–A, as Reported by Oliver Cowdery." The Joseph Smith Papers. josephsmithpapers.org/paper-summary/discourse-27-february-1835-a-as-reported-by-oliver-cowdery.

———. *Teachings of Presidents of the Church: Joseph Smith*. Salt Lake City: The Church of Jesus of Christ of Latter-day Saints, 2007.

Smith, Joseph F. In Conference Report, Apr. 1902, 85–87.

———. *Gospel Doctrine*. 5th edition. Salt Lake City: Deseret Book, 1939.

Smith, Joseph Fielding. *Doctrines of Salvation: Sermons and Writings of Joseph Fielding Smith*. Vol. 1. Compiled by Bruce R. McConkie. Salt Lake City: Bookcraft, 1954.

Smith, Preserved. *The Life and Letters of Martin Luther*. Boston and New York: Houghton Mifflin, 1911.

Spafford, Belle S. *A Woman's Reach*. Salt Lake City: Deseret Book, 1974.

Taylor, John. "Discourse." *Deseret News*, Sept. 30, 1857, 238–39.

Teaching, No Greater Call: A Resource Guide for Gospel Teaching. Salt Lake City: The Church of Jesus Christ of Latter-day Saints, 1999.

Thomas, Robert K. "Cultural Clues to the Abundant Life." *Ensign*, Aug. 1971, 59–60.

De Tocqueville, Alexis. *Democracy in America*. Vol. 1. Translated by Henry Reeve. New York: Georg Aldrad, 1839.

True to the Faith: A Gospel Reference. Salt Lake City: The Church of Jesus Christ of Latter-day Saints, 2004.

Twain, Mark. *The Adventures of Huckleberry Finn*. New York: P. F. Collier & Son, 1918.

_____. *Mark Twain's Aquarium: The Samuel Clemens Angelfish Correspondence, 1905–1910*. Edited by John Cooley. Athens: University of Georgia Press, 1991.

Uchtdorf, Dieter F. "A Matter of a Few Degrees." *Ensign*, May 2008, 57–60.

Weaver, Sarah Jane. "The Lord Sustains, Supports His Children in Missionary Service." *Church News,* July 12, 2015, 7.

Wixom, Rosemary M. "Stay on the Path." *Ensign*, Nov. 2010, 9.

Wordsworth, William. "Ode: Intimations of Immortality from Recollections of Early Childhood." In *Selected Poems of William Wordsworth*. England: Oxford University, 1919. 461–66.

Young, Brigham. *Discourses of Brigham Young*. Compiled by John A. Widtsoe. Salt Lake City: Deseret Book, 1925.

_____. *Teachings of Presidents of the Church: Brigham Young*. Salt Lake City: The Church of Jesus Christ of Latter-day Saints, 1997.

Zobell, Albert, ed. *The Parables of James E. Talmage*. Salt Lake City: Deseret Book, 1973.

INDEX

Aaronic Priesthood, 9
Abinadi, 109
Action, inviting others to, 120
Active learning, 266–68
Adultery, 235–36
Adventures of Huckleberry Finn, The (Twain), 258
Alma the Elder, 60
Alma the Younger, 17–18, 53, 139, 155
Ammon, 155–56
Amulek, 152
Analogies, 47, 103–4, 122–23, 125–26, 156–58. *See also* "Like unto" principle
Angel(s): ministering of, 9; teaches Nephi, 108
Answers: questions serving as effective, 155; listening to, 163–64
Apostasy, 102–4, 125–26
Araujo, Fernando, 190–92
Archaeological discoveries, 130
Archimedes, 277
Arnold, Mervyn B., 190–92
Art, 251–57

Atmosphere, for inspired discussion, 165–66
Atonement, 61–62, 82–84, 124, 159–60, 205–6
Awkward silences, 164
Axmen, parable of, 273–74

Ballard, M. Russell, 127–28, 141, 156, 252
Baptism, 102
Baptism for the dead, 90
Bednar, David A., 38, 67, 142, 170, 210–11
Benjamin, King, 60–62
Benson, Ezra Taft, 64, 101
Bodies: as temples, 231, 235; and modesty, 236–37. *See also* Morality
Book of Mormon: anachronisms in, 130; and answering difficult questions, 133–36; receiving testimony of, 158; introducing, 172–74; authors read, with sons, 204; Oliver Cowdery receives witness of, 225–26
Brother of Jared, 159

INDEX

Burke, Edmund, 290n5
Burroughs, John, 222
Bush, George W., 276

Caesar, tributes paid to, 113
Cake analogies, 122–23, 125–26
Calculus, and rising to expectations, 146–48
Callings, for less active and inactive members, 193–94
Callister, Douglas, 245
Callister, Nathan, 201–2
Callister, Rebecca, 219–20
Callister, Reed, 178
Callister, Rick, 209–10, 216–17
Carson, Ben, 15–16
Carson, Sonya, 15–16
Celestial glory, 234
Change, inspired by love, 177–80
Charity, 182–84
Child, Paul C., 8–9
Children: teaching, 2, 61; parents' responsibility to teach, 12–14; parents' influence on, 15–19; quality time with, 19–20; teachers' role in teaching, 20; and importance of parenthood, 20–21; and teaching clearly and simply, 70–71; stories and teaching, 109; used in object lesson, 113–14; expectations for, 146–49; discovering interests of, 201–2; teaching power of prayer to, 202–4; reading scriptures with, 204; teaching doctrine to, 204–7; wayward, 207, 208–9, 212–13, 240–41; teaching wise use of time to, 212; never giving up on, 212–13; serving as example for, 218–19; helping, recognize promptings, 223–28; importance of teaching morality to, 229–30. *See also* Home, teaching in; Informal teaching; Morality; Parents
Choices, making, 100–101
Church materials, 132–33
Church of Jesus Christ of Latter-day Saints, The, leaving, 136–37
Circumcision, 286n7

Clarity, in teaching doctrine, 70–71
Clark, Emily, 125–26
Clark, J. Reuben Jr., 69–70, 138, 247
Clark, Rachael, 125
Class members: getting to know, 183–84; focusing on, 184; inactive and less active, 186–95; technology and seeing, 196–98
Clothing, 236–37
Coin, parable of lost, 190
Comfort, in doctrine, 56–57
Commandments, 124
Commitment, questions heightening level of, 153–54
Common-sense method of scriptural interpretation, 92–93
Comparison. *See* Analogies; "Like unto" principle
Compliments, 177–78
Confidence, in class discussions, 163
Consecration, 76–77
Consistency, 210–11
Cook, Quentin L., 248
Corianton, 155, 235
Cornelia, Mother of the Gracchi (Kauffmann), 251–52
Cowdery, Oliver, 225–26
Cowley, Virginia Pearce, 74
Creativity, 115
Crises, spiritual preparation for, 59–60
Cultural refinement: as religious pursuit, 245–47; developing, 247–49; in home, 249–59; in classes, 250–59
Curiosity, 270–71

Dalebout, Angela, 196
Darwin, Charles, 246
Daughter of Jairus, 67–68
David (Michelangelo), 22–23
Dead: Lazarus raised from, 67; daughter of Jairus raised from, 67–68. *See also* Baptism for the dead
Death, 57, 66
Decision making, 100–101
Determination, 209–10
Devils, casting out, 158
Dew, Sheri, 271

INDEX

Difficult questions: need to address, 127–28; principles governing answers to, 128–33; Book of Mormon and, 133–36; lost faith due to, 136–37
Discouragement, 213–14
Discussion / Discourse, 107–8; teacher's role in, 162; encouraging confidence in, 163; increasing quality of, 163; listening to answers in, 163–64; handling awkward silence in, 164; involving hesitant class members in, 164–65; domination of, 165; environment for inspired, 165–66; continuing, to natural end, 166–68; ending, on spiritual note, 168; assessing, 168–69; in home, 208–10
Divine worth, 230–31
Doctrinal relationships, 81–82, 84–85, 286n7; and plan of salvation, 82; and Atonement, 82–83; and doctrine of Christ, 83–84; summary of, 84
Doctrine: as foundation of gospel teaching, 1–2; in lesson plan, 45–46; impact of, 51–54; converting power of, 53–54; Holy Ghost invited by, 54; counters falsehoods, 54–56; comfort in, 56–57; salvation and perfection through, 58; and teaching levels, 58–61; on Atonement, 61–62; scriptures as primary source for teaching, 63–67; patterns in, 67–68; listing questions about, 68–69; teaching undiluted, 69–70; teaching, clearly and simply, 70–71; and scripture memorization, 72–73; of Christ, 83–84; relationship between testimony and, 138–40; teaching, to children, 204–7; on morality, 230–34; acting on, 276. *See also* Doctrinal relationships; "Like unto" principle; Principles; Repetition
Durant, Will and Ariel, 232–33

Earrings, principle regarding, 79–80
Enabling power of Atonement, 83
Enlightened understanding, 226–27
Enos, 208
Entertainment level of teaching, 59
Environment, for inspired discussion, 165–66
Escalante, Jamie, 146–48
Eternal marriage and family, 233–34
Exaltation, 231. *See also* Redemption; Salvation
Expectations, 149–50; set by Jesus Christ, 145–46; rising to, 146–49
Experience, drawing upon, 27
Eyring, Henry B., 54, 152, 154–55, 215–16, 263

Faith: versus works, 87, 88–89; and unanswered questions, 129, 131, 136–37; integrity toward existing, 132
Faith-promoting stories, 110
Falsehoods, countered by doctrine, 54–56
Families, eternal, 233–34
Family prayer, 203–4
Farrar, Frederic W., 258
Faust, James E., 23
Featherstone, Scott, 209
Featherstone, Vaughn J., 195, 208–9
Fleming, Alexander, 275
Follow-up questions, 156–58
Fornication, 235–36
Friendship, in spirit world, 10–11

Garbage-can lesson, 208
Garcin, Bob, 179–80
Garfield High, 146–48
Generosity, 216
Gifts of the Spirit, 27–28, 182–83
God: nature of, 55–56, 65–66, 89, 92; "man of," 66–67; love of, 182; works in subtle ways, 223–24; becoming like, 230–31, 263; creation in image of, 231; creations of, 291n2
Godhead, doctrine on nature of, 55–56, 65–66, 93–94
Godhood, 149–50
Good, intent to do, 226

INDEX

Grace, 88–89
Grand Canyon, 245–46
Grandma Moses, 276
Grant, Heber J., 101
Gravity, 123–24
Groberg, John H., 25–26
Guiterman, Arthur, 35

Habits, 171
Hales, Mary, 141
Hales, Robert D., 271
Hallstrom, Diane, 291–92n16
Hammerstein, Oscar, 183
Handcart companies, 110–11
Handel, George Frideric, 250–51
Hard work, 210
Harmony method of scriptural interpretation, 93–94
Healing, 57, 77–78, 118–19, 158, 190
Heart, questions penetrating, 152–53
Helaman's stripling warriors, 17
Hinckley, Gordon B., 6, 34, 35, 271
Hobab, 194
Holland, Jeffrey R., 43, 59–60, 132, 164
Holy Ghost: assistance of, 25; power of, 31–32; teaching by, 31–32; preparing and teaching by, 32–43; and recording impressions, 41; teaching with, 43; invited by doctrine, 54; doctrinal questions on, 68–69; and teaching clearly and simply, 71; scriptural confirmation by, 94–95; in missionary work, 114; inspiration for creative ideas through, 115; witness of, 131–32; invited by testimony, 141; and extending inspired invitations, 170–71; love as evidence of, 182; and informal teaching, 218; importance of recognizing promptings of, 221–23; helping children recognize promptings of, 223–28. *See also* Impressions, recording and organizing; Promptings; Revelation
Holzapfel, Richard, 162

Home: dedicating, 212; cultural refinement in, 250–59
Home, teaching in, 2, 14, 16–17; discovering children's interests, 201–2; teaching power of prayer, 202–4; reading scriptures with children, 204; teaching doctrine to children, 204–7; regular scripture study, 207–10; teaching value of hard work, 210; consistency in, 210–11; sharing church lessons, 211–12; teaching wise use of time, 212; as lifelong pursuit, 212–13; feeling overwhelmed and discouraged, 213–14. *See also* Children; Informal teaching; Parents
Humility, 42–43, 268
Hyde, Orson, 64
Hymns, 254–56

Iceberg analogy, 156–58
Impressions, recording and organizing, 39–41, 271–73. *See also* Holy Ghost; Promptings; Revelation
Inactive and less active class members: reaching out to, 186–88; never giving up on, 188–92; searching for cause of inactivity of, 192; using class members in reactivating, 192–93; as needed, 193–95
Inadequacy, feelings of, 23–24
Individual study, 273–74
Individual worth, 120
Informal teaching, 215–19
Informational level of teaching, 59
Ingersoll, Robert G., 262
Inspirational level of teaching, 60–61
Inspired invitations, 170–73
Inspiring others, 2–3
Interests, discovering children's, 201–2
Invitations: to action, 120; inspired, 170–73

Jairus, daughter of, 67–68
James, William, 247–48
Jared, Brother of, 159
Jeremiah, 54

INDEX

Jesus Christ: conversion to, 3–4; following example of, 4–5, 6–8; becoming like, 33–35, 42, 145; used scriptures to teach doctrine, 63–64; doctrine on nature of, 66; heals man on Sabbath, 77–78; doctrine of, 83–84; teaches with repetition, 99–101; object lessons of, 113–14; creativity of, 115; "Like unto" principle used by, 117–21; divine Sonship and mission of, 120–21; as Savior, 133; expectations set by, 145–46; testimonies of, 154; as example of extending inspired invitations, 170; love of, 179; parables of, 188–89, 190; information teaching moments of, 216; artistic portrayals of, 252; focuses on individual, 280; and teaching with inspiration, 280–81; and rich young ruler, 288n1. *See also* Atonement

Johnson, Cindy, 192–93

Joseph of Egypt, 235

Joy, in learning, 277

Judgment, exercising, 100–101

Justice, 123–24

Kauffmann, Angelica, 251–52

Kennedy, John F., 278

Kimball, Spencer W., 177, 178, 207, 248, 254, 291n16

Kingdom of heaven, 119

Lamoni, King, 155–56

Language, 208

Law of consecration, 76–77

Law of Moses, 76, 77

Law of multiple witnesses, 89–90, 91–92

Lazarus, raising of, 67

Leadership: Jesus Christ as example of, 6–8; and teaching methods, 8–11

Learning, 277–78; ongoing, 261–63, 275–76; responsibilities in, 264–66, 273–74, 277–78; active, 266–68; humility for, 268; prayer for blessings in, 268; preparation for, 268; and class participation, 269–70; and asking questions, 270–71; and recording impressions, 271–73; through observation, 274–75; and acting on doctrine, 276; joy of, 277

Lee, Harold B., 3, 19–20, 41, 267, 273

Les Misérables (Hugo), 258

Lesson plan, 44–45; preparing written, 41; doctrinal principles in, 45–46; scriptures and words of living prophets in, 46; questions in, 46–47; other resources for, 47–48; organizing, 48–49; focusing on people versus, 184

Lewis, C. S., 87, 94

"Like unto" principle, 115, 124–26; used by Jesus Christ, 117–21; examples of, 121–24. *See also* Analogies

Linford, Steven T., 156–57, 166–67

Literature, 257–59

Lost sheep, parable of, 188–89

Love, 184–85; as essential to teaching, 177; as inspiring change, 177–80; of Jesus Christ, 179; expressing, 180–81; as evidence of Spirit, 182; of God, 182; acquiring, of Christ, 182–84; and focusing on people, not lessons, 184; Holy Ghost and increased, 227; for wayward children, 240–41

Luther, Martin, 87

Madsen, Ann, 180–81

Madsen, Truman, 247–48

Maeser, Karl G., 246

Majority-wins method of scriptural interpretation, 91

Mandarin translator, 94–95

Markham, Edwin, 189

Marques, José de Souza, 190–92

Marriage, eternal, 233–34

Marriott, Daniel, 219

Marriott, Neill F., 218–19

Martha, 154

Maxwell, Neal A., 24, 35

INDEX

McConkie, Bruce R., 10, 110, 139–40, 257–58, 265, 273
McConkie, Joseph Fielding, 274
McKay, David O., 1, 101, 184, 186, 281
Meat, principle regarding sacrificial, 79–80
Memorization of scriptures, 72–73
Menlove, Mary, 188
Mercy, 123–24
Messiah, The (Handel), 250–51
Michelangelo, 22–23
Milton, John, 47, 91
Mind, questions stimulating, 152
Misbehavior, 178–79
Modesty, 236–37
Monson, Thomas S., 8–9, 101, 162, 177, 253–54
Morality: repetition in teaching, 105; importance of teaching, 229–30; doctrine on, 230–34; laws and blessings of, 235–39; and wayward children, 240–41; and dealing with temptations, 241–43; timing of teaching, 243–44
Morning prayer, 203
Mortality, purpose of, 233–34
Mosaic law, 76, 77
Moses, 194
Mothers, as teachers, 219–20. *See also* Parents
Motivational level of teaching, 60
Multiple-witnesses method of scriptural interpretation, 91–92
Music, 250–51, 254–57

Naaman, 190
Natural man, 119–20
Nelson, Dantzel, 19–20
Nelson, Russell M.: on teaching in home, 2; as husband and father, 19–20; on revelation, 26; draws upon personal experience, 27; on receiving impressions, 40, 41, 285n16; on principles, 78–79; teaches with repetition, 101; on Holy Ghost, 221; teaches using art and music, 250–51; on literature, 257; on spiritual growth, 267; on Gordon B. Hinkley's curiosity, 271
Nephi, 108
Nibley, Hugh, 28
Numbness, spiritual, 238

Oaks, Dallin H., 4, 104, 182, 241, 257
Object lessons, 113–14
Observation, 274–75
Offense, spiritual, 241–43
"Of God," 66–67
One, rescuing, 188–90, 253–54
Ordinances, principles and, 84–85
Overwhelmed, feeling, 213–14

Pace, Mark L., 83
Packer, Boyd K.: on Jesus Christ as example, 6; on teachers, 7–8; on gift of teaching, 24; on Atonement, 61; story about handcart company told by, 110–11; parables told by, 112; uses "like unto" principle, 122–23; on repentance, 125; on apostates, 136; on bearing testimony, 142; on wayward children, 213; on listening for promptings, 222; and *Winged Victory*, 252; as active learner, 267; on class participation, 269–70; on teaching with inspiration, 280–81
Palsy, man sick of, 158
Pancakes, 217
Parables, 112–13, 118, 188–89, 190
Parents: responsibility of, to teach, 12–14; influence of, 15–19; quality time with, 19–20; importance of, 20–21; as examples for children, 218–19; as teachers, 219–20; honoring calling as, 279–81. *See also* Children; Home, teaching in
Parker, Ann, 110–11
Parker, Arthur, 110–12
Parker, Robert, 110–11
Participation, 269–70
Pasteur, Louis, 275
Patriarchal blessings, 10
Patterns, in doctrine, 67–68

INDEX

Payson Utah Temple, 218
Peace, and recognizing Holy Ghost, 225–26
Pearl and the box, parable of, 112–13
Penicillin, 275
Perfection, 58, 145–46
Perry, L. Tom, 24
Personal experience, drawing upon, 27
Peter, 145, 154
Philip, 279
Philosophical level of teaching, 59–60
Plan of salvation, 51–53, 82
Poetry, 257
Pondering, 37–39
Pornography, 237–39
Porter, L. Aldin, 104–5
Pratt, Parley P., 141–42
Prayer, 35, 187, 197, 202–4, 268
Preparation: for spiritual crises, 59–60; to respond to questions, 127–28; to learn, 268
Priesthood blessings, 57
Priesthood power, 157, 216–17
Priestly, J. B., 266
Principles: focusing on, 75–76, 104; versus rules, 76–77; examples of teaching, 77–80; governing answers to difficult questions, 128–33. *See also* Doctrinal relationships; Doctrine; "Like unto" principle; Repetition
Priority method of scriptural interpretation, 87
Procreation, 231–33
Promptings: importance of recognizing, 221–23; helping children recognize, 223–28. *See also* Holy Ghost; Impressions, recording and organizing
Prophets: use scriptures to teach doctrine, 64; speak with repetition, 101; use "like unto" principle, 121–23
Prophets, words of, 46
Purity, 229, 239

Questions: in developing lesson plan, 46–47; about doctrine, 68–69; power of, 151–52; that enlighten mind and penetrate heart, 152–53; eliciting self-evaluation, 153; heightening our level of commitment, 153–54; inspiring testimony, 154–55; serving as effective answers, 155; determining levels of understanding, 155–56; follow-up, 156–58; stage-setting, 158; building self-reliance, 159–60; structuring good, 160–61; quality of, 163; awkward silence following, 164; giving heads up for, 198; asking, 270–71. *See also* Difficult questions

Rattlesnake analogy, 237–38
Reactivation, 186–95
Reason / Reasoning, 59, 71, 92–93, 94, 286n8
Redemption, 83. *See also* Exaltation; Salvation
Repentance, 57, 123–24, 125
Repetition: Lord teaches with, 99–101; prophets teach with, 101; employing, 101–4; need for, 104–5; as beneficial for teacher, 106; in telling stories, 109; and law of sacrifice, 287n7
Restoration, 102–4, 125–26
Resurrection, 66
Revelation, 25–26, 36–39, 41, 152, 227. *See also* Holy Ghost; Impressions, recording and organizing
Richards, George F., 257
Rich young ruler, 288n1
"Riding the wave," 166–68
Rigdon, Sidney, 12–13
Roberts, B. H., 71
Romney, Marion G., 36–37, 267
Rules, principles versus, 76–77
Russell, Bertrand, 246
Ruth, Babe, 217–18

Sabbath, 77–78, 91, 118–19, 218–19
Sacrament, 219

INDEX

Sacrifice, repetition applied to law of, 287n7
Salvation, 58, 87, 88–89, 92, 118, 276. *See also* Exaltation; Redemption
Science, 130
Scott, Richard G., 39, 72, 76, 165–66
Screen sharing, 198–99
Scripture chains, 65–67
Scriptures: as teaching tool, 26–27; learning directly from, 36–37; and planning lesson, 46; as primary source for teaching doctrine, 63–67; introducing, 64–65; memorizing, 72–73; interpreting, 86–87; man-made methods of interpreting, 86–91; God's methods of interpreting, 91–95; and teaching children, 109; reading, with children, 204; holding regular study of, 207–10; individual responsibility to study, 273–74
Self-control, 232, 290n5
Self-evaluation, 153
Self-reliance, 159–60
Sermon on the Mount, 34
Shakespeare, William, 261–62
Silences, 164
Sin, 123–24
Single-witness method of scriptural interpretation, 89–90
Sit-ups, 209–10
Small and simple things, 210–11
Smith, George Albert, 255–56, 269–70
Smith, Joseph: Lord's counsel to, 12–13; on teaching principles, 75; on spiritual confirmation of scriptures, 95; on creative ideas, 115; and testimony of Book of Mormon, 133–34, 135; Parley P. Pratt's testimony regarding, 141–42; and revelation given to Oliver Cowdery, 225–26; on revelation, 227; on recording impressions, 272; on ongoing learning, 275
Smith, Joseph F., 138–39, 276
Smith, Joseph Fielding, 32
Snow, Lorenzo, 101
Socrates, 267

Spafford, Belle, 269–70
Spanish: missionary struggles with, 148–49; author practices, 217
Spiritual curiosity, 270–71
Spiritual experiences, sharing, 216–17
Spiritual gifts, 27–28, 182–83
Spiritual growth, 129–30, 267
Spirituality, culture and, 245–47
Spiritual man, 119–20
Spiritual numbness, 238
Spiritual offense, 241–43
Spiritual trailers, 172–74
Spiritual transformation, 119–20
Spiritual wave, riding, 166–68
Spiritual witness, 131–32
Spirit world, sociality in, 10–11
Sports, 201–2, 248
Square-peg-in-the-round-hole method of scriptural interpretation, 90
Stage-setting questions, 158
Stories, 109–12
Stripling warriors, 17
Survival level of teaching, 58–59
Swainston, Erika, 192–93
Swimming lessons, 197

Table manners, 246
Talmage, James E., 112
Taylor, John, 59, 70, 141–42
Teacher(s): mission of, 2–4; influence of, 4; Christlike attributes and skills in, 4–5; Jesus Christ as example for, 6–8, 33–35; and teaching children, 20; qualification of, 24–25; revelations for, 25–26; testimony of, 138–39, 141; role of, in discussions, 162; and reaching out to inactive and less active class members, 186–95; mothers as, 219–20; ongoing learning of, 261–63; responsibilities of, 264–66; honoring calling as, 279–81
Teaching: as great trust, 1–2; methods for leaders, 8–11; ability for, 22–24; qualification for, 24–25; Holy Ghost's assistance in, 25; revelation for, 25–26; using scriptures in,

INDEX

26–27, 36–37; drawing upon personal experience in, 27; using testimony in, 28–29; by Spirit, 32–43; levels of, 58–61; testimony as essential to, 141; love as essential to, 177; responsibilities in, 264–66. *See also* Home, teaching in; Informal teaching

Technology: and seeing students, 196–98; practicing using, 198; technical difficulties in, 198; and screen sharing, 198–99; and encouraging video feed use, 199

Temples: Spirit's lesson concerning, 218; bodies as, 231, 235; pictures of, 254, 291–92n16

Temptations, 241–43

Testimony: as teaching tool, 28–29; of others, 132–33; relationship between doctrine and, 138–40; as spiritual exclamation point, 140; impact of, 141–42; blessing of bearing, 142; timing of bearing, 142–43; questions inspiring, 154–55; of Book of Mormon, 158; strengthening, 194; and recognizing promptings, 221–22; and helping children recognize promptings, 224; and scripture study, 273

Thomas, Robert K., 247

Thoughts, unclean, 239, 241–43

Time, wise use of, 212

Timotheus, 286n7

Tithing, 101

Tocqueville, Alexis de, 130–31

To Kill a Mockingbird (Lee), 258

Trailers, spiritual, 172–74

Transformation, spiritual, 119–20

Tree of life, 108

Trials, spiritual preparation for, 59–60

Tribute money, 113

Trumpeter, and harmony in scriptural interpretation, 93

Trust, teaching as great, 1–2

Truths: unrevealed, 129–30; scientific versus religious, 130; secular versus spiritual, 131; learning secular and spiritual, 262–63

Tunnel-vision method of scriptural interpretation, 88–89

Turner, Joseph Mallord William, 253–54

Twain, Mark, 178, 258, 272

Uchtdorf, Dieter F., 27, 121–22

Unanswered questions, 128–31, 136–37

Unclean thoughts, 239, 241–43

Understanding: questions determining levels of, 155–56; Holy Ghost and enlightened, 226–27

Video feed, 199

Virtual technology. *See* Technology

Virtue, 239

Walters, Archer, 110–12

"Wave, riding," 166–68

Wayward children, 207, 208–9, 212–13, 240–41

Whitney, Newel K., 13

Whitney, Orson F., 249

Widow's mites, 216

Wilkinson, Ernest L., 1–2

Williams, Frederick G., 12

Winged Victory, 252–53

Wise man and foolish man, parable of, 118

Witness: spiritual, 131–32; divine, 227–28

Witnesses, law of multiple, 89–90, 91–92

Wixom, Rosemary M., 244

Word of Wisdom, 101

Work, 210

Works, versus faith, 87, 88–89

Worth, individual, 120

Young, Brigham, 26, 31, 247, 262

Zoramites, 211–12